D0896760

Saamaka Dreaming

Saamaka Dreaming

Richard Price and Sally Price

DUKE UNIVERSITY PRESS

Durham and London 2017

© 2017 Duke University Press
All rights reserved
Printed in the United States
of America on acid-free paper ∞
Designed by Amy Buchanan
Typeset in Quadraat and Quadraat Sans
by Westchester Publishing Services

....

Library of Congress Cataloging-in-Publication Data
Names: Price, Richard, [date] author. |
Price, Sally, author.
Title: Saamaka dreaming / Richard Price
and Sally Price.
Description: Durham : Duke University Press, 2017. |
Includes bibliographical references and index.
Identifiers: LCCN 2016059668 (print) |
LCCN 2017003772 (ebook)
ISBN 9780822369660 (hardcover : alk. paper)
ISBN 9780822369783 (pbk. : alk. paper)
ISBN 9780822372868 (ebook)
Subjects: LCSH: Saramacca (Surinamese people) |
Saramacca (Surinamese people)—Social life
and customs. | Saramacca (Surinamese people)—
Folklore. | Maroons—Suriname.
Classification: LCC F2431.S27 P753 2017 (print) |
LCC F2431.S27 (ebook) | DDC 988.3/3—dc23
LC record available at https://lccn.loc.gov/2016059668

....

Cover art: Gravediggers on the river.
Photo: Martha Cooper.

Most serious and productive artists are "haunted" by their material—
this is the galvanizing force of their creativity, their motivation.
It is not and cannot be a fully conscious or volitional "haunting"—
it is something that seems to happen to us, as if from without.

JOYCE CAROL OATES

CONTENTS

....

PREFACE (ix)

CHAPTER 1   Testing the Waters (1)

CHAPTER 2   On Trial (13)

CHAPTER 3   A Feast for the Ancestors (28)

CHAPTER 4   Going "Outside" (34)

CHAPTER 5   On Nai's Doorstep (40)

CHAPTER 6   Under Kala's House (51)

CHAPTER 7   The Sika (58)

CHAPTER 8   What Month Is It? (62)

CHAPTER 9   The Captain's "Granddaughter" (71)

CHAPTER 10   Upriver (74)

CHAPTER 11   At the Ancestor Shrine (86)

CHAPTER 12   The Cock's Balls (100)

CHAPTER 13   Nai's Rivergod (103)

CHAPTER 14   Agbago's Seagod (108)

CHAPTER 15   Kala's Snakegod (114)

CHAPTER 16   A Touch of Madness (123)

CHAPTER 17   Playing for the Gods (132)

CHAPTER 18   A Tree Falls (139)

CHAPTER 19   Sickness (144)

CHAPTER 20   Death of a Witch (155)

CHAPTER 21   Chasing Ghosts (173)

CHAPTER 22   Death of a Child (179)

CHAPTER 23   Returns (190)

CHAPTER 24   Foto (202)

CHAPTER 25   Looking at Paper (205)

CHAPTER 26   The End of an Era (215)

NOTES (231)

BIBLIOGRAPHY (243)

INDEX (247)

PREFACE

Although we speak a number of languages, the one we learned during the 1960s while living in the Suriname rainforest is the one—other than our native English—that we most often use with each other. It's also a frequent dream language for us both. Our hosts, the Saamaka Maroons, call it Saamakatongo, or simply Saamaka. (Saamakas are the descendants of Africans brought to Suriname in chains who rebelled and escaped in the late seventeenth and early eighteenth centuries and established an independent society in the tropical forest.)[1]

For political reasons (death threats from the dictator/president of the country), we haven't been able to set foot in the Republic of Suriname since 1986. Since then, our ongoing fieldwork with Saamakas, the source of our knowledge about present-day life in their villages, has been conducted from the somewhat excentric perspective of neighboring Guyane (French Guiana). Following the Suriname Civil War of 1986–1992, about a third of Saamakas moved there permanently, returning periodically for visits to their home villages in Suriname. That turns Saamaka territory, as we knew it in the 1960s, 1970s, and early 1980s, into something of a dreamworld for us.

Yet we're still haunted by our Suriname experiences, preserved in ethnographic fieldnotes as well as recordings and photos . . . and memories. This book revisits the life we experienced in Saamaka, particularly during our initial fieldwork of the 1960s—scenes of our youth and a Saamaka world considerably different from that of today.

Among the many Saamakas who dealt with the arrival of the two young outsiders in 1966, receiving them with a mixture of curiosity, suspicion, ambivalence, hostility, and fascination, there were three people who played especially pivotal roles.

Agbago Aboikoni, in his early eighties when we first met him, was the dignified paramount chief (*gaama*) of the Saamaka people. In office since 1951, he presided over a period of increasing pressures from the colonial government to integrate his people into the wider society. It was Agbago who ultimately bore responsibility for deciding whether we should be allowed a trial period of residence in a Saamaka village, with permission for our longer stay to be decided in due course by divination with gods and ancestors after they'd had a chance to assess our intentions. A tall lanky man whose deep bass voice bespoke authority and wisdom, he struck a regal figure, conducting audiences with a combination of solemnity and gentle good humor, always punctuated by proverbs and esoteric allusions. Born in Dangogo, the last village on the Pikilio River, he ruled from the tribal capital of Asindoopo, just a half hour downstream by paddle.

Agbago's brother Kala, nearly seventy, was the senior village captain (*kabiteni*) of Dangogo, a village split on either side of the Pikilio, with about three hundred residents. Once our house was built in his neighborhood, he became responsible for us on a day-to-day basis, making sure that we were holding up our end of the bargain that allowed us to stay in Saamaka. Universally known for his "fierceness," Kala closely monitored our adherence to basic rules, most importantly Sally's monthly isolation in the menstrual hut at the edge of the village, and he did his best to act as the gatekeeper for Rich's interviews with particular people. Kala was proud and vain, despite having a mildly crippled leg from an old tree-felling accident. In his relationship with us, he lived up to his stormy reputation, though the ups and downs of our encounters gradually produced an underlying acceptance, and eventually something approaching real friendship.

Their nonagenarian sister Nai had, like her brothers, been raised in Dangogo. During our stay in Saamaka she was the oldest person on the Pikilio and the undisputed doyenne of their matrilineage. No longer able to travel to the camp where she had enjoyed maintaining gardens ever since moving back from her husband's village after his death forty years earlier, she stayed in Dangogo where she was treated as a kind of nerve center for local events. Pregnancies and births, marriages and divorces, trips to and from the coast, and rituals of every kind were routinely brought to her doorstep for her reactions and advice. The placement of our own house facing that doorstep, just a few yards away, gave us special access for keeping up with the latest events . . . and also allowed her to keep an attentive eye on our own activities. Over time we became very close. Our adoptive kinship relationship was the normal one for people separated by two generations: Rich and Nai were ritualized "husband" and "wife," while Nai and Sally addressed each other as *kambo*, a playful version of *kambosa* ("co-wife"). When we left in late 1968, Nai—thinking toward her coming death, and concerned that Sally had not yet become pregnant—vowed that when she died she would serve as the *neseki* (namesake, spiritual genitor) of our future child.

Our relationships with Agbago, Kala, and Nai led to others that contributed importantly to our experience in Saamaka. The trials and tribulations of Agbago's three wives—the aging Apumba, her co-wife Gadya, and their younger rival Kaadi from a Christian village downstream—came under frequent discussion. Kala's ultra-possessive guardianship of his wife Anaweli's nubile granddaughter Maame ("Mah-may") led to some of the most dramatic moments of our stay in Saamaka. And the children and grandchildren of Nai's deceased daughter were omnipresent in our daily lives.

Faced with stories, observations, and commentaries that filled thousands of pages of fieldnotes we have decided to give this book focus by limiting it to experiences that involved this threesome and their immediate families.

....

It would be futile to attempt a list of traditional "acknowledgments" to individuals and grant organizations who have provided intellectual and financial assistance at some point over the fifty years covered in this book. But we would like to thank John Collins and Peter Redfield for their helpful comments on a draft and Marty Cooper for sharing her precious photos of the *gaama*'s funeral.

FIGURE PREF.1. Rich with a fish he caught. Photo: S. Price.

FIGURE PREF.2. Sally with a pet monkey belonging
to Nai's great-granddaughter Dyam.
Photo: R. Price.

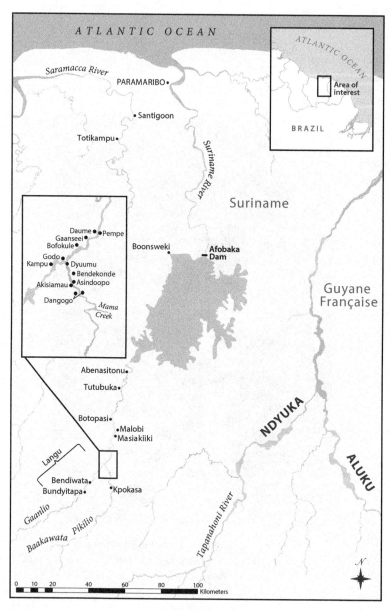

MAP 1.1. Some places mentioned in the text.
Map drawn by Nicholas Rubin.

....

CHAPTER 1

Testing the Waters

Despite physical discomforts, periods of boredom, ailments ranging from funguses and dysentery to malaria and hepatitis, and periodic ridicule for being culturally clueless, we have always loved ethnographic fieldwork. We recently found a typescript, dated 1972, intended for a book that we started writing in New Haven but never finished. It began:

> Whether it's an indication of a certain alienation from our own society, a basic function of the ethnographic process or—as seems likely—some combination of the two, we have always felt life most viscerally while doing fieldwork, whether in Peru, Martinique, Andalusia, Chiapas or, most particularly, Saramaka. For us, in the field, there is a remarkable openness to reality, a switching on of all one's senses, and a fantastic investment in human relations. Life becomes delightfully refreshing.

This retrospective confessional continued, "We truly lived for the summers, spending autumns digesting, writing up, and publishing our last summer's work, and the springs preparing for the next." That was the mindset that set the course for our professional, and in many ways personal, lives for many decades.

In 1964, the idea of Rich doing dissertation research with people known as "Bush Negroes," the descendants of self-liberated slaves in the Dutch colony of Suriname, had begun to grow on us. We knew that Melville Herskovits, the founder of Afro-American studies, had considered Suriname's six Maroon "tribes" at one end of his "Scale of Intensity of Africanisms" in the Americas (with Harlem Negroes at the other, most assimilated, end). We'd read about the research that Dutch anthropologists had recently undertaken among the Ndyuka Maroons of eastern Suriname. And we'd seen the magnificent photographs by French geographer Jean Hurault of proud Aluku Maroons who since the late eighteenth century had lived just over the border with Guyane.

But there was a potential problem. In the 1960s, anthropology was still viewed largely as the study of people who, in that pre–politically correct era, were classified as "primitive," and the Harvard department specified that the Ph.D. could be awarded only to students who had carried out at least three months of fieldwork in a non-Indo-European language. Saamakas, despite their "primitiveness" on almost every other criterion, were ruled out, since at the time scholars considered that all creole languages—including the one spoken by Saamakas—were the bastard offspring of Indo-European languages such as English, French, Portuguese, and Dutch. (That meant that a student could not get a Ph.D. in anthropology at Harvard with a dissertation about, say, Martinique or anywhere in Afro-America. As Caribbeanist Sidney Mintz is said to have joked, "If they don't have blowguns and you can't catch malaria, it's not anthropology.") Rich managed to slip through only thanks to a bizarre loophole. The two summers we'd spent doing fieldwork with Zinacanteco Indians in Mexico, who spoke a Mayan language called Tzotzil, officially met the non-Indo-European language requirement, and he was thus authorized to undertake dissertation fieldwork with Saamakas.

By 1965, we had begun corresponding with Dutch scholars, who warned us that the recent damming of the Suriname River by Alcoa and the colonial government, which had flooded out six thousand Saamakas from their villages in central Suriname, might make the colonial government wary of anyone doing research in the area. But we decided to give it a try. In the summer of 1966, after brief fieldwork in Mexico, we picked up a string hammock in the Yucatan and flew to the Dutch colony, with a brief stop in Papa Doc's Haiti. Our goal: securing permission to carry out fieldwork among the Saamaka, then some twenty thousand people living in seventy villages along the upper Suriname River.

Our memory of the two-week bureaucratic marathon in Paramaribo is of countless hours sitting on wooden benches in lonely government waiting rooms. It was clear early on that our fate depended directly on

District Commissioner Jan Michels—a man whom, we later learned, Saamakas called Tu-Buka-Goni (double-barreled shotgun) because he spoke out of both sides of his mouth. Michels eventually gave us the go-ahead on the condition that we not spend time with the communities displaced by the dam. He also offered to arrange our transportation to the *gaama*'s village and to provide proper letters of introduction.

With our upriver departure set for the following week, we began to be bombarded with well-meant advice by everyone from old government hands who had visited the interior to storekeepers, the East Indian family who'd rented us a room, and the chief of police who had impounded our passports "just in case." We were not taken in by their tales of a jungle teeming with snakes and jaguars and rivers swarming with bloodthirsty piranhas. But we did take the advice of merchants who had outfitted previous mining and scientific expeditions to the interior, purchasing knee-high boots (essential protection against snake bite, they said), U.S. army surplus nylon-and-net zip-up hammocks like those being used in Vietnam ("against vampire bats and malarial mosquitoes"), and certain types of cloth and rum that they claimed were preferred by "Bush Negroes." Once in Saamaka, we learned better. We never once donned the clumsy boots (instead going barefoot throughout our stay) or slept in the coffin-like hammocks. The only resemblance between the cloth we'd bought and that used by Saamakas was that it contained stripes, and the 150 proof rum was much stronger than anything Saamakas drank or even used for libations.

On the morning of our departure we set out in a government jeep for the sweaty, bumpy ride that brought us after several hours to the massive hydroelectric dam at Afobaka. The district commissioner's three Saamaka boatmen—Neiso and his two assistants—were there waiting for us and helped transfer our gear, now covered (like ourselves) with red-brown bauxite dust from the road, to a government motor canoe for the trip upriver. It was only as the boatmen pointed the slim craft out into the artificial lake that we looked back and saw the immensity of the construction, the broad sweep of concrete in between hundreds of meters of high packed red earth, looming up from the fetid water.

At last we were on what Saamakas were still calling "the river," negotiating a tortuous path lined on either side with the bare grey tops of forest giants, standing as skeletal sentinels in a vast space of death. As we followed the course of the twisting, ancient riverbed, far below us,

FIGURE 1.1. Mamadan shrine to the Wentis. O. J. R. Jozefzoon, *De Saramaccaanse wereld* (Paramaribo: Varekamp, 1959), 28.

the Saamaka steersman would point and call out to us the name of each submerged village, buried forever beneath the muddy waters—houses, shrines, cemeteries, gardens, and hunting grounds, places where great battles had been fought and famous miracles effected.

After four or five hours in the eerie silence of the lake, we heard a low roar that grew louder as we approached. Suddenly we broke into the exuberance of the bright green forest and plunging waters of the most famous rapids on the Suriname River, Mamadan, "Mother of all Rapids." The river rushed at us from all sides, the foaming water coursing through numerous channels and plunging over giant boulders. After the boatmen poured libations on shore at the shrine to the Wentis (gods of the rapids and the sea), we spent a fitful night's sleep on an island in the midst of this liquid plenitude.[1]

It was still early the next morning when we arrived upstream at Abenasitonu, Neiso's home village, and one of the first of the Saamaka villages that had not been sunk by the dam. Our gear was deposited in the house of the Moravian schoolteacher, away on summer vacation, and we were told to wait there while the boatmen continued several days upriver to the village of Asindoopo to ask Gaama Agbago whether they could bring these whitefolks into Saamaka territory. Four days later, the boatmen returned with formal permission to proceed, and we set out again upstream.

At the time, no outsiders—whether from the government or elsewhere—ventured into Saamaka territory without this nod to the principle that the *gaama*, on behalf of his people, maintained full territorial control. The government's unilateral decision to build the Afobaka dam had, of course, slashed a deep wound into this long-respected sovereignty. But in 1966, any non-Saamaka setting foot in their territory still did so as a guest of the Saamaka people. For them, the treaty that their ancestors concluded with the Dutch crown in 1762 not only ended decades of bitter warfare but also established three inalienable principles: freedom (from slavery), independence (from the colonial society—the right to govern their own society as they wished), and control over their own territory, stretching from Mawasi Creek (some fifteen kilometers downstream from the dam) to the headwaters of the Suriname River. Gaama Agbago was fond of repeating the litany, "From Mawasi on up, the forest belongs to us."

During the rest of the upriver journey, we stopped for brief visits in village after village, seeing bits and pieces of a way of life that looked more exotic than anything we'd ever imagined—libations being poured before a gabled coffin as women shrieked in mourning, men sporting shiny gold earrings, bright patchwork capes, embroidered neckerchiefs, umbrellas, variously curved machetes, tasseled calfbands, multicolored beaded sashes across their chests, and hats that varied from berets and fedoras to panamas and pith helmets—evoking for us visions of seventeenth-century pirates of the Caribbean. Between villages, sometimes for an hour at a stretch, we glided next to forest walls of breathtaking beauty, seeing only the occasional fisherman or a woman paddling a small dugout canoe laden with garden produce. Over and over, we passed through foaming rapids, marveling at the boatmen's skills and knowledge of every twist and turn and rock in the river. Throughout the voyage, we pestered them about Saamaka words, building on our knowledge of Sranantongo (the coastal Creole), which we had learned from a Dutch radio course, and which they spoke as a contact language. Rich was already getting used to being called "Lisati" (the Saamaka pronunciation of Richard) while Sally's name, easier for Saamakas to pronounce, remained intact.

On the afternoon of the third day, we arrived at Tuliobuka ("Mouth of Two Rivers") where, over a mighty rapids on our right, the Gaanlio flowed into the Suriname. We entered the left-hand, quieter flow of the Pikilio, which led to the *gaama*'s village several kilometers upstream. A messenger had been sent ahead that morning to alert him of our arrival, but we were told to wait in the canoe until we received permission to disembark. After a half hour baking in the sun, we were led ashore and into Gaama Agbago's council house, a kind of throne room that took our breath away. Michels had told us that during the reign of Atudendu, Agbago's immediate predecessor, visitors literally crawled through the doorway until being signaled to rise. The Herskovitses wrote about their arrival in what they called "the Court of the Granman" in 1929, greeted by multiple shotgun salutes and much "hallooing of the women," and devoted more than half a dozen pages of their book to a description of the council house and its ceremonial stools, umbrellas, and other accoutrements. Even in 2015 a blogger wrote of visiting the Saamaka "King" in his "Royal Palace."

Our boatmen ostentatiously wiped their feet on the large doormat and bowed down as they entered, and we followed suit. The *gaama* was reposing on a large, cushioned steel chair, flanked on either side by a dozen wicker armchairs set on a platform. He wore a fedora, a tailcoat made from a bright Union Jack, green and blue pinstripe pajama pants, and red high-top basketball sneakers, unlaced. In one of the armchairs, a young man who we later learned was a foster child of the chief named Line ("Lee-nay"), was casually thumbing through a Dutch movie magazine.

The *gaama* motioned to us to come forward, and indicated the two adjoining armchairs. After an exchange with the boatmen about the trip, he recounted some of the history of outsiders visiting Saamaka territory and poured a libation of rum, informing the ancestors of our arrival and asking that they protect us during our stay. Hearing that we'd lived in Martinique, he told us how, in his youth, he had shipped out on a steamship from Belém and how he and his fellow sailors, on shore leave in Fort-de-France, had been arrested and spent time in jail in the wake of a political assassination. He boasted about the size of that ship and gave a vivid imitation of the sounds of its powerful, chugging engines and its foghorn.

When we were finally given an opening to explain the reason for our visit, Rich summoned up his best effort at Sranantongo to outline our goals, saying we wished to learn how Saamakas lived and mentioning gardening, hunting, woodcarving, and of course language. But because the several weeks we could stay on this visit would be far too short, he said, we wished to return some months hence and stay for two years. Later we realized that he'd been far too direct—as newcomers we had little sense of the subtleties of Saamaka etiquette, let alone the linguistic tools to produce it. The *gaama* answered graciously but non-committally, offering us the use of a wood-frame guesthouse he maintained for government visitors, and inviting us to join him in a ride back to the coast in three weeks, when he was due in Paramaribo for official business. We presented him with several of the gifts we had brought and our meeting was over.

The next morning, we met again with the chief, asking him whether we might arrange to eat our meals with a local family—as we'd done in previous fieldwork in Peru, Martinique, Spain, and Mexico. He answered cordially, but refused, explaining that people moved around a great deal to forest camps and spouses' villages, and offering instead to obtain for us whatever food we needed. He had apparently heard from the boatmen how mosquitoes had been attacking us through the open mesh of our Yucatecan hammock, and generously offered us a sturdy Brazilian substitute.

Our first days in Asindoopo, a village of several hundred people, included frequent periods of boredom and frustration. Complete outsiders, we were tolerated as amusing curiosities by some and as possible sources of tobacco or trinkets by others, but also left alone for long periods. No one seemed to want to take responsibility to engage us. Despite our requests, no one agreed to teach us anything about canoeing or cooking or gardening. Rich spent most mornings fishing in the river and most afternoons with a group of young men playing soccer at the nearby Moravian mission, after which they drank beer and listened to calypsos and soul music on a battery-driven phonograph while pouring over a deck of Nu-Vu playing cards. Sally, visiting village women, was frustrated by quick shifts from cordiality to hostility when she asked questions about harvesting rice, sewing clothes, or carving calabashes. Our handwritten notes from the period report such gems as "Bought one fish from a little boy for 2 fishhooks, but Sally dropped it in the river as she was cleaning it. No one saw." Children sometimes burst into tears at the mere sight of us—once, when a little boy cried

FIGURE 1.2. Abatili. Photo: R. Price.

at seeing Rich, one of the *gaama*'s wives teased him, "Better get used to it. That's what you'll see when you go to the city." When young men or women took us to nighttime dances in nearby villages, our Saamaka clothes evoked loud hooting and clapping as people pulled and adjusted them to show us exactly how to wear them. Women must have retied the knot of Sally's waistkerchief a hundred times. And late evening visitors to our house would encourage us to get into our hammock if we were tired, saying they would just stay and watch.

Slowly, however, we began to forge relationships. Abatili, a thirty-some "grandson" of the *gaama* who lived in Dangogo, the *gaama*'s natal village a few kilometers upstream, and one of Rich's new soccer-playing friends, took a special interest in us and began sending us small gifts—a bird he'd shot, a carved comb, two eggs. As one of the *gaama*'s official boatmen, he took advantage of his access to an outboard motor to bring us to Dangogo several times. There we met his grandmother

Nai, who gave us a bucketful of oranges on our first visit, and with whom we participated in a large feast in honor of her deceased mother a few days later.

Dangogo was divided between a hilly site where Nai, Kala, Abatili, and their closest relatives lived and a flatter part of the village across the river. Between them rushed a rock-strewn rapids and on either shore there were flat rocks where women cleaned fish, washed hammocks, did their dishes, and engaged in relaxed conversation. Just downstream, on either side, were numerous canoes, all intricately carved on their prows, sterns, and seats, tied up to stakes on the sandy banks. On both sides of the village large clusters of houses, separated by lines of bushes, belonged to particular kin groups, each with its own ancestor shrine. Fruit trees—oranges, limes, breadnuts, mangos, guavas, coconuts, palepu palms brought back from Guyane—calabash and cotton trees, and many varieties of medicinal plants dotted the village.

With the *gaama*'s permission, Abatili took us by paddle for a four-day visit to Kpokasa, his sisters' garden camp on the upper Pikilio. Kpokasa was our first glimpse of a world dominated by natural beauty, plentiful crops, game, and fish—a world treasured by Saamakas as an escape from the tensions of village life. During our stay, we were included according to our abilities and stamina in hunting, cutting roofing materials, house building, rice harvesting, and food preparation along with the close-knit family group, including Abatili and his wife Ina, as well as his three sisters. Naina was a premenopausal woman with striking facial cicatrizations who seemed somewhat skeptical about the two new visitors; Akobo, in her forties, expressed enthusiasm about teaching us Saamaka things; and their younger sister Beki was pretty much a full-time mother for her two sons—ten-year-old Elima, perpetually misbehaving, and Bane ("Bah-nay"), a lively one-year-old still often tied onto her back with a length of cotton cloth—and her outgoing five-year-old daughter Poi. Naina's thirty-year-old son Dosili was also there with his young wife Dyeni and his daughter Seena, whose mother had died giving her birth. In the evening, we all ate our meals together (women in one group, men in another, but within hearing distance) and, when folktales were told around the smoldering fire, we even managed to contribute a crude version of Cinderella in our fast developing but still rudimentary Saamakatongo.

FIGURE 1.3. Dosili. Photo: R. Price.

Our notes from that stay record beautiful nights, our hammock slung in an open-sided shelter under the full moon with, off in the distance, mysterious, somewhat frightening sounds. Rich took the precaution of slipping his machete under our hammock, but they turned out to be agoutis calling out one night, howler monkeys the next. (We never met the jungle beasts we imagined roaring, though later—twice during our time in Saamaka—jaguars came within a few feet of our house in Dangogo and were shot during the night by Dosili.)

Upon our return from upriver, we talked to Abatili about the possibility of living in Dangogo instead of Asindoopo, which because of its political role and relationship to the outside world we thought would give us an atypical view of Saamaka life. He agreed to help us make this request to his grandfather.

When the *gaama* interrogated him about our stay in Kpokasa, Abatili described how many "hands" of rice Sally had cut, what kinds of birds

Rich had shot, how we'd participated in rice hulling and house building, and how we had eaten food from the same pot as his sisters. Apparently satisfied, Agbago said that the next day we would all go to Dangogo and pick out a site for our future house. He also announced that he was taking a government plane to the city in four days, so we would need to leave Saamaka at that point as well. He was clearly skeptical that we'd ever return, despite our having left a cash deposit with Abatili for the house that was to be built in Dangogo during our absence.

Throughout our stay, Gaama Agbago was generous, showering us with gifts almost daily—enamel basins filled with cocoa, tea, condensed milk, cookies, and sugar from the city and kilo upon kilo of rice from local gardens. He included us in the distribution of hunting kills— portions of tapir and wild boar that were routinely presented to him when any man on the Pikilio made a significant kill. One evening he sent a wrap-skirt to Sally and a bottle of cold beer to Rich from his kerosene-powered refrigerator.

By the time our three-week stay was over, we had participated in a variety of rituals—a funeral, a feast for the ancestors, the installation by the *gaama* of a new village captain, ceremonies for snakegods and forest spirits, and numerous rites at the ancestor shrine. We had seen a good deal of spirit possession. We had visited a number of neighboring villages, often being given a raucous welcome by dozens of women and children clapping and hooting all around us. We had attended secular and ritual dances, some lasting all night. We had gathered much preliminary information about gardening, learned the names and locations of the forty-three villages that had disappeared underneath Alcoa's lake, and begun to understand the rudiments of material culture, from calabash carving to house construction. More important, our initial use of Srananтongo had shifted into a workable command of Saamakatongo.

The final page of our joint notebook from that summer contains a list of what to bring when we returned: a twelve-gauge shotgun, fishing gear, a machete, a small hammock for use in the menstrual hut, dozens of lengths of cloth, and a kerosene lantern, as well as a portable typewriter, paper, and carbon paper. Our visit to the Pikilio had lasted several days longer than that of the Herskovitses, who wrote *Rebel Destiny* on the basis of their trip, but we were well aware that we'd hardly scratched the surface.

On our way downstream, a couple of kilometers above the site of Mamadan, our canoe slid down through a final rapids to meet the flat brown waters of the artificial lake. Although the surrounding forest was still as green and vibrant as when we'd come upstream, the "Mother of All Rapids" had disappeared forever beneath Alcoa's rising waters.

....

CHAPTER 2

On Trial

We spent the next five months in Cambridge (Mass.) learning Dutch, reading the literature on Suriname, and (for Rich) completing pre-dissertation requirements for the Ph.D. In February Sally went to New York to handle final preparations, including instructions from a friend on how to load shotgun shells from scratch (primer, black powder, shot, cardboard and paper wads . . .). Rich flew to Paramaribo to tackle the bureaucracy (permissions from police and immigration, a license for his shotgun), and meet with Michels, other district commissioners, officials at the U.S. Embassy, the head of Moravian missions, and pilots from the Missionary Aviation Fellowship. By chance, Gaama Agbago was in the city for a couple of days as a guest of Prime Minister Pengel, in anticipation of national elections to be held later that month—for the first time a voting booth would be set up on the upper river. After visiting with the *gaama*, Rich wrote back to Sally, "What a wonderful smile! He was truly glad to see me, extremely gracious . . ."

After his first week in the city, Rich lied to a pious missionary pilot that there was no alcohol or tobacco in his baggage, which allowed him to catch a ride on a Cessna to the hospital airstrip near Asindoopo, just a couple of days before the prime minister's visit. (Overflying Dangogo during the descent, Rich wrote: "From 1500 feet up, Dangogo hardly shows at all—it's just a tiny hill by a strip of white water in the midst of a vast forest broken by fields.") Asindoopo had been transformed—city officials spilling out of every available accommodation, crowds of Saamakas from surrounding villages dressed in their best, Saamaka captains and their assistants in full uniform—as three planeloads of

FIGURE 2.1. Kala splitting reeds for
our house. Photo: R. Price.

cityfolk, including the prime minister and his entourage, arrived for
the pre-election visit. Pengel's people doled out drinks and sweets by
the case. Saamakas performed the requisite dances for the TV crews.
We were later told that Pengel's party garnered more than 96 percent
of the local vote.

Once the village had returned to normal, Rich accompanied Abatili
and Line to Afobaka in one of the *gaama*'s freight canoes (to refill barrels of gasoline) and took a minibus to the city, where Sally had arrived
from New York. After a few days of shopping (pots, pans, and similar
supplies), we met up again with them and headed upstream, sleeping
in several villages on the way, to be back before election day.

In Dangogo, our house had been finished except for the roof, so we
slept in Abatili's and ate meals cooked by Ina, who had a house of her
own facing his. On our first day back a man named Asopi arrived bearing
the ear of a tapir that he'd killed in a gun-trap during the night, so Kala

FIGURE 2.2. Roofing our house. Photo: R. Price.

arranged for a canoe to go upstream to bring back the kill. With Kala supervising, the animal was butchered, meat was distributed throughout
the village, and the head was dispatched by canoe to the *gaama*.

Two days later Kala took Rich fishing for several hours (first with
the canoe tied to a fallen tree, then with Rich's foot holding onto the
stem of a water plant, and finally standing on rocks in the middle of the
river—not a single bite), while Sally visited his wife Anaweli, an Aluku
Maroon who had arrived a few years earlier with Kala and her adolescent granddaughter, Maame. Rich helped him with the final French-
inspired painting (*bleu, blanc, rouge*) of his two-story house, and Kala, who
had been impressed by a building in Guyane with "La Mairie" engraved
over the door, imitated it, painting "ALMERI" on the front of his. He
also helped Rich trim the sheet of glass we'd bought in the city to provide a bit of light inside our house so we could read and write. And
he showed Rich the private area behind his house where he'd built a
gangplank up to a fallen tree, and offered him the use of it—a welcome
gift since men were normally expected to limit defecation to nighttime
squatting on river rocks. At twilight, fishing from shore, Rich caught a
large *mbooko*, which he presented to Kala, saying that his first Dangogo
fish belonged to the captain. Kala looked pleased.

As the holder of a silver-tipped staff dating from the original 1762
peace treaty, Kala took on the role of guardian of First-Time values and

FIGURE 2.3. Kala with Poi and Dosili's daughter
Akinesi dancing. Photo: R. Price.

morality. He presided over a village that had a blanket prohibition on
any outsider, black or white, staying overnight. And everyone felt vulnerable to the wishes of the gods and ancestors who regulated village
life and who were likely to be very unhappy about two whitefolks living
among them. So Kala found himself in an awkward position once his
older brother, the *gaama*, sent us to live under his immediate authority. (It was only much later that we learned how alarming our presence
was for people in Dangogo. Many believed the two of us were advance
scouts for a foreign military that would one day bring airplanes to pour
burning oil on their villages—hardly unreasonable, given that this was
during the Vietnam War. And, to our shock, Nai, with whom we had
come to be quite close, apparently feared for her life during the first
year, imagining that we might come and kill her in the night.)

Although we were quickly integrated into the kinship system
through terms of address ("brother/sister" or "brother-/sister-in-law"
with most villagers, but "husband" and "wife" or "co-wife" for the elderly), we remained very much on trial for the first couple of months. A
day hardly passed when Kala didn't give one or the other of us a speech
about taboos on our stay. Sally must go to the menstrual hut upon the

first sign of blood each month, and Rich must not discuss anything having to do with First-Time. We must never walk on the path across the river that leads by the shrine of Awoonenge, which honors the First-Time ancestors, those who shed their blood for freedom. Kala even tried (unsuccessfully) to ban us from having our own canoe on the idea that we might use it to violate this restriction. And he reiterated the *gaama*'s insistence that we not travel upriver to Baakawata, the creek where the Saamakas' ancestors had lived during the wars of liberation. During those early weeks, Kala prayed almost daily at Bongootu Pau, the oldest ancestor shrine in the village.

> Whitefolks have never come to Dangogo. The ancestors always said that whites must never come to Dangogo. No outsider [black or white] has ever slept in Dangogo. The Old-Time People cannot "see" [tolerate] whitefolks. The war we fought, it's not finished yet. . . . What in the world are we to do with these people? I have never buried a white person. If they die, how will I know how to bury them?

Kala's fears were shared. Through overheard conversations, we became aware of the "fierceness" of many older men, the deep anathema they harbored toward outsiders, and the degree to which their identity was predicated on the opposition between freedom and slavery. As these men liked to remind each other, "If we forget the deeds of our ancestors, how can we hope to avoid being returned to whitefolks' slavery?" Or "This is the greatest fear of all Maroons: that those times [slavery and the struggle for freedom] shall come again." For Saamaka men, talk about First-Time was very far from being mere rhetoric. Rather, First-Time ideology lived in their minds because it was relevant to their own life experience—it helped them make sense, on a daily basis, of the wider world in which they lived. For more than a century, every Saamaka man had spent many years of his life in coastal Suriname earning money by logging, construction work, and many other forms of low-paid wage labor. There, he would meet *bakaas*—"outsiders," white and black—who treated him in ways that fit comfortably into a First-Time ideological framework. Asipei, a dignified man in his sixties, described to Rich how, when he was a boy visiting the city with his mother's brother, an urban Afro-Surinamer derisively called him a "monkey," to which his uncle replied angrily but with pride: "Where you live, you pay to drink water, you pay to have a place to shit; but in the forest where I live, I drink the finest water in the world whenever I like, and I defecate at my leisure."

Early on, we learned that the final decision about whether we would be allowed to stay lay with an oracle called Gaantata ("Great Father"). A couple of times a week, we would be awakened shortly after dawn by Kala, stopping to give morning greetings to Nai and then to us, on his way to the shrine just behind Bongootu Pau where Gaantata held forth. (Sundays were the sacred day for Gaantata, but he could be consulted on Wednesdays as well.) Rich would pull on some clothes and make his way up the hill, taking his place on a wooden stool among the other men (sometimes four or five, sometimes twenty) to await the oracle's arrival. Two of the older men, often including Kala, would enter the shrine and emerge, balancing the sacred bundle attached to a plank of wood on their heads, one in front, one behind. Doote, Gaantata's elderly priest, would pose questions to the oracle, and it would move its two bearers forward (to say Yes) and backward (to say No).

Gaantata, we later found out, was a god that had first appeared among the neighboring Ndyuka Maroons around 1890. Quickly gaining a reputation as a finder, and punisher, of witches, its cult spread to other Maroons. Before the start of the twentieth century, Bongootu, then captain of Dangogo, made the long journey to the Ndyuka capital on the Tapanahoni River and persuaded the oracle's high priest as well as Ndyuka Gaama Oseise to give him "a piece" of the god to bring back to his village. What he brought back and established in a new shrine in Dangogo lacked the witch-finding powers (which Saamakas were afraid to unleash), but it became the central arbiter of daily life. Dangogo's Gaantata not only has his shrine, in the form of a house, but also, down a path from the village, a shaded glen and prayer-site, where flags are raised and libations poured to him. It's a magical place sheltered by an umbrella of tall trees, with the sound of the rushing rapids rippling through the foliage.

We knew that, across the river on the other side of Dangogo, there was a similar-looking oracle who served a similar purpose—Mamagadu ("Mother God"), whose origin was purely Saamaka. At the same time as Gaantata's cult was developing among the Ndyuka, a Saamaka man named Kodyi who founded a village on the border between Guyane and Brazil, where many Saamaka immigrants were working as canoemen in the gold rush, created his own carry-oracle, Mamagadu. And around

1920, he gave "a piece" of it to a Dangogo man to bring back to his village, where that man's sister's son is its priest today. Mamagadu and Gaantata are frequently consulted about the same matters, often on the same day, and tend to cooperate with each other. Two of Mamagadu's specialties are supervising pregnancies and consecrating men's axes before they undertake the dangerous task of felling trees for gardens.

During the first sessions we witnessed in front of Gaantata's shrine our own situation was mentioned briefly, but the oracle said he would deal with it on another day. As he answered questions and walked among the spectators, he would sometimes go off through the village and point at someone's house, indicating that its owner was responsible for some illness or other misfortune. We felt acutely vulnerable, always wondering whether we would be next. After ten weeks, Gaantata had still not agreed to consider our situation, despite the fact that it was frequently brought up by both Kala and Doote.

Meanwhile, our days were busy with everything from the construction of the braided palm-frond roof and dirt floor of our house, to a range of local ceremonies, including a commemorative feast in Dangogo for Boo (rhymes with "law"), the mother of Agbago, Kala, and Nai, which allowed us to learn much about ceremonial cuisine, prayer, and drumming. And we were making a series of adjustments to Saamaka life. We became used to sleeping in a hammock, quickly coming to prefer it over a bed for both sleeping and sex. Sally had mastered the technique of periodically scraping clean the area around our house with a short-handled hoe and received approving remarks by the women who watched her progress (though her attempts to adopt a proper Saamaka posture for the task, bending at the hip, were far from successful). And she did her best to adopt Saamaka standards for the cleanliness of pots and pans, which were expected to be scoured with fine wet sand until they sparkled like new (though Abatili's ten-year-old daughter, Dyam, often reprimanded for her own efforts, took pleasure in criticizing Sally's, pointing out the occasional crevice under a pot handle where she hadn't fully succeeded). At the same time, she developed a leisurely approach to riverside tasks, following the lead of village women who used their time at the landing as much for relaxed conversations and animated gossip as for dishwashing, laundry, and the preparation of fish and game. Sometimes the setting provided surprises. Akobo once killed a venomous stingray at water's edge and threw it into the

FIGURE 2.4. Women at the landing place. Photo: R. Price.

bush, for which she was soundly reprimanded by Doote, who said she should have saved the tail so he could use it in an *obia*. And another time a woman spotted a poisonous snake slithering out of the water just behind Sally, who was washing dishes, and quickly shoved it back in with a paddle.

One day, Assistant Captain Takite ("Ta-kee-tay") arrived from across the river with a freshly sewn breechcloth to present to Rich, having decided that he should undergo, even if a bit too late, the rite de passage of manhood that would normally have been performed in adolescence. And after our neighbors kept asking Sally why she always wore tops with her wrap-skirt, she swallowed enough of her self-consciousness to go bare-breasted like other women for the rest of our stay in Dangogo, covering up only for trips downriver and for the camera. And the men of our immediate neighborhood were quick to include Rich in the meals that they ate together with Kala.

Rich got formal permission from the *gaama*, and then Kala, to conduct several-hour-long interviews in our house—as long as he didn't venture into First-Time or *obia* ("magical") information. (He proposed paying his interlocutors for their time at the going local rate for day labor at the Dyuumu mission, an arrangement that was accepted without further discussion.) He was soon sitting down with various men, but most frequently with Asipei, a middle-aged, well-respected neighbor, once or twice a week, getting the backstories to events he had witnessed and exploring aspects of Saamaka life from agriculture and woodcarving to marriage and religion—things everyone in the village knew but us.

But we were also making notes on every facet of our new physical, cultural, social, and ritual environment. We each kept a small notebook handy and tried to use it with discretion, since some people were clearly uncomfortable when they saw us writing things down.[1]

From the first, we set our ethnographic goals much more expansively than we had in past fieldwork, where we had used one or two summers' stay for the investigation of a particular subject—trial marriage in the Peruvian Andes, fishing magic in Martinique, courtship in Andalusia, land tenure in Chiapas. Knowing that we would be spending a couple of years in Saamaka, we set our sights on a comprehensive embrace of all aspects of life. Our model was thoroughly Malinowskian—indeed, a copy of *Argonauts of the Western Pacific* joined a few other anthropological classics such as Evans-Pritchard's *The Nuer* on the shelf we built across the rear of our house.[2] That latter book, with its photos of lanky leopard-skin chiefs and other Nilotic men with their lengthy male members, aroused considerable interest. Kala, Abatili, and Asipei, peering at the photos, remarked to a man, "We've lost it! Look at how those Africans were hung!"

Along with the rest of the village, we had a scare when Kala was reported missing after he'd gone off hunting to provide meat for a feast in honor of Agbago's former wife Peepina, who had died a few days earlier. The next day Rich was part of the search party that found him safe and sound in the forest where he'd lost his way after killing two peccaries.

On Suriname's election day we went to Asindoopo, where we found the village in a state of commotion—there'd been a spectacular pre-dawn assassination attempt on the *gaama*. A council house built in the nineteenth century that was used to store stools, flags, uniforms, and other accoutrements of office had been burned to the ground, but the *gaama* was unharmed, since he'd been sleeping in a different house. The attempt on his life, intended to disrupt the elections, led to complex supernatural entanglements as well as intervention from the city justice system, as a policeman had been present in the village when the act was committed. The would-be assassin, a man from a nearby village who was considered mentally disturbed, claimed to have been directed in the attempted murder by the voice of Gaama Dyankuso, who died in 1932. After burning down the building, he ran into the nearby ancestor shrine, a holy site where no fighting is allowed, but at daybreak the men of the village pulled him out and gave him a thorough beating before the policeman, sent for the elections, tied his hands behind his back and took him to the city.

Over the next few weeks we paddled down to Asindoopo frequently to participate in the complex series of purificatory rituals involving the clan of the perpetrator and the *gaama*'s people. One morning when we arrived, Line showed off a thick poisonous snake he'd just killed near his house, a fer-de-lance. On another day, specialists who had traveled from the Langu region on the Gaanlio organized a large-scale ritual.

Their leader was Baala, an elderly man described in Rich's fieldnotes as "living like a hermit, hung all over with *obias*, smeared with broad bands of kaolin, the most ritually prepared man we've ever seen."[3] Baala directed two men to dig a broad four-foot-deep hole in front of the new building, near which they placed a large clay pot, a basket overflowing with leaves, roots, and barks, balls of kaolin, and some calabashes to use as scoops. He then asked women to bring buckets of water from the river and to place them near the hole. Finally, he directed the pouring of a libation of rum at the edge of the hole and the sprinkling of kaolin all around it. The vegetable ingredients were then mashed and added to the clay pot with kaolin and water.

After the Langu people were washed, Baala asked who had discovered the fire and when a woman stepped forward he had her kneel next to the hole. One of the Langu men brought a chicken, dipped it in the clay pot, and passed it twice down each side of her body. She screamed that it was scratching her, so they tied its legs and wings. A hammer was removed from the pot and touched to her forehead, right shoulder, left shoulder, and knees, and these gestures were repeated three times. The man took two bundles of branches, moistened them, and passed them over her twice from head to toe. Then he used a calabash to pour liquid from the pot over the woman's body several times, as she rubbed it all over. After that it was the turn of the people who had helped extinguish the fire—the same treatment, with chicken, hammer, branches, and liquid. Everyone who'd been in Asindoopo the day of the fire received the whole sequence. The two of us were washed twice, at an hour-long interval. By our second washing, there were two Langu men working full-time, and it took them three hours to finish. Everyone was given a taboo on bathing in the river for the rest of the day, which meant staying covered with kaolin and bits of leaves (and the attendant flies) until the next morning.

Rich had also helped over several days as the replacement for the old council house was built, roofed, and consecrated. And we witnessed the botched show trial of the would-be assassin by judges and lawyers in black robes who had flown in from the city, intended to show Saamakas how "civilized" justice worked. In the process, the *gaama* was publicly humiliated by the prosecutor, and the perpetrator, who in the end was accused only of arson, was sentenced to just one-and-a-half years in jail. Saamakas were scandalized and the trial had quite the opposite effect from that intended by the urban participants.

On one of our first days in Dangogo, Rich and a new friend, a young man named Baala, on their way upstream to gather palm fronds for the roof of our house, spied a deer swimming near the riverbank, and as Baala paddled furiously, Rich discharged his new shotgun for the first time, balancing unsteadily in the fast-moving canoe. They quickly overtook the animal, Baala gave it a blow to the neck with his machete, and they pulled it over the gunwale. Arriving back in the village, they laid out the animal on the sand by the landing place, and Baala announced that Lisati had shot a deer. Rich, who wasn't at all sure he'd hit the mark, told Baala that it was probably his machete blow that had killed it. But Baala bent over the carcass and pointed to a place just behind the eyes, insisting that he could see spots of blood where the bird-shot had penetrated. Kala supervised the butchering and distribution of portions of meat, keeping the skin for himself to make a drumhead, while Faansisonu, the headcaptain who lived just up the hill, kept the deer's nose and hoofs to make an *obia* for his hunting dog. (Like

Baala, we were given a whole hind leg, a piece of liver, and an additional chunk of meat.) Everyone who received a share of meat concluded that Rich was a useful addition to the village, and from that day on, we were fully included in the sharing of fish and game.

One day Headcaptain Faansisonu, the *gaama*'s most trusted advisor, invited us to join him across the river for a forest-spirit ceremony, with drumming, dancing, and possession. It would be held on the upper path, not far from Awoonenge, he said, but as long as we stayed at the ceremony that would pose no problem. Excited, the two of us dressed in our finest and paddled over in the canoe that we'd bought the week before. We were greeted at the shore by an assistant captain with a message from Kala: we would have to go home because our destination was too close to Awoonenge. We felt angry but turned our canoe in the other direction. Back on our own shore, several people said it was ridiculous, that we were being treated too harshly, that Kala was singling us out unfairly. But given his position and his personality, his word was final— no one, not even the *gaama*, stood ready to cross him directly.

It wasn't till ten weeks after our arrival, Rich having sat through more than two dozen oracle sessions, each several hours long, that Gaantata finally agreed to hear our case. After several cases of illness and pregnancy had been handled, Kala began to interrogate him about us. His standard "Whites have never come to Dangogo" speech was followed by an assertion that "Lisati doesn't fool anyone into thinking his gun is for game," at which point Doote chimed in that whites had even invented a kind of gun (a pistol) to use when you were too close to a person to shoot him with a hunting gun. Kala then addressed the oracle, who had listened impassively up to that point:

> Well, Father, what shall we do with them? Should they simply go back to their own country immediately? (No) Can they simply live here until they're finished with their work and then go home? (No) [murmurs from those attending] Can they live here? (No) [puzzled looks] . . . Must we perform rituals? (Yes)
>
> Kala continued for some time, attempting to discover the nature of the rites and offerings Gaantata required.
>
> Must there be a payment [offering]? (Yes) Will you tell us how much? (Yes) Lengths of cloth? (Yes) One? (No) Two? (No) Fourteen? (No) Did we go too high? (Yes) One? (No) Two? (No) Twelve? (Yes)

At this point Nai, sitting on her ancient round stool, laughed aloud and clapped her hands, exclaiming "Good god!"

With something else? (Yes) Rum? (Yes) One bottle? (No) Sixteen bottles? (No) Did we go too high? (Yes) One? (No) Two? (No) Three? (Yes)

Gaantata runs into Bongooto Pau.

Should we raise a flag there? (Yes) One? (No) Two? (No) Three? (No) Four (Yes)

When Kala then asked Gaantata exactly where the cloths should be distributed and the rum poured, he indicated the *gaama*'s ancestor shrine, the Awoonenge shrine for the First-Time ancestors, Bongootu Pau, and various shrines in Asindoopo, and specified the manner in which various classes of ancestors should be informed. Kala:

> Should I say "They didn't come to do evil, they must live, have children, and then when they're finished, they should go back?" (Yes) I'm glad you want me to say that, Father. Because if they died here, I wouldn't know what to do. I have never buried a white person.

When Gaantata had finally been returned to his shrine, Kala addressed Doote. "So, we'll do the necessary ceremonies once they get the offerings together. And we'll pray for them to live. They must learn what they need and then leave. Let them learn the language but no one must teach them 'traditional' things. And they must never, ever go to the Upper Pikilio."

At six-thirty the next morning Abatili and Rich went to Asindoopo to inform the *gaama* of Gaantata's verdict. They found him in his council house talking with people from several downstream villages and eventually moving on to the fenced-in ancestor shrine where he spent close to an hour pouring libations to former *gaamas* and other ancestors, spraying a mist of rum on the belly of a pregnant woman, raising a flag for a man about to leave for work on the coast, and taking care of a number of other matters. Once back in the council house, Rich presented a carefully prepared report on Gaantata's verdict about our situation, addressing Captain Amonipina, who supplied the formal replies as the *gaama* listened. As soon as Agbago heard the size of the payment, he expressed surprise and said to the captain that it was much too high. "Didn't people in Dangogo object?" he asked. "Who were the bearers when Gaantata specified the payment? They should raise him again and ask him to lower the amount. Let them set it at six cloths instead of twelve, and one bottle of rum. Lisati shouldn't have to spend all his money on this and have none left. People will say that Saamakas don't live well with him. After all," he said, "when I introduced zinc roofs for the first time, I only had to pay six cloths. Six cloths would be enough for the three shrines in Dangogo, two for Asindoopo, and one to keep in reserve for Gaantata." And to Abatili: "Go back to Kala and ask [Captain] Aseni and [Assistant Captain] Tando to raise the god again."

That evening at dinner, Abatili reported the *gaama*'s reaction. Kala was livid. "If the payment is only six cloths, I'll have nothing to do with it," he hissed. "We're not talking about a zinc roof. This is about someone with white skin coming to Saamaka! Their being here won't bring us any advantage at all. If they have a child they wouldn't even leave that for us here. I'm going to go to the *gaama* myself tomorrow and give him a piece of my mind!" Speaking softly, Abatili told him that wouldn't be necessary . . . that he would take care of transmitting the message.

The next day Abatili took the two of us to Asindoopo, where he offered the *gaama* a toned-down report of Kala's reaction. "All right," Agbago replied (understanding very well what his brother's rant must have been like), "If *he* won't budge, I will. After all, when someone gets a jail sentence in the city, they appeal to have it reduced. And, as I often say, there's nothing on the face of the earth that can't be fixed." Abatili, protesting that he was only a child, charged with supporting Kala's position, reminded the *gaama* gently that it wasn't Kala who set the payment . . . it was the god. "OK," said the *gaama* with determination, "but then I'm going to contribute half of it." And, indicating that the conversation was over, he called Abatili to accompany him to his storehouse to gather up the necessary items.

Kala was never told that his brother had helped with the payment. We spent a good bit of time over the following days witnessing the prayers, the raising of flags, and the libations (though not those, of course, at Awoonenge). As Kala addressed the ancestors at each site, he would remind everyone that until a generation before, whitefolks were forbidden to walk near *any* ancestor shrine and that it was only because the district commissioner had intervened with the *gaama* that this rule had been relaxed. "Whites used to believe Saamakas had tails," he said "and we don't want these people to go home and say they lived with dogs." The assistant captain who was pouring the libation as Kala spoke interrupted to say that Assistant Captain Apaasu of Dangogo "still doesn't fully understand that the whites are no longer at war with Saamakas. When he sees a government policeman, like the other day in the *gaama*'s village, he runs for his machete and needs to be forcibly restrained, just like an original runaway!"

The final day of this round of ceremonies was conducted by Gaantata himself. After Kala had addressed him with his usual diatribe about whitefolks, Gaantata indicated that we should be seated on a new cloth, part of our payment. The cloth was laid on the ground before the shrine and one of the priests encircled it with kaolin. We were then each led onto the cloth and seated on it, legs outstretched. Gaantata signaled to the priest to open the first of two bottles of Heineken in which we would be "washed." The bottle cap landed cork side down, which indicated a problem, so that bottle was set aside. The second landed "open." On Kala's request, Gaantata explained that the reason the first cap had fallen inauspiciously was that one of our promised offerings had still not been made. Kala agreed to take care of it, and the god signaled him to proceed. Under Gaantata's direction, the priest anointed us with beer, telling us to rub it all over, and sprinkled on a layer of kaolin. The priest then raised us up and led us under the sacred bundle and into the interior of the shrine, while the god was interrogated about our taboos for the rest of the day. Among other things, we were forbidden to wash until the following morning, leaving us sticky and fighting off flies and wasps for the rest of the day. As we came outside, Kala made yet another speech about how Rich had a gun that was obviously not for game.

Our original welcome in Dangogo had not exactly been with open arms. But after ten weeks, we felt that we had managed to wriggle our way through the initial test and were well on our way to an exciting adventure.

....

CHAPTER 3

A Feast for the Ancestors

During our first trip to Saamaka, Abatili brought us to Dangogo in the *gaama*'s official motor canoe (Saamakas' Air Force One), along with Gaama Agbago, one of his grown daughters, Analisi, our friend Line, and Captain Ketema of Asindoopo. Nai had invited us to participate in a feast in honor of her mother, Boo. She'd told us that they usually conducted this ceremony once a year but had been remiss for the last two, and Gaantata had told them to get on with it.

The feast Nai organized was the first of some two dozen such rites that we participated in, though a number of others were held in the village during our stay as well. We soon learned that for Saamakas, food offerings (*tuwenyanya* or *nyanyatuwe*) are a required part of certain events such as funerals, a man's successful return from wage labor on the coast, and the enstoolment of a *gaama*, captain, or assistant captain, but they are also one of the most frequently recommended rites when a problem is brought to divination. Most often made to ancestors, they are also proffered to gods and *obias*. (Ruminating once about how frequently divination prescribed food offerings to snakegods and forest spirits, the elderly Kandamma shook her head and marveled to Rich, "Isn't it amazing how similar gods are to humans?") Giving food to the ancestors means fulfilling an obligation but it is also a joyful event, fun for young and old.

A few days earlier, Abatili and Dosili had gone hunting for the feast and killed two peccaries and some birds, and the day before the feast Doote and Kala, in Nai's presence, had poured libations of water, morning and evening, in front of the captain's house, inviting the ancestors to "come share a little cassava" with them. Once we'd climbed the hill

FIGURE 3.1. Dangogo women preparing an ancestral feast.
Photo: R. Price.

to the village and greeted Nai, Rich went off with Line to visit Abatili, who'd been bitten by a poisonous snake on his way back from hunting and was still hobbling on a very sore foot. Analisi and Sally prepared some cocoa in Nai's house and brought it to the men who were listening to 45s on Abatili's wind-up phonograph—the Mighty Sparrow ("A Death of Kennedy," "Congo Man"), Ray Charles, Nat King Cole, and Jim Reeves (whose recent death in a plane crash they much lamented)—and shuffling though a deck of playing cards that featured nude pictures of Marilyn Monroe ("Look at that ass!" "What a pair of tits!"). Sally visited women in various houses where cooking for the feast was getting started, savoring the tastes of peccary, white rice, and peanut rice (a delicacy reserved for ancestral feasts) that they offered her. By midmorning, everyone had assembled in front of Nai's house, where individual bowls of these festive foods were served. When more canoes arrived carrying captains and assistant captains from downstream villages, all dressed in their best, the men joined the others at Abatili's, where they were offered shots of rum, while the women set off for the open-sided cook-house, to help with the massive pots of rice, peanut rice, fish, fowl, and game that were bubbling away on wood fires.

By late morning, some forty or fifty people have gathered in front of Kala's house, on carved stools or folding chairs imported from the city. Abatili and Line sit with us on a fallen tree off to the side. The *gaama* is seated near the captain, on the stool carved at the turn of the twentieth century by Nai's husband that is reserved exclusively for him, always covered with a cloth to mark his status. People are chatting and joking, the atmosphere relaxed.

Headcaptain Faansisonu, in a provocative mood, opens an animated debate by asking, innocently, "Is there any fish that isn't supposed to be used for an ancestral feast? I," he claims, "use them all!" Doote expresses shock.

There are lots of fish that are prohibited: piranha, eel, *pendefisi*, *deema*. And as for game, you can't use deer, iguana, anteater, porcupine, "animals of the above" [monkeys, sloths, etc.], agouti, or *kapasi* and *kamba* [two of the three kinds of armadillo Saamakas know], though turtle is OK. The hawk family—the whole bunch—is out. But toucans, bushfowls, and curassows are fine. The trumpeter is OK, except if the deceased was the medium for a forest spirit.

People interrupt Doote to ask why armadillos are prohibited while a turtle, which also has a shell, is all right. "We don't know why," he smiles. "That's just the way it is." Another man volunteers that iguana is neither a bird nor a fish nor an animal. He isn't sure what it is but to him it seems most like a bird. Others argue. Doote points out that it's important for birds not to outnumber mammals in a feast for the ancestors.

Meanwhile, women have set out several dozen enamel or ceramic bowls containing the various dishes they've prepared, in front of the house on the clean-swept earth and, standing at a massive aluminum pot, they call children, and anyone else who wishes, to "burn their hands." The kids come running in a wild melee to dip their hands quickly in a calabash of cool water and then receive a steaming double-

FIGURE 3.2. Doote. Photo: R. Price.

handful of peanut-rice to gobble up before the official ceremony begins.

Captain Ketema, sitting on a low bench with a kerchief tied around his head, then begins the ceremony. First he washes his hands in a carved calabash and pours water over a large wooden winnowing tray set on a banana leaf on the ground, inviting the ancestors to wash their hands and join the living for the feast. He then offers them water from another calabash. "You, old people, don't you see? We've prepared a bit of cassava for you today. Come join us!" He addresses Boo directly, telling her how her children think about her each day, and how they're working in the same gardens she loved. He calls on some fifty or sixty ancestors by name—those from the matrilineage but also former *gaa-mas* and other notables—speaking to them in a relaxed tone and often reminiscing about particular incidents from times they'd spent together. As he prays, he slowly loads up the winnowing tray with chunks of food, using both his hands and a calabash scoop, and carefully including a little of each delicacy. By the time the prayers are finished, stewed peccary, fish, birds, okra sauce, white rice, peanut rice, and pieces of cassava cake form a giant heap on the tray. Faansisonu takes a bit of each kind of food from the tray—a piece of cassava cake that he has dipped in broth, some white rice, peanut rice, meat, and fish—and tosses it all with his cupped hands onto the banana leaf for the ancestors to eat. Then he and Assistant Captain Tando take double handfuls of peanut rice and distribute them into the waiting hands of Nai, Agbago, Analisi, Kala, Naina, Beki, Akobo, Abatili, Dosili, and ourselves to be gobbled up, however messily—greasy and delicious, with a lot falling onto the earth. Akobo shovels food into a large dish, spilling much on the ground, and someone asks her why she's wasting food like that. Tando interrupts, "What do you mean, wasting? Isn't this a feast for the ancestors?" Portions are set aside for several distinguished kinfolk and villagers who were unable to attend because of illness, and gifts of cloth are draped over the shoulders of Nai, Agbago, Kala, and Analisi to honor their akaas ("souls"). When Ketema calls out to the children to take another turn with the food, they scream and rush for the still heavily laden tray, scrambling to grab as much as they can. Kabuesi, a woman from up the hill, pours some palm oil into the remaining rice on the tray and rubs the mixture all over Analisi's body.[1]

Repeating the opening gestures of the feast, Ketema washes his hands and offers the ancestors water from a calabash, first to wash their hands and then to rinse their mouths. He pours libations of Parbo beer followed by rum, asking Boo and the other ancestors to accept what they have been offered and to protect the villagers in the future. The tray, now largely empty but coated with grease, is overturned on the banana leaf, as adults avert their eyes and rush children from the scene, since this is the dangerous moment when the ancestors are said to be physically present. Ketema then alerts the ancestors that it's time to leave by tapping the bottom of the tray three times with a stick and then rights it on the banana leaf once more.

Tando, who has arrived from the other side of Dangogo, makes the rounds, offering each person a swallow of rum from a porcelain cup. Faansisonu follows with colored soft drinks, doling them out in a tiny goblet. Dosili turns on his tape recorder and soon the children and a few adults are dancing to seketi songs—the popular Saamaka music whose lyrics recount current village scandals and other news. Meanwhile, one of the assistant captains from downriver starts to smear peanut rice and other leftover food all over Analisi, covering her with the gooey mess from her face and breasts right down to her toes, and over several other women as well, amid laughter and joking. As they leave, some of the women who'd done the cooking load leftovers into small pots to take home. Before we leave to return to Asindoopo, we're surprised by being profusely thanked by the people of Dangogo—the Saamaka custom of thanking a visitor hadn't yet become routine for us.

The next day Abatili told us that Kala, with Nai and her granddaughters present, had poured morning libations to Boo, thanking her for coming to their feast and asking her to carry them safely through another year.

Soon after our return to Saamaka, Nai held another feast in honor of her deceased daughter Dyamati (mother of Naina, Akobo, Beki, and Abatili) in front of her house. Once again, we participated, eating our fair share of the festive dishes. While people were still sitting around at Nai's doorstep, Sally was hit with a violent bellyache and went inside to our hammock. Rich was forced to let people know, even though he suspected what their reaction was going to be. His notes record how Kala first ran back to his house to fetch a special *obia* that he was very proud of but which looked like ordinary dirt to us. Taking a bit in his mouth to show it wasn't poison, he offered a handful to Sally who felt she had no choice but to swallow some of it. (Akobo whispered to Rich that she believed it had been made in Daume, the sacred village forbidden to *bakaas*.) He told her to rub kerosene on her belly button, but then, thinking better of it, ran back to his house to get a vial of oil of wintergreen he'd bought in a Chinese store in the city and said to use that instead. Nai then came into our house and laid her hands on Sally's belly, rubbing them around and intoning, "You must get better, you must get better, your belly must get cool, it mustn't hurt anymore, it must get better." But the cure wasn't over yet. Akobo arrived with a bottle containing a vile-looking green mixture and explained that a man in the city had once given it to her for a bellyache. Rich pulled the cork, peered into the bottle, and saw a jumble of multicolored mold. The stench was overwhelming. Deciding it was time to call an end to our neighbors' generous help, he thanked them profusely and said that if Sally didn't recover quickly she would certainly try the mixture. A two-hour nap took care of the problem.

....

CHAPTER 4

Going "Outside"

Even before our arrival in Suriname, we knew that fieldwork with Saamakas was going to require Sally's periodic isolation from village activities. Both the Herskovitses and a physician named Morton Kahn had described menstrual seclusion as best they could understand it from their brief visits to Saamaka villages in the 1920s.

However, handwritten notes from our exploratory trip in 1966 make no mention of beliefs and practices involving menstruation (other than a note to buy a small hammock for Sally's time in the menstrual hut when we came back). During our four-day stay in the Kpokasa garden camp, we made a schematic map of the structures there, labeling one of them "rough storage shed" and learning only the next year that it was the shelter for women during their periods. It's as if (in retrospect), the two-and-a-half-week visit was brief enough so that our hosts could exclude the white woman from the normal system. Other outsiders were given the same pass, and in any case, we had spent very little time in Dangogo, a village where requirements in this realm were particularly iron clad.

When we returned for a longer stay, it was a different story. From our very first day, the need for rigorous compliance with the rules of seclusion was stressed and re-stressed. If we wanted to stay in Dangogo, we were told, there were two absolute requirements: adherence to the rules of menstrual seclusion, and a promise not to set foot anywhere near Awoonenge, the shrine across the river that honored the ancestors who fought the original war of liberation. Sally made a first priority of recording the essentials: Do not enter structures other than the

FIGURE 4.1. The living area at Kpokasa. The *faagi* is on the right.
Photo: R. Price.

one designated for menstruating women—in Dangogo a rudimentary structure next to the path leading into a small clearing that women and children used as a toilet. Do not cook for anyone but yourself. Do not speak to anyone who has undergone recent ritual activity. Never travel in a canoe with a man. When it's over, wash your hammock and return to normal life. Later Kala made a special trip to our house to underscore the need for compliance, and filled in more of the rules, showing us, for example, which paths, river rocks, and ritual structures were to be avoided.

And yet, ten days later, when the much-anticipated moment arrived for Sally to deal with her polluted state, she botched it. Darting into the house that Beki was letting us use until our own was finished, she grabbed two pots, a Primus burner, a box of matches, a bar of soap, a bag of rice, and a wrap-skirt, and carried them off to the dilapidated structure at the edge of the village, feeling ethnographically virtuous. A few minutes later we heard loud cries of alarm. Beki was livid: "How could you have entered my house in that condition?!" she screamed. "You should have sent a child in to take your things. Now I'll have to conduct purificatory rites to undo the contamination you've caused!" And she stalked off, shaking her head.

Over the next two years, Sally's stays in the *faagi* helped to fill in the full picture of restrictions. When she once handed a notebook to Rich, a neighbor told her that she should have placed it on the ground for him to pick up. When she took up a stool, she was handed an old board to sit on instead, and she also became accustomed to sitting on a rag on the ground. Women with babies made sure that she didn't touch them. When Rich shot a monkey, she was told not to cook a piece of it for herself since that would have meant that Kala couldn't accept his share. Her days in the *faagi*, it was explained, were the best time to have cicatrizations cut or re-opened. It would have been a bonding experience, several women getting together away from the gaze of men . . . with an older woman using a razor blade to define the decorative patterns, then staunching the blood, and rubbing irritants (special leaves and finely sifted ashes) into the wounds to create the raised keloids that Saamakas consider essential for sexual pleasure. But in the end she decided to draw the line of ethnographic immersion at bodily interventions. She often shared the hut with one or sometimes two others, but many women would take their canoe and go off to their garden camp during their periods, since they were prohibited from engaging in activities in the village, and the atmosphere in the camps felt more relaxed. Our fieldnotes occasionally mention times when the hut became especially uninviting: "Lionu was bitten on the foot her second night in the faagi, but couldn't say whether it was a rat or a bat," and "Dyeni found a snake in the faagi." One night when it was raining hard Nai told Sally that if her period was almost finished and she couldn't find anyplace to tie her hammock without getting dripped on, it would be OK for her to bathe by the side of her house, sleep in her own house, and go through the normal procedures for emergence the next morning, though it's not clear whether Kala would have allowed that if he had been told. As for the ritual of emergence, it was Nai who offered to apply the purificatory kaolin on Sally's body once she had washed at the river.

The association of sexual activity with the first night out quickly became clear, as people would greet her with the euphemistic "Big feast today!" Indeed, emergence from the *faagi* was taken as an especially propitious time for conceiving a child. The woman's husband was expected to sleep with her, rather than any of his other wives, that night, and neighbors often kept a vigilant eye out to see that that principle was respected. Once when Sally finished her time in the *faagi*, Nai called out to Rich: "Oh, husband, you'll be leaving me tonight!"

Women engaged in frequent calculations aimed at the relationship between menstruation and pregnancy. When two or three women met in the *faagi*, the absence of one of them the next month would spark discussion. Since Nai no longer maintained gardens in the upriver camp and lived within view of the hut, she was in a particularly good position to keep track, and would speculate on a woman's chance of being pregnant if she figured that more than four weeks had gone by. Her concern for us to conceive a child was often expressed as a sigh of disappointment when she saw Sally setting off for the *faagi*.

Menstrual prohibitions were both physically and socially determined. "Apron girls," roughly between the ages of ten and thirteen, whose dress consisted of a frontal apron secured by a waist tie, were exempt until they underwent the ritual in which their relatives presented them with the wrap-skirts marking their adult status and marriageability. Until then they handled periods by tucking a small piece of cloth in their vaginas. Right after being given the skirts of adulthood, they would be ritually "pushed" into the hut, usually by a senior female relative, and then come right out. During a girl's first time in the hut the rules were relatively relaxed, and women would cook for her, and when she emerged at the end, they would pat kaolin on her body to mark her return to an unpolluted state.

The fact that some men from Dangogo had wives from Christian villages downstream led to frequent friction during our stay. When Abatili took a wife named Emma from the Christian village of Botopasi, her advanced pregnancy when she arrived in Dangogo allowed her to be greeted warmly and treated as a valued member of the neighborhood. But in general, the wives who came from Christian villages were viewed with suspicion, and made to feel less than fully welcome in Dangogo.

Gaama Agbago's youngest wife Kaadi, who like Emma was from Botopasi, was the frequent target of gossip, with speculation centering on whether she was really old enough to be menopausal as she claimed. The consensus, fueled in part by feelings of solidarity with her two senior co-wives, was that she systematically cheated by hiding her periods.

The daily activities of Beki's daughter Poi, who is present on nearly every page of Sally's notes, not only show how early children take on the roles they'll need to play as adults, but also reflect women's feelings about menstrual seclusion. At five, Poi danced gracefully for snakegods and did convincing imitations of being possessed. Her secular dancing was equally accomplished. In addition to making fires to cook her mudpies, she used Nai's to boil real food (eggs, plantains, etc.), used a sharp knife to cut full bunches of rice in the garden, hulled small amounts of rice with a mortar and pestle, and knew the names of popular cloth patterns and enamel dishes. Nai could count on her for updates on the state of rice fields being worked by her mother and aunts in their upriver garden camp. Poi played expertly at mafiakata divination and would challenge her playmates to settle disagreements by going to kangaa, the ordeal that determined guilt or innocence by inserting a feather through the tongue to see if it would swell. She got Dosili's son Konfa to tie hammock pieces in a calabash tree for simulated sex. And she often played at being pregnant (tying a calabash onto her belly), giving birth (lying on the ground and grunting), and being a mother (with a gourd baby held on her back by a cloth). But not once did she pretend to be "outside" (as the Saamaka expression puts it).

During Sally's days "outside" she often found herself feeling mildly out of sorts. She considered it ethnographically instructive, but not especially fun, to be excluded from normal activities, and she did not count nights (often alone) in the rundown shelter at the edge of the forest among the most exhilarating aspects of her fieldwork. But for her, it was the feeling of being socially ostracized that grated the most. The frequent gossip about women cheating was one of many indications that her feelings were shared by Saamaka women, whose careful compliance with the restrictions reflected a sense of civic responsibility and fear of the potential consequences of their failure to do so, rather than any enjoyment of the custom.

It was interesting, then, when we returned to academic settings in the United States, to discover the promotion of a vision of "the menstrual hut" as the exhilarating site of sisterly solidarity. A feminist-driven wave of interest in menstrual seclusion was gaining steam, and the tone was distinctly celebratory. " 'There should be celebration around menstruation. If done right it could be wonderful!' . . . Some have urged us to revel in menstrual blood and make it a matter of spiritual delight by developing new rituals, 'bleed-ins.' "[1] At a session of one meeting of the American Anthropological Association devoted to the subject, we heard a panelist voice a fervent desire for the privilege to experience life in a menstrual hut at some point in her life. The consensus among interested academic women was that menstrual seclusion had been badly misunderstood by sexist male observers, that in fact it represented a much appreciated opportunity for feminist bonding, an escape from the patriarchal constraints of the rest of their lives. The energetic promotion of a positive attitude toward menstruation was being fueled by books like Germaine Greer's *The Female Eunuch* ("If you think you're emancipated, you might consider the idea of tasting your menstrual blood; if it makes you sick, you've a long way to go, baby")[2] and Annie Leclerc's *Parole de Femme* ("Watching and feeling the warm, tender blood that flows downstream from its source once each month is happiness . . . to be this vagina is bliss").[3] *Blood Magic*, a collection of anthropological essays published in 1988 on menstrual seclusion in societies around the world, emphasized variation, but leaned heavily toward the celebratory view (partly by a motivated selection of sources).[4]

As Saamakas (and other Maroons) have been adapting more and more fully to life in the towns and cities of coastal Suriname and Guyane, understandings about the power of menstrual pollution have survived intact. With no designated structures for their seclusion, women simply sleep apart from their husbands and refrain from cooking for them, but other aspects of their life are sometimes impacted as well. We've witnessed women in Cayenne with long-standing plans for a return to Saamaka reluctantly unpack their bags and cancel their travel arrangements because they've "gone outside" and thus cannot ride in a bus with men. And men exercise caution, for example avoiding restaurants and takeouts, since they have no way of knowing whether the food was prepared by a menstruating woman—one restaurant in eastern Suriname hires an all-male kitchen staff on Saturdays in order to give Maroon men a once-a-week opportunity to enjoy eating out.

....

CHAPTER 5

On Nai's Doorstep

Suffering from chronic back pain, Nai leaned on a walking stick and ventured infrequently into other areas of the village, so the front of her house served as an active reception area for the reports and discussions that people brought on births, sicknesses, deaths, interpersonal disputes, sexual scandals, marital tensions, gardening activities, trips to and from the coast, ritual activities of every sort, and more. Men would bring her meat when they returned from hunting. Women would come by to give her some okra from their garden. Others would buy an egg or two from the chickens she raised next to her house. Dreams would be analyzed for their potential warnings about how to handle particular decisions (whether to cancel travel plans, change the date for an upcoming ancestral feast, and so on). And neighbors would come by simply to chew the fat. In addition, although Nai was no longer strong enough to pound rice with mortar and pestle, we would often see her sitting, legs outstretched, on a cloth on the ground, making small contributions to food production—breaking palm nuts with a rock to make cooking oil, shelling peanuts for an upcoming feast, or salting a fish that a grandson had brought her.

On the day when Kala failed to return from a hunting foray in the forest, Nai's "doorstep" (a massive block of wood that extended the full width of the house, used as a bench) was the site of animated speculation about his fate. Nai argued that he might have been chasing a peccary until night fell, but that he would never have gotten lost. Dosili brought up a taboo, in the area where Kala would have been, against hunting on Wednesdays, the day of his disappearance. And while a

FIGURE 5.1. Left to right: Beki with Bane, Poi, Nai, and Akobo in front of Nai's house. Photo: R. Price.

number of people took pains to console Nai about her brother's fate, Akobo strode around loudly declaiming, "Kala is dead!" until people made her stop. Of course when Kala was brought back to the village the next day by the search party, Nai's front door was the site for his indignant and angrily repeated denials that he, a man of the Matyau clan, could ever lose his way in the forest.

The ups and downs of conjugal relations were frequently on the agenda, and the active sex lives of men such as Dosili and Abatili provided ample fuel for discussion. Each time a new wife was brought to the village, her appearance and behavior—even her voice, her posture, and her way of speaking—would be scrutinized carefully by Nai and others, and they showed no hesitation to voice their opinions. One day shortly after Dosili had officially split with his wife Betemuyee (much to the relief of Nai and others, who had campaigned actively against her), he complained to Nai that his wife Dyeni was giving him the silent treatment and refusing to cook for him. "I certainly won't be quick to forgive her," he said. He told Nai that because of the way she was acting he had spent four nights with his wife Ozili, and then three nights with his wife Amindi, and that he was going upriver with Amindi the next day. Before, when Dyeni was a good wife, he reminisced, he used to steal an extra night from his other wives' three-night turns to sleep more with her. But he's also having trouble with Ozili, who's angry that he's taking Amindi upriver. Doesn't she remember, he says indignantly, how well he treated her when she was a new wife? Later we heard Amindi, who had come by to see Nai, gloating about the fact that Dosili wasn't giving Dyeni any of the porcupine that he shot, and then launching into a sarcastic imitation of Betemuyee's voice.

But conjugal relations also came up for praise. We had heard frequent disapproval of Abatili's young wife Koopi, but when Abatili went through the ritual of showing Nai and her granddaughters Koopi's thank-you for the traditional marriage basket he had given her some months earlier, the tone changed. They exclaimed approvingly as they examined the embroidered cartridge sack and neckerchief, the two patchwork capes, the pair of calfbands, the dance apron, and the large bottle of palm oil. And they all agreed that her gesture confirmed her commitment (though Abatili, already losing interest in her, made a point of looking distinctly uninterested). Another day a similar scene was played out when Anaweli presented Kala with a hammock sack, a breechcloth, a patchwork cape, a bottle of palm oil, a shoulder cape, and several other items. These presentations were always shown to neighbors and relatives, and were greeted with the same excitement as the lavish gifts that men presented to wives upon their return from wage-labor trips to the coast.

Children were a constant part of the scene in front of Nai's house. Little girls would be given dishes to take to the river to wash for her, sometimes bringing her a small bucket of water on the way back. A girl's first attempt at sewing and a boy's at woodcarving often took place at her doorstep, where it would be critically evaluated and either warmly complimented or sarcastically ridiculed by the adults present. There were almost always other adults around, so babies were nursed, cuddled, and sung to; toddlers were toilet trained; disobedient children were yelled at and whipped; and little boys and girls were encouraged to dance to the rhythm of handclapping by adults who were there simply to pass the time of day. Beki's son Elima, who frequently slept at Nai's, sometimes woke up in a bloody hammock after vampire bats had bitten his toe because he refused to sleep with the Saamaka version of a mosquito net.[1] Each time, Beki would give him a sound beating and send him to the river to wash the blood out of the hammock and Nai would shake her head at how impossible he was to raise. But he was also honing skills that he'd soon need in earnest. In August 1967 our notes record that he'd built an open structure and roofed it with palm leaves—smaller than the others in the village, but big enough for Seena, Dyam, and Tumbui to make three small fires that they used to heat mud pies in little tin cans. And like other boys his age, his fishing contributed significantly to meals for Nai and others in the kin group, just as little girls took on much of the dishwashing and even some of the cooking. (When Sally was in the *faagi*, Seena, who was about eight, took responsibility for preparing Rich's meals.)

Adults liked to joke sexually with little children, sometimes pulling gently at a toddler's penis and asking him what he could do with it, and children's sex play with each other was a frequent source of amusement. We heard many stories about children listening outside houses at night to hear the sounds of lovemaking or little boys bending over to get a better view of a young girl's genitals. When Poi complained that Bane had tried to "stick his finger in my pussy," Beki and her sisters laughed and asked her to show them where her pussy was. Beki then reported finding the three-year-old Ambii in a hammock with Bane, pulling his penis toward her crotch despite his active protests. We saw two- and three-year-olds miming sex with each other, encouraged by laughing adults. And everyone assumed that Elima and his age-mates were already at it in earnest.

Because our own front door faced Nai's at a distance of ten to twelve feet, we had a front-row seat to the scene of these ongoing dramas. One day, just two weeks after our arrival, Sally heard Nai telling Beki about something Kala had reported when he came back from visiting the *gaama* the previous day. Kaadi (the *gaama*'s youngest wife, the one from a Christian village) had cooked a pot of rice, set it on the floor, and straddled it. Her co-wife Gadya caught her performing this dastardly

FIGURE 5.2. Seena (Dosili's daughter), Tumbui (Ina's adopted daughter), and Poi bringing meals to their play husbands (Adiante, Ayumbakaa, and Rich). Photo: R. Price.

act and knew that it might prove deadly to the *gaama* if he ate any of the rice. But because Gadya was afraid of Kaadi, Nai explained, she held back from giving her a beating, and simply told the *gaama* what she had witnessed. Nai and Beki speculated about whether Gadya might have made up the story out of jealousy, but in the end both decided that it was probably true. Everyone knows, they said, that Kaadi steals money from the *gaama* but he's so hopelessly in love with her that he won't tolerate any criticism.

Women's sedentary activities often took place on Nai's doorstep. One day, for example, we saw Naina planning out a narrow-strip shoulder cape for her husband. Having brought a sack of left-over trimmings from wrap-skirts she'd sewn and spread literally hundreds of them out on the earth, she was trying different combinations before settling on the final composition. Beki, Nai, and a woman named Godofutu from another part of the village were all adding their two cents on different possibilities, commenting on the juxtaposition of colors, the alternation of warp and weft, the width of the strips, and the names that had been given to particular cloth patterns—making a cape was always a cooperative aesthetic enterprise.[2] On other days several women would bring their partly finished calfbands to Nai's doorstep and work on them together while they discussed everything from their gardens and neighborhood children to local gossip and the day's ritual activities. Other times, a woman would bring five or ten freshly boiled and scraped calabash shells and, sitting on a cloth on the ground, use a piece of broken glass to carve designs into them—also benefitting from aesthetic commentary from the others present. And few days went by without someone having her hair braided in any of a dozen popular patterns there.

The older women of Dangogo, especially those who no longer had husbands, were frequent visitors at Nai's. Akonda, an amply proportioned woman in her sixties, was known for compulsive stealing, the only way she had to satisfy her addiction to snorting tobacco.[3] (She blamed this craving on the Apuku that habitually possessed her—forest spirits all love tobacco.) But Akonda also had the power of *mafiakata*, a form of divination performed by coating the hands with sacred clay and vigorously rubbing them together until they "catch," which signals a positive response to a question being posed. Nai regularly called on her to discover the cause for minor ailments such as particularly bad back pain or a toothache, each time making a small payment, often an egg, for the service. Or again, Konoi, a woman almost as old as Nai from just up the hill, would come by to share graphic descriptions of her diarrhea, check plans for upcoming ritual activity, complain that Kala's cats were eating food in her larder, or reminisce about how she and Nai used to make earthenware pots.

Nai received strong support from her grandchildren, who gave her produce from their gardens, brought buckets of water from the river, shared their hunting kills, and came by every day to see how she was. And yet, as an elderly woman without a husband, she maintained a certain frugality, cooking spoiled meat after washing out the worms and sleeping in a frayed hammock even after Agbago had given her a new one. A few days after a government anti-malaria campaign arrived in the village with bags of amodiaquine-laced salt for each household,[4] we saw her carefully washing a bag of the bright yellow salt, which she then spread out on a winnowing tray to bleach in the sun. After an hour, when the first washing didn't get the salt white, she repeated the whole process. Konoi had been the first to use the free salt in cooking, but announced that it tasted awful. Others tried it and agreed. And several people claimed that after eating food cooked with it they felt ill. So the women developed a technology to return it to its un-medicated state— and even then used it only for salting fish or game for preservation, never for cooking. (We once saw people trying to poison an anthill with it, though it failed to accomplish the task and had to be followed up with a kerosene fire.) As Nai later said to Kabuesi, "If they want to give us something, why don't they bring us something useful like kerosene or sugar?"

Sexual scandals provided abundant fodder for the exchanges on Nai's doorstep. One day we heard a half dozen people laughing hysterically about the shockingly active sex life of an "apron-girl" from the other side of the river. Nai: "She'll be the death of us all!" A neighbor: "There's only one way to handle her. . . . Give her skirts [to mark her marriageability]." Another: "No way! No man will marry her . . . she screws around too much." And Konoi, shaking her head thoughtfully, provided a philosophical assessment of the situation: "Each person has her own particular cunt." The nighttime activities of men from the matrilineage, who often took their canoes off to another village to sleep with someone else's wife, were followed with care and disapproval. Nai once expressed concern that Dosili's younger brother would have special difficulty finding a wife since Dosili, she said, had already slept with virtually every woman on the upper river. And the beatings that Abatili occasionally received at the hands of men from a clandestine lover's matrilineage were sometimes brutal enough to require weeks of recuperation in the care of Nai and her granddaughters.

Many of the conversations on Nai's doorstep turned on the specifics of pregnancies and births, a matter of heightened interest in this society in which each girl is strongly encouraged, from an early age, to contribute babies to her matrilineage. One focused on a woman from the other side of the river who was accused of washing in leaves designed to promote her pregnancy if the baby was a girl, but to abort it if it was a boy. And Dyeni, one of Dosili's wives, came up for complex discussion almost every week for the full nine months of an unusually problem-ridden pregnancy, with countless forms of divination seeking the causes of the problems, and prayers, rituals, and herbal baths being prescribed to deal with them. Although Nai was now too old to supervise the births themselves, her relationship with the rivergod, Tone ("Tow-nay"), meant that she was the ultimate authority in the matter for the whole Pikilio, and she was consulted on virtually every pregnancy in the immediate region.

One day Gaduansu came to report that his wife Simoni had gone into labor at night while they were in her upriver garden camp. Rushing to get back to the village, he carried her on his back until she told him to set her down, and very soon, in the bushes at a place called Tyamandeku, she'd given birth to a baby girl. The little group that had gathered at Nai's doorstep express satisfaction, as Nai claps her hands and does a little dance of joy. Gaduansu mentions that while they were upriver he had shot at some peccaries but missed. Konoi offers that if he hadn't missed they could have named the baby Pingo-Muyee (Peccary-Woman), but Kala declares that she should be called Tyamandeku-Muyee. Plans for birth-related activities, including special prayers at the ancestor shrine and a hunting expedition to provide meat for the new mother, begin to be organized immediately.

Once in a long while Nai would pick up her walking stick and make the rounds of the village, often with Sally. Not only was it a good way of keeping up with village happenings, but visits were seen as a generous gesture of friendship, and always thanked. Nai's duties, as she conceptualized them, included both instructing us about our behavior (for example, coaching Sally on the rituals of emergence from the menstrual hut and teaching her the importance of sweeping the "dirt"—physical, but more importantly spiritual—from the house and the doorstep each morning), and maintaining the village's reputation by protecting us from misbehaving villagers.[5] Ansebuka, an elderly woman remembered by senior men as having once been a striking beauty, often stopped by at Nai's house to discuss village happenings, but she was second only to Akonda in her quest for tobacco, and Nai showed no hesitation to reprimand her about her behavior. One day when she came to our house to beg, Nai saw her and called out: "What kind of money did you bring them?" Ansebuka paid no attention and stepped boldly into our house where we were working on notes. Nai: "Turn around and look at me when I talk to you! Did you bring money to buy the tobacco?" Ansebuka: "No, I didn't. But last week I brought them a coconut!" Nai: "Well, was that because they came to your house and begged you for a coconut? And didn't I hear that they gave you some tobacco just last week?" When Ansebuka turned around, Nai softened her tone and called her to come sit down. "After all," she said, "let's not kill each other over a silly thing like tobacco."

Nai had no hesitation to call on us when she felt we could provide support. For example, knowing that Rich was a friend and occasional hunting partner of her grandson Abatili, she once asked him to help persuade Abatili not to break up with his young wife Koopi, with whom he was having a serious falling-out. And she occasionally assumed the role of expert when others had esoteric questions about us. She sometimes explained to visitors to the village that what we were doing, when we were sitting quietly in our house, was "looking at paper." And when one woman expressed perplexity about the fact that Sally's breasts had not yet "fallen to her chest" even though she was well past adolescence, Nai wisely counseled patience: "Believe me, give them some time and I assure you that they will."

Some of the incidents that enlivened the space in front of Nai's house involved us directly. One happened in June 1967 when a fishbone got stuck in Sally's throat. We offer a near word-for-word transcription of Rich's notes on the aftermath.

Nai recommends eating some dry cassava cake. Or, she says, Sally should put a plate on her head. She then appears with a large flat stone, very heavy, on which she's made some marks with kaolin, tells Sally to set it on her head, walk on the path until she can see the river, and then return, keeping the stone balanced on her head. Sally does what she's told, but the bone hasn't budged. [At this point several neighbors have come to see what's up and are discussing possible solutions to the problem.] Nai then sends Bodi [an "apron girl"] to get the leaves of a bembe plant so she can use it for a cure. But no one can find any bembe in Dangogo. The news has now reached Ansebuka's neighborhood and she arrives bearing a handful of wet leaves. She tells Sally to throw back her head and squeeze the liquid into her throat, re-moistening the leaves at intervals of a few minutes and squeezing them into her throat until the bone disappears. Bystanders begin suggesting that she should stick her hand into her throat to pull the bone out, but that just produces vomiting. Ansebuka warns Sally that doing that will make her throat "split in two," and follows with a lecture on how we should've prepared the fish so the bones would be too small to get stuck. More people arrive and assure us that the bone will eventually come out. And then . . . down goes the bone. Ansebuka is in ecstasy. Nai pleads with her to share the name of the leaves she used, but Ansebuka refuses, saying that her deceased husband had taught her the *obia*. [Assistant Captain] Kasindo takes the leaves and sniffs at them but can't identify them. Ansebuka sits on the doorstep and beams broadly, bursting with pride. We pay her with tobacco, and after it's over, Nai runs over to Sally to conduct a *madyomina* exchange (the ritual of payment).

Sally's notes record that Nai later expressed confidence she'd be able to convince Ansebuka to trade one of her own *obia* secrets for Ansebuka's fishbone cure. Kasindo also wants it. And four days later Ansebuka is still coming by, asking how Sally is and whether we aren't impressed by her cure.

Not surprisingly, Sally lacked experience in a number of the skills required for a fully Saamaka lifestyle—she'd never prepared monkey stew or skinned a sloth before coming to Saamaka and it took several weeks of practice before she was comfortable balancing a heavy bucket of water on her head, carrying it up the steep path from the river several times a day. Nai was often the person who served as her coach in such matters. Under Nai's watchful eye, she became adept at mounding a bowl of rice into a perfectly smooth hemisphere before taking it to the men's meal and learned the subtleties of proper behavior during her periods.

We both felt real affection for Nai, and she clearly cared about us too. At the very end of our time in Saamaka she even showed Sally her private "wrestling belt"—a supremely intimate accessory originally composed of six strands of colored beads, held flat by beaded cross-strands, which she had reduced to four strands after her husband died—and let her make a sketch of it on the condition that she swear not to let Rich see it. We'd been told how such a belt, designed for tactile pleasure during love-making, would be presented to each girl about to be married for the first time by the women of her matrilineage, and how it would sometimes be given to a husband to keep with him during his time on the coast as a sign of fidelity. And when one was being laid in the coffin of an elderly woman along with her other belongings, we'd seen the way everyone made a point of averting their eyes. Sally took Nai's offer as a touching gesture of trust.[6]

But she was also firm about maintaining certain realms of Saamaka knowledge secret. In April of our second year in Dangogo, Sally heard Takite chatting with Nai on her doorstep. At one point he declared, *Nouna!* And then he repeated it even more emphatically: *Nouna!* Nai nodded knowingly: "I once said that to Kala and he agreed." Takite then said triumphantly: "First-Time hasn't been lost! *Nouna* . . . never forget it!" and Nai countered, "It's always with me." The next time Rich interviewed Asipei, he asked him about *Nouna* and was told the basic plot of the folktale that encapsulates this key element of Saamaka ideology. (In short, a hunter skilled at killing mythical animals called "Bush Cows" is almost stymied by a beautiful woman—a Bush Cow in disguise sent to learn his secret—but his mother warns him just as he's about to reveal it to say *Nouna*, a meaningless word, instead of its real name, thus saving the day.)[7]

A few weeks later, during a visit to Dangogo, Agbago came to visit Nai and sat down at her doorstep on the special carved stool reserved for his use. He was of course aware that Asipei, who was there, had been serving as a teacher for Rich, and he addressed him about how to handle that role. "I've heard about six Surinamers who've gone to the Queen's country to learn things there. Well, it's just like these people. They've come here to learn our ways. I want Dangogo to treat them well, share meat with them, and teach them everything—everything, that is, except *Nouna*."

In 1968, when we left Saamaka to return to the United States, Nai offered us a patchwork hammock sheet that she had been given decades earlier by her sister-in-law, Agbago's wife Apumba, and reiterated her promise to serve, after her death, as a *neseki* (spiritual genitor) for the child she was so eager for us to have.[8]

CHAPTER 6

....

Under Kala's House

For the first seven months of our 1967 stay—until Kala left for Guyane—Rich, like other men of the neighborhood, ate most of his meals (morning, mid-day, and evening) with the captain in the open space under his two-story house. Sally and other wives provided the food and dishes, each bringing a tray with carefully mounded rice, a side dish of meat, fish, or okra sauce, a hand-washing calabash, and a small, shiny teakettle of cool water. Men would serve themselves a bit of food from each woman's dish, though the first few times they left Sally's contributions untouched and only gradually, over the early weeks, began including what she'd cooked in the full rotation. The evening meal was generally a time of relaxation, though village business sometimes intervened—Nai stopping by to remind Kala that he should pour a libation the next morning at Bongootu Pau to alert the ancestors of an upcoming feast in their honor, a nephew seeking Kala's advice about acceding to the demands of a woman he was clandestinely sleeping with for a second gift of a hammock (Kala said no), and other diverse requests. It was often a privileged moment—sometimes stretching on for an hour or two—for men to exchange talk about women and sex. On a typical night, according to Rich's fieldnotes, it went something like this:

Dosili (who worked with Abatili as an official boatman for the *gaama*) told about how he interrupted a recent minibus ride from Paramaribo, where he had been in the hospital for a hernia operation, to Afobaka, to catch the canoe for the trip upriver. "There's this plump girl, a real looker, who gets off at my stop. Asks me to walk with her along the path to the village. We get to the creek and she reaches into her bag and hands me a towel. Would I hold it for her while she bathes? I'm just standing there watching while she pulls off her blouse, then her skirt, then her slip, and then her underpants. Stark naked. The cicatrizations on her ass sparkle in the sunlight and she very slowly washes all over." "Wooh! That woman is killing you," says Kala. "She slowly walks over to the side of the stream, squats, and shits. [He imitates the sound.] Then she pisses [more sound effects]. She comes back, takes the towel and dries off, slowly puts back on each piece of clothing, and says, 'Let's go.'" "She's really killing you now," laughs Kala. "When we get to the village she points and says, 'This is my house and I sleep alone.' I give her a smile and say 'See you around.'" (Dosili's operation barred him from having sex for several weeks.)

Kala said this reminded him of a time when a woman from across the river asked him if he would take her upriver to her garden camp the next day.

> We went in separate canoes and met at the mouth of Mama Creek. We each tied up our canoe and took the path together. After a while, she said I walked too fast and she was hot. "Would you mind if we stopped for a minute for me to cool off in the creek?" I stood there and watched as she slowly took off each of her skirts. After she'd washed and dressed again, we walked on without a word. We got to the garden camp, went into a house, and I sat down on a stool and just stared at her for a long while. Finally, I just couldn't stand it anymore and took her right there.

Dosili (who had three wives at the time, including one new one) followed quickly with a report about the previous evening. He'd borrowed the *gaama*'s canoe to go far up the Gaanlio to Bundyitapa for an all-night play. He noticed a girl he'd never seen who was staring at him from the crowd. When he got up from where he was sitting, he saw her distinctly lick her lips (he demonstrates). So he sat back down. When he got up again, she batted her eyelashes at him (he again mimes her action). Later, during the drumming and dancing, another girl came to him with the message that the first girl wanted him. He followed her to the other girl's house and spent the better part of the night in her hammock.

Often enough, talk about sex turned to talk about hunting, the second most favored activity of men. It rarely recounted the actual chase, focusing more on the mysteries of the forest. One time Dosili told how he went hunting that morning up Tio Creek and wandered into the Balon Creek basin. "Boom, boom, boom," he heard, just like a drum. He knew it was only water dripping into a hole but he was always scared when he came near that place. And then he arrived at the rapids in the creek where a caiman was perched on top of a boulder, just staring at him. It really scared him. "Who wouldn't be scared?" Kala asked. "That's one *baad* stretch of forest!"

This story reminds the captain of a time when he was in the forest in the territory of the Matawai Maroons. He happened upon a clearing a good fifty yards wide, as if leaf-cutting ants had swept through the place. Abatili interjects that if it had been him, he'd have called out "Hello! Is anyone around?" After turning round and round trying to find a path out, Kala finally succeeded and got to a Matawai village, where he went to sleep. Soon, a beautiful woman came to his hammock saying she'd seen him that day when he'd visited her village. The forest-spirit woman! She said that if only she were human, she'd take him back to her village as her husband because he's the finest looking man she's ever seen, his teeth are the whitest, his shape the most attractive. But she couldn't make love with him because she wasn't human. At dawn, she got out of the hammock and left. When he awoke, he could still feel where she'd rubbed up against his chest.

Kala tells Dosili and Abatili to talk with Fosumii, a man his age, about the forest near Tio Creek, where he cuts gardens for his wife. That area has amazing boulders and places where you must not speak—last year a man took his son to it and went too close to a certain boulder. The son died before the week was out. A forest spirit lives there who's a gifted thief. If you leave a flashlight in the garden camp, you'll be lucky to find it half a mile away the next day in the forest. Or maybe you'll never see it again.

"And once, on the Oyapock," Kala goes on, "a man got lost hunting but finally came upon a village. An old man told him, 'Don't be afraid, I'm a living person. You can sleep in this house over here. But first, come have something to eat.' After dinner, the man told him to go to the house and said he'd soon send an apron-girl to spend the night with him. When she knocked and he beckoned her to his hammock she said no, she'd rather sleep in her own. He pleaded with her. She was so beautiful! But she said she couldn't because in her land, a man could have only one wife, and if he took her, he could never take another woman. The man wanted her so much that he stayed in that place day after day. Every night, the same thing. She still didn't let him have her. Finally, he swore faithfulness forever, and she joined him in his hammock. After some months, he said he wanted to make a quick visit to his old village. He promised his new wife to be back in three days. When he came to his village, what a celebration! They fired salutes, held a dance . . . and after washing in the river he came ashore to sleep with his former wife. Soon he forgot all about his promise to return. And then one day, when he was urinating at the edge of the forest, his forest-spirit wife appeared before him and then quickly vanished. The next day all the things his wife had decorated her house with came crashing to the ground. Not long after, he was struck with leprosy and soon he died. Apuku women can be just as jealous of their co-wives as humans!"

Kala ended the evening session by boasting that there was nothing he didn't know about women. "I've had nine wives since I last came back from working on the coast, including an Amerindian. I gotta tell you, all women are the same."

Often enough, other mysteries were discussed. One evening Assistant Captain Tando showed up from across the river, asking us if we knew anything about an obsolete five-franc French banknote that he'd found floating in his drinking water calabash while he was upriver that morning. Kala almost choked, throwing down his spoon and saying I should go on eating but that he was done. (Rich later learned that he had a taboo about hearing anything related to witchcraft while he was eating.)[1] Tando said if he couldn't clear this up in Dangogo, he'd seek help in Bendiwata (where the most powerful of all Saamaka oracles resides). Tando continued his story. He'd gone upriver to cut palm fronds for his roof. When he returned to his canoe to eat, he saw the bill, with little holes burned in it, floating in his calabash. The next day, he'd ask around in Asindoopo. And if no one confessed, he'd tell the gaama. He added that the day before, his gun had fallen off its peg in his house and the hammer was knocked off. Next, they'll try to kill him!

The following morning Rich was in Asindoopo, where the gaama's new council house was being roofed and a crowd was standing around watching. Tando appeared carrying a pot with the mysterious banknote on top. At first, no one had the courage to handle it. Finally, one of the captains, who had spent much of his life in Guyane, picked it up and declared it to be obsolete, no longer acceptable even at a bank in Cayenne. No one could see a date on it—Rich saw only a reference to a law of 1901.

Over the next few days, Tando's banknote was often discussed, as people tried to figure out if it was a sign of witchcraft or perhaps simply that someone had left it as a mark to say that they were going upriver. He later placed it, under a bottle of Heineken, on a plank in Gaantata's house for safekeeping. But when the oracle was asked about it, there was no reply. A few weeks later, Tando had ninety-three guilders stolen from his sack while buying cloths in the city. Some days after that, Gaantata was asked about Tando's problems. Has he done something wrong? Offended a god? Does someone want his wife? All got No for an answer. Is someone trying to kill him? Yes. Someone from within the Pikilio? Yes. He had better take precautions![2]

Canoe-making was another frequent topic of conversation. All men carved a multitude of wooden objects, elaborately decorating them as presents for their wives (and sometimes kinswomen)—combs, stools, paddles, winnowing trays, mortars and pestles, peanut-grinding boards, calfband forms, food stirrers, architectural decorations, and more. But besides constructing attractive houses, building handsome canoes was what made men most proud. From finding an appropriate tree in the forest, felling it, dragging it with the help of others to the river, floating it to the landing place, hollowing it out with precision, and opening it with fire in a delicate operation, to finally carving the prow and stern, the seats, and other parts with sinuous decorations—all this was something men loved to reminisce about. They made canoes for each new wife and every three or four years for their other wives. The exact length of a canoe, where it came from in the forest, whom it was made for, its life history (for example, how one got loose from the landing place during a night's high water and was found three days later far downstream)—Kala and the younger men who ate with him recounted and discussed their canoe-building experiences with enthusiasm.

When a man returned from a stint of wage labor at the French missile-base in Kourou, Guyane—where nearly half of the men from the Pikilio were off working during our stay—dinner conversation turned to the details of wages offered and prices paid for the myriad goods they'd brought back to Dangogo and which they'd use as gifts to wives, as payments for rituals, and for daily living until their next trip several years away. Early in our stay, Dosili's brother Amombebuka came home from Guyane to a villagewide welcome. Beki hugged him, saying she remembered that he had left when the palepu palm nuts were last ripe, and now they were coming ripe again—a full year had passed. Boys from throughout Dangogo carried loads from the freight canoe to Dosili's house and women gathered to examine the haul. Kala and Faansisonu opened a bottle of Amombebuka's rum, said a brief prayer of thanks, and offered a drink to everyone standing around. Rich scribbled down a partial list—a marriage basket bought at an Amerindian village on the way back (since he was planning to take his first wife); seven crates of French soap; a sewing machine; six colorful enamel buckets; a large crate with various shiny aluminum pots; two crates of Martiniquan rum; a large oil drum of kerosene (used for women's tin lamps and men's lanterns); two large sacks each of salt and sugar; a tape recorder; batteries; an umbrella; a machete; plastic jewelry; spools of thread; a large box of soap powder; two folding chairs; some rope; several hammocks; boxes of shotgun cartridges; a wrist watch; four metal trunks loaded with lengths of cloth; a crate of Rountree's cocoa; a pack of Nu-Vu playing cards; bread; and several dozen letters and tapes from men he'd worked with to deliver to their wives and kin in various villages. In the evening at Kala's, he described how he'd found work for seven of his eleven months away—first laying cement for houses at the missile base, later cutting a path through the forest for a pipeline. He said he'd cleared the equivalent of $850. And then there was talk of prices—for each item, from soap to tape recorder to kerosene, including the fact that instead of the 12-franc umbrella he'd bought he really wanted a 17.50-franc one that folded up but he'd run out of money by that time.

Sometimes Kala led extended boasting sessions. He'd been thinking a lot about outboards lately, since Headcaptain Faansisonu had a government-issued one and he didn't. "There's no one who knows more about motors than I do," he claimed (quite ludicrously). "The other day I was riding in a flotilla with the *gaama* up the Gaanlio. I told him that the third motor to the left of us would soon be in trouble and he just laughed. Sure enough, five minutes later it caught fire and exploded and everyone in the canoe had to jump in the river. I could tell by the sound it was making." Abatili followed with three stories about how various people doubted his competence in repairing a motor but he ended up being right. And Kala once proudly asserted, "I may be old but I don't pee more than three times in twenty-four hours—and never at night. Most men my age go every little while, drip, drip, drip."

One night, Kala boasted to Rich that his captain's staff was the oldest—and most powerful—on the river, and that he has not one but two golden breastplates adorned with coats of arms, while most captains have none.[3] District Commissioner Michels, he says, is concerned that he does so much more work than Faansisonu even though Faansisonu, as headcaptain, gets a higher government stipend and an outboard motor. It's true that Agbago loves Faansisonu more than him, he says, but everyone knows that he should be considered the higher of the two. Nai, on being told of Kala's boast, later remarked, "There's not a single captain who's not jealous of Faansisonu, but when it comes to Kala, forget about it—it's over the top!"

CHAPTER 7

....

The Sika

We often went weeks at a time feeling that our relations with neighbors couldn't be better. But there were also days when latent hostilities broke through to the surface. One particularly painful incident occurred halfway through our first year in the field, a time when we thought that our friendships were well established.

Rich is sitting around with Kala on stools as Abatili and his nephew Amombebuka squeeze sugarcane juice from Dangogo's only remaining press. (Beer had come into general use for libations, but certain ceremonies still required *apenkusu*, fermented cane juice.)

They're laughing about something called a *sika*, and ask what Americans call it. Rich says he can't say because he's never heard that word. Kala looks incredulous. "Lisati, those people you pay, what is it they teach you? They certainly don't teach you our language. You pay them, but look at the result—you don't even know what a *sika* is!"

There follows a discussion about how it's not language Rich is asking people about. "He asks about the names of rapids in the rivers and the names of clans," says Abatili. Kala: "He asks about the relationship of Dangogo and [the village of] Akisiamau in olden times." Abatili: "What he's really trying to learn is First-Time history." Kala laughs derisively, addressing Rich, "They won't take you far. They're just tricking you. . . . Didn't you come here to learn the language? Then you have to point to an object [indicating a bottle lying on the ground] and ask what it's called. 'Bottle.' 'What kind? 'Liter bottle.' But instead you ask how many bottles Dangogo has, how many Akisiamau has!"

Feeling vexed at the hostile tone (as well as the uncanny accuracy of Kala's understandings of ethnographic inquiry) Rich replies a bit testily. "Maybe I don't *want* just to learn language . . ." Kala to Abatili: "Did you hear that? He says he wants to learn 'things.' Well, then, all he'll end up with is lies. People will take his money but teach him nothing. After all, when you go to school, don't you have to learn A, B, C before going on to anything else? If you want to learn, you have to start with every word in the language. I may not be able to read and write but I have more things in my head than all of Lisati's books put together." Rich is by now quite exasperated. "Actually, I'm rather pleased with my progress so far. I understand perfectly well that there's a lot to learn, and it'd be ridiculous to think I could know everything after just six months."

Kala explodes: "Enough! Precisely! Now you've said it! Nothing more to say. You're exactly right. You're learning perfectly!" A long silence, as Kala stares at Abatili and Amombebuka, looking like a volcano about to blow. Then he launches into a story about a man he once worked for in Paramaribo who tried to cheat him out of money, thinking he couldn't count. "City people write things down, but I can count to ten as well as anyone. They can't fool me. They think we're animals. We may not go to school but we have the same heart that they do."

That evening after dinner, Kala formally addressed Dosili in the presence of Abatili, Amombebuka, and another kinsman, announcing that he was going to explain something about insults and the thing called *bakaa* (outsiders).

We all know that white-skin people don't like black-skin people. Only two kinds of people had slaves—Americans and Dutch. They came to Africa with big ships. But they never fought to get the slaves; all they did was cheat them. Don't fool yourselves into thinking blacks would enslave blacks! The whites just came the way Lisati has come to us. They sat down and ate with them, gave them drink, invited them to dance, and then carried them off to the ships. Not one captain on the whole river would host Lisati. I'm the only one. Botopasi! Tutubuka! Abenasitonu! Dyuumu! [Christian villages]— those are places where he should be welcome, *bakaa* with *bakaa*. But a Saamaka village: Never! All the other captains say to me, "Kala? Why in the world are you hosting a *bakaa* in Dangogo?" But Gaama

Agbago has sent him to me! "If he's got to live somewhere, let's keep him in our own family. That way we'll be able to keep an eye on him."

Kala has only just gotten started. Rich is sufficiently upset so that the next morning, he pours the whole diatribe into his fieldnotes, as far as he can remember the details:

The *gaama* can't tell me what to do. I'm the one who runs Dangogo. No one here finds the slightest benefit from Lisati's presence. I charge him two guilders for chickens that cost six in the city, but he still buys his chickens from someone else. When a *bakaa* sleeps over in Asindoopo, the *gaama* charges him a guilder but Lisati stays here for free. Of all the captains on the river, I'm the one who's responsible for Lisati if he gets sick and I'm the one who will have to bury him if he dies. We in the Matyau clan know about the people called *bakaa*. We the people of today may have forgotten a bit of what our ancestors knew, but we haven't forgotten much. The things *bakaas* did to us during slavery, those we'll never forget.[1]

Look, Lisati has done two very bad things since he came. If he does a third, we'll throw him out. One day he was fishing at the river and Maame called him over to take a piece of meat she found floating in the river to use as bait for piranhas. He took it and returned to fishing. But then he threw it back to Maame. If Anaweli hadn't been bending over at that very moment to scrub a pot, it would have hit her! And then today, Lisati insulted us. He insulted us deeply. I've never heard such a terrible insult! When I told him that the people who are teaching him weren't doing their job because they hadn't taught him what a *sika* is, he told me that he was learning exactly what he wished and that I should mind my own business. Who sends him the people who work for him? Me! Who tells them what to teach him and what not to? Me! If Lisati asks about slavery-time things I won't let them say a word. If we told him all the things *bakaas* did to us then . . . Do you know why *bakaas* ask us about those things? It's so they'll know how to put us back into slavery. If anyone discloses those things to a *bakaa* it would kill me on the spot. The ancestors do not want it. Those are not things for whitefolks' ears.

If Lisati wants to learn Saamaka language, he must learn the Saamaka way of life. Dosili, you must sit down with Lisati and teach him about the thing Saamakas call "insults." Abatili, you should do the same. Make sure he never insults us again. Because if he does, he'll be forced to leave. OK. My speech is finished.

Dosili asks Rich, rhetorically, if he's "heard."

> Yes, I've heard. And I'd like to respond. The captain is right, what he says is true. Everyone here has been most gracious to us. For all they know, I came to learn about them, go back to my country, and bring back soldiers and airplanes to kill them all. They can only judge us by what they see. By now, they should know our hearts. It's very hard to learn another way of life. A little child learns for so many years. People scold him, whip him until he learns to live properly. You look at me and see a man but in some ways I'm like a little child—I'm still learning how to live here and it's not always easy, I can't do it all in one day.

He explains that if Dosili came to the United States and teased an older woman the way he teases Nai, people would be shocked at his lack of respect. "The Maame 'insult' was unintentional—I thought she was teasing me and I tried to tease her back. Yes, I am responsible for two 'insults.' And for these, I beg forgiveness. I'll do my best to live better from now on."

Kala answers formally that there's nothing more to say, adding that he's already forgiven Rich. We all go home, but before getting into the hammock, Rich looks up *sika* in the mimeographed Donicie and Voorhoeve Saamakatongo-Dutch *woordenschat*. It's a flea.[2]

....

CHAPTER 8

What Month Is It?

Perhaps being "fast" was simply in Kala's DNA. But fast about what month it is?

Saamakas, like other people who use a lunar calendar, have a practical problem—lunar months last roughly 29½ days, so that twelve "moons" last 354 days, rather than the 365¼ that it takes the earth to circle the sun. So over time, to keep the calendar synched with the seasons, adjustments are required. Ancient Jews, following Exodus 12:1–2, had their Council of Judges identify and sanctify each new moon as it appeared. Saamakas instead determine its identity, in large part, by argument and negotiation.[1]

At dinner one night, when we were well into Pikideeweiliba (the fourth named month of the year), Kala declared that it was now Sebitaaliba (the fifth). A couple of days later, when a number of men were helping to roof the *gaama*'s new council house, there was a lively argument, with Kala boasting loudly, "I've been a captain for seventeen years and never once has the district commissioner said I was wrong about what month my paycheck should come." Most of the participants were persuaded by Kala that it was, indeed, Sebitaaliba. Later in the day, alone with the *gaama*, Rich asked him what month it was, and he said that the new moon we would see in a few days would be Sebitaaliba. (When Rich mentioned this to Kala, he muttered, "Even the *gaama* can get confused.")

Sebitaaliba is known for bringing the year's heaviest rainfall. It also carries a blanket prohibition on making important *obias*, since its rain is said to be evil, so no one should use the leaves that have received its moisture. Indeed, a week after the new moon, Asipei, who'd said a couple of days earlier that it was now Hondimaliba (the sixth moon), corrected himself, saying that the heavy rainfall of the past few days had changed his mind—it must be Sebitaaliba. Toward the end of that moon, however, Dangogo faced a crisis. Gaantata had found that an Apuku was sickening many people in the village and a major ceremony had to be performed as soon as possible to appease it. After much discussion about how they couldn't do this during Sebitaaliba, Nai and other elders declared, "Well, it must now be Hondimaliba!" And Kala, at dinner, announced firmly, "The cassava you see in the sky [a cassava cake is large, round, and white] is Hondimaliba."

Then, when Hondimaliba was nearly full, Beki proclaimed that it was Baimatuliba (the seventh moon), time for men to start getting ready to clear new gardens for their wives and sisters. And a couple of days later, Nai said to Konoi, squinting up at the sun that was trying to break through the early morning fog, "It looks like a dry season morning but the rains aren't quite through yet. Once this moon is 'dead,' it'll be Tanvuuwataliba [the eighth moon] and the better sort of men will start clearing gardens. It's almost time for the menfolk to start sharpening their machetes!" Both women were engaged in wishful thinking—speeding up the succession of moons to hasten the day when women could get back to the garden work that they so loved.

In the middle of Tanvuuwataliba (the eighth moon), we heard Kala insisting to Nai that it was now Wayamakaliba (the ninth). Then toward the end of Wayamakaliba, Doote, the elderly priest of Gaantata, told Nai that the moon she saw "dying" up there was Wayamakaliba and the new moon would be Tenimu. "Perhaps," she murmured, "perhaps. "Since I've stopped going to Kpokasa and don't do garden work anymore, I really can't keep track of the months. But I have a strong feeling that the months are going by too quickly." Doote: "That's because you listen too much to Kala! He thinks he knows what month it is, but he's always 'fast.'" The two of them reminisce about how Nai's mother's brother, Captain Bityenfou, used to know the months without fail. "He would always tell us when to plant, when the rains would come." Pomala, a young man from across the river, jokes that if Kala weren't leaving very soon to deliver Maame back to her Aluku family, we might be startled any day now to hear gunshots from near his house, to celebrate New Year's. "In a year like this, when Kala doesn't cut a new garden, he's always way too fast."

Each year, once Saamakas hear that it's almost time for the annual Suriname national holidays of Christmas (which has always been considered a dangerous, evil day by non-Christian Saamakas) and New Year's (which they celebrate like their city brethren), they, in effect, reset their clocks. At New Year's they look to the sky to decide whether they should call the current moon Yailiba (New Year's moon). (Our observations suggest that if on January 1 the moon is anywhere in its first three quarters, they'll call it Yailiba. If it's waning and in its final quarter, they'll call the next moon Yailiba.)[2] So, each New Year's the annual cycle is reset, and by the fourth month or so, the arguments about what month it is begin again.

Knowing what month it is matters to Saamakas. Success in farming, hunting, fishing, and certain rituals depends on it. Each named month is associated with particular features of climate, the visibility of certain constellations, the cutting of gardens, the ripening of particular crops, the behavior of certain animals, birds, and fish (often tied to the ripening of their favorite foods), and much else. Some examples at random: The Pleiades, which Saamakas call Sebitaa, dips below the horizon as the month called Sebitaaliba ends. (The black slugs known as Sebitaa, apparently named after the month, also come out in quantity at that time.) Hondima, the constellation comprised of the three stars in Orion's belt (for Saamakas: the hunter, his dog, and his game) disappears below the horizon during the month named for it. Bakayailiba is sometimes called Kapasimiiliba ("Armadillo baby month") because, during that month, nine-banded armadillo mothers walk along the forest floor with their young following in single-file. Wayamakaliba ("Iguana month") comes during the time when iguanas lay their eggs, which are much appreciated by Saamakas. Between Gaanliba and Sebitaaliba, when yellow mombin fruits ripen and drop to the forest floor, tapirs get fat on them so it's the season for setting gun-traps for these prized catches; by the final two months of the year, tapirs are skinny and their flesh black and tasteless. But the main correlation between the Saamaka months and the natural world is climate, rain, and sun.

For Saamakas, the calendar begins with New Year's, toward the end of the short rainy season, a slow period in the agricultural year, though toward its end women begin the hard work of preparing their rice gardens for planting with a short-handled hoe. This is followed by the

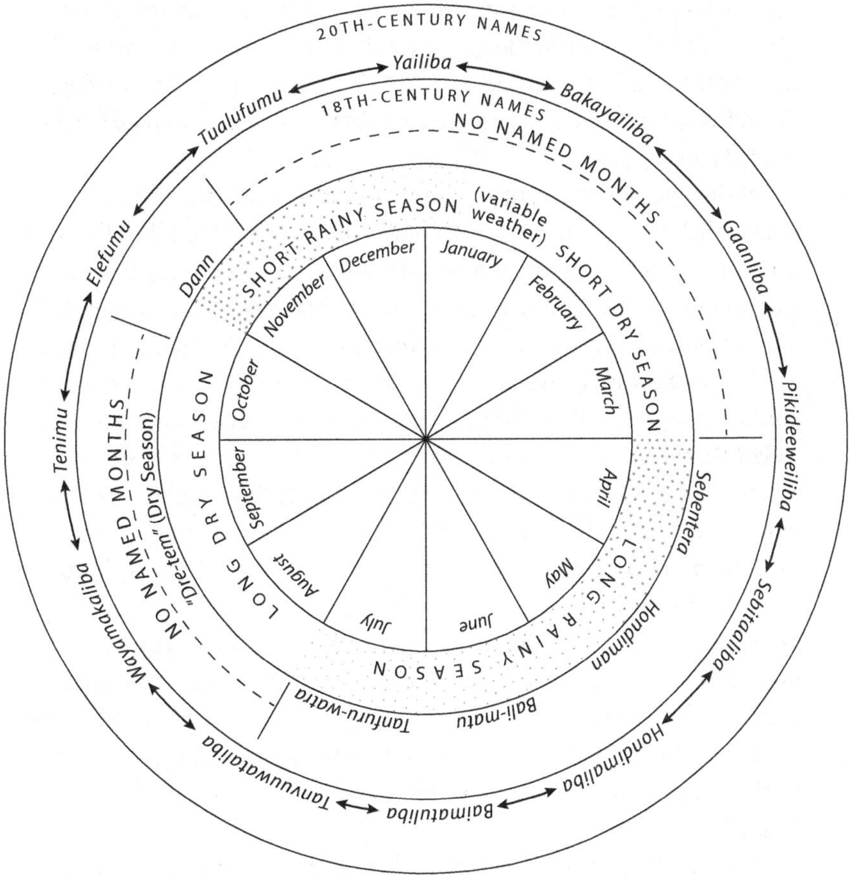
20TH-CENTURY NAMES
Yailiba
Bakayailiba
Gaanliba
Pikideeweiliba
Sebitaaliba
Hondimaliba
Baimatuliba
Tanvuuwataliba
Wayamakaliba
Tenimu
Elefumu
Tualufumu
18TH-CENTURY NAMES
NO NAMED MONTHS
Sebentera
Hondiman
Bali-matu
Tanfuru-watra
Dann
NO NAMED MONTHS
"Dre-tem" (Dry Season)
SHORT RAINY SEASON
(variable weather)
SHORT DRY SEASON
LONG RAINY SEASON
LONG DRY SEASON
January
February
March
April
May
June
July
August
September
October
November
December

FIGURE 8.1. R. Price, drawing from "To Every Thing a Season," 64.

short dry season (the months of Bakayailiba, Gaanliba, and Pikideeweiliba), the key moment for preparing the fields and planting a variety of crops—first corn, okra, taro, sugarcane, sweet potatoes, cassava, watermelon, pepper, peanuts, tobacco, and diverse greens, then the staple food, rice. In the middle of the long rainy season (Sebitaaliba, Hondimaliba, Tanvuuwataliba), men scout out sites for cutting new gardens, and in its final month, when the rains have pretty much ceased, they begin working with their machetes to clear the underbrush; by the end of the period women are harvesting rice. As the long dry season (Wayamakaliba and Tenimu) begins, men start the heavy work of felling trees with axes, and in its waning days, before the rains start up again, they burn the fields. Women, meanwhile, are harvesting rice, sweet potatoes, sugarcane, and other crops in their older gardens. The rains soon return and garden work slows, as people prepare for the start of a new year.

In the eighteenth century, the Moravian missionary Christian Ludwig Schumann (living in a Saamaka village) described the climatic cycle in precisely the same terms and noted that "months are reckoned from one new moon to the next."[3] Yet the Saamaka calendar puzzled him, as only certain months had names at all, and Saamakas "did not even know how many months compose one year." Schumann and his confreres reported that the Saamakas' calendar began with a month called Dann (usually about October/November), and that they recognized its arrival by the beginning of the Short Rainy Season. The next named lunar month (which usually came about April) was Sebentera (Schumann derived the name from "seven stars," the Pleiades), recognized by the beginning of the Long Rainy Season. The following three rainy-season months (about May, June, and July) were named Hondiman, Bali-matu, and Tanfuru-watra—essentially the same names that are used today. The Long Dry Season months which followed were unnamed, and the cycle would begin again with the coming of the small rains—the moon then in the sky would be designated Dann.[4]

Brother Schumann was surprised to find that Saamakas began their year at a different moment from Christians, thus marking "the end of the Long Dry Season or the beginning of the Short Rainy (planting) Season, with the previous months being considered as belonging to 'last year.'" But he noted that this "New Year" moment usually fell in October. We surmise, then, that eighteenth-century Saamakas were still sufficiently close to the experience of slavery to have synched their New Year moment to Rosh Hashana, as celebrated by their Portuguese Jewish former owners. And that sometime during the nineteenth century, as their relations with the coast became closer and less hostile, Saamakas instead began synching to the date on which Paramaribo celebrated New Year's.

Lucky thing Saamakas retained a way to synch their lunar months with the Western calendar! If not, Kala would be planting when he should be felling trees, somewhere over in the other world.

While our Saamaka neighbors argued about what month it was, the two of us were puzzled by a related dilemma (which was of no concern to Saamakas). Why did Saamakas call Friday "Dimingo" and conceptualize the week as beginning on that day, when their Portuguese-speaking owners must have called *Sunday* "Domingo" and begun the week on that day?

Some scholarly spadework allowed us to demonstrate that this two-day shift took place in the forest, sometime before the 1762 peace treaty, while the ancestors of the Saamakas were still at war with the whites (see table 8.1) The sequence Pikisaba/Gaansaba/Domingo ("Little sabbath"/"Big sabbath"/"Sunday"), which on Jewish plantations referred to Friday/Saturday/Sunday, came in the forest to refer, instead, to Wednesday/Thursday/Friday, with the rest of the sequence kept in order. During our time in Saamaka, Gaansaba ("Big sabbath," our Thursday) brought numerous restrictions and taboos—no heavy garden work, no starting a trip, no major rituals. In other words, Saamakas have maintained the *sequence* or order of days, as well as some of their "meaning," since the time their ancestors labored on plantations, but soon after they rebelled they seem to have "lost" two days. How could this have happened?

We can think of three competing explanations—there may be more. First, since day names were conceptualized as a series and, in contrast to month names, were "arbitrary" for Saamakas—unrelated for them (unlike their Jewish owners) to ritual events—their ancestors in the forest may at some point during the war years have simply been sufficiently isolated to lose track of the "correct" day and, by process of argument (much as with month names) agreed that it was, say, Domingo on a day that whitefolks were calling Friday. A second possibility is that the shift was somehow related to the 1752 change from the Julian to the Gregorian calendar that forced people, for example in England and the British colonies, to agree to "lose" eleven days. (There are two problems here: first, the Saamaka shunt is one day too many to be explained in this way—unless one imagines that their ancestors erred slightly in the way they effected the change—and second, Suriname seems to have operated, at least officially, on the Gregorian calendar from the beginning of the Dutch takeover in 1667, even as the British colonies stayed

Table 8.1

ENGLISH	DYUTONGO 1690S*	SAAMAKA 1770S	SAAMAKA 1820S	SAAMAKA 1960S
Sunday	Domingo	?	Drie-dakka-foe-sabba ("3rd day after sabbath")	Sonde (from Dutch or English)
Monday	Tu daka ("2nd day"); Portuguese, Segunda-feira	?	Voe-dakka-voe-sabba ("4th day after sabbath")	Fodaka ("4th day")
Tuesday	Dri daka ("3rd day"); Portuguese, Terça-feira	?	5 dakka voe sabba ("5th day after sabbath")	Fefidaka ("5th day")
Wednesday	Fo daka ("4th day"); Portuguese, Quarta-feira	Pikkien sabba ("Small sabbath")	Pikien sabba	Pikisaba
Thursday	Fefi daka ("5th day"); Portuguese, Quinta-feira	Grang sabba ("Big sabbath")	Gran saba	Gaansaba
Friday	Pikinsaba ("Small sabbath")	Domingo	Demingo	Dimingo
Saturday	Grangsaba ("Big sabbath")	?	Toe-dakka-voe-sabba ("2nd day after sabbath")	Sata (from Dutch) or Tudaka-u-saba ("2nd day after sabbath")

* Dyutongo ("Jew language") was spoken by those Africans enslaved on Sephardic Jewish plantations, as were the great majority of those who became Saamakas. It developed into Saamakatongo once those ancestors escaped. For discussion of Dyutongo, see Smith "History of the Suriname Creoles." The 1770s names are from Schumann's 1778 dictionary, which reports only three names of days for Saamakas. The 1820s names are from van Eyck, "Algemeen verslag," 5–6.

with the Julian version.)[5] A final possibility is that the shift was an attempt by one or more Asante-descended or Asantephilic Saamakas to coordinate the day name sequence with one of the new laws proclaimed by High Priest Komfo Anokye upon the descent of the Golden Stool from the heavens at the end of the seventeenth century, one of which was that "Thursday is to be observed as a holy day—work in the fields, embarking on war, and so forth is forbidden."[6] In that case, Gaansaba ("Big sabbath")—the Jewish owners' Saturday—would have become the (Afrocentric) Saamakas' Thursday, as indeed it now is. Which of the three seems most likely? We'd opt for the first, be unsurprised if the second somehow turned out to be correct, and be amazed if the third was in fact what happened.

FIGURE 9.1. Kala and Maame. Photo: R. Price.

....

CHAPTER 9

The Captain's "Granddaughter"

The photo, posed according to Kala's wishes, quickly became iconic.[1] There he was in his official uniform with his house in the background, standing proudly beside Maame, his wife's granddaughter, dressed in her best—both unsmiling, as was the Saamaka ideal for photos in the 1960s.[2]

Kala's relations with women were famously fraught. He'd had relatively few Saamaka wives because, people told us, his stormy reputation was so widely known. And both of his wives who were no longer alive had already become *kunus* (avenging spirits) against his lineage.[3] His first wife died in childbirth soon after he threw her out of their hammock during a violent argument. The other one became a *kunu* even before his mourning period for her was up. When we arrived in Dangogo, he'd been with Anaweli five years or so, frequently threatening to send her back to her Aluku village, and everyone was telling us that when she died, she too was sure to become a *kunu*, given the way he treated her— and given what he was doing with Maame.

Even Nai said it was obvious why Kala hadn't yet given Maame her skirts of womanhood in the requisite ceremony at the ancestor shrine. Clearly, he wanted to keep her for his own pleasure which, it was widely rumored, he was already enjoying with his wife's reluctant complicity.

Meanwhile, Kala's jealousy knew few bounds. Maame had a crush on Kasindo, and when Kala once caught her chatting with him, he lit right into him and forced him to pay a hefty fine for having transgressed his authority. On another occasion when Kala was in his garden camp,

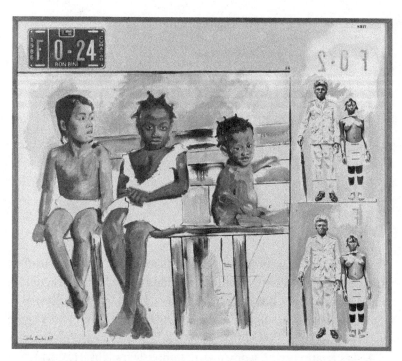

FIGURE 9.2. Carlos Blaaker, Fo-2. In 1989, attending the opening of an art exhibition in Cayenne, we saw to our surprise an artistic replay of the photo in three oil paintings, dated 1988, by the Surinamese-Dutch artist Carlos Blaaker. (For the two other Blaaker paintings that play with the Kala/Maame photo, see van Binnendijk and Faber, *Beeldende kunst in Suriname*, 44–45.) Photo by Roy Tjin. Collection of L. Bijlhout, Suriname.

a visitor from Ndyuka came to ask Anaweli for Maame's hand. When Kala heard, he kicked him out of the house and forced him to spend the night in the forest. Once we heard tremendous shouting from Kala's house—he was ranting at an elderly man who was chatting with Anaweli. And another time, Kala became incensed when he discovered a place in front of his house where the weeds had been flattened, inspiring him to accuse Maame of making love to someone there. Neighbors later explained that two pre-adolescent girls had been wrestling in that spot earlier in the day but he continued ranting and forbade the two children to appear in his sight for the next two months.

Sitting around one morning at the ancestor shrine, waiting for Kala to arrive, Rich heard a long discussion about how many men had come to ask for Maame's hand, only to be sent off with curses. They joked: "What was the Great God thinking when he made Kala?"

In early 1968, Kala was part of a delegation that went to Paramaribo to welcome the *gaama* back from his trip to the Netherlands, where his arthritis had been looked after by specialists (though Saamakas gossiped that the hospital stay was really to cure his erectile dysfunction). While in the city, an elderly Aluku from Maame's matrilineage came to Kala saying that they'd heard he had treated her well, but that it was certainly time for the ceremonial presentation of the skirts of adulthood—though they didn't want her to be given a husband until she was back with her lineage. When Kala returned to Dangogo and prepared for the trip to Aluku, he waited until the month before his departure and conducted the ceremony quietly in Nai's house rather than publicly at the ancestor shrine. He was afraid, everyone said, that men would come running to take her. And in spite of his militant position about menstrual pollution, he prevented her from going to the *faagi* that last month, fearing that a man might rendezvous with her there.

A particularly dramatic incident involved Headcaptain Faansisonu's son, Adiante, who was about twenty. A skilled hunter, he'd noticed animal tracks under a maripa palm out in the forest several hundred yards behind Kala's house, and planned to set a gun trap. Meanwhile, Beki was interested in the ripe fruits on that same tree, and asked Maame to help her harvest them for making cooking oil. With two children in tow, Beki and Maame walked back to the tree and were surprised to find Adiante examining the tracks. Beki, sensing trouble, scolded him violently for coming so close to Kala's house and quickly returned to the village with Maame, where she let out piercing screams exactly like those made upon learning of a close relative's death. As people came running, Beki continued her wails. When other women finally succeeded in calming her down, she assured everyone that Adiante hadn't lain a finger on Maame, that she and Maame had simply gone to gather fruits and found him snooping around, and that she had not in any way set up a lovers' tryst. Later, Kala, in a rage, summoned Adiante's uncle Kasindo to castigate him, making him promise to instruct Adiante about the gravity of his intrusion. A couple of days later, when Kala saw Adiante for the first time since the event, he grabbed his machete and chased him around the village, bum leg and all. Adiante was quicker. But it made us think of the Keystone Cops.

....

CHAPTER 10

Upriver

During the first two weeks of our 1966 exploratory visit, Abatili invited us upriver, far past Dangogo, for a several-day visit to Kpokasa, the camp where his sisters maintained their gardens. The magical allure of that forest setting—for our hosts as well as for us—was palpable, but it was only the following year, with greater immersion in Saamaka life, that we really came to appreciate the multiple roles that such sites played in subsistence, ritual life, and the Saamaka imaginaire.

The upper Pikilio belongs to the Matyau clan (which is based in Dangogo), so around the turn of the twentieth century when members of the Watambii clan (based in Akisiamau and historically a client clan of the Matyaus) wanted to clear gardens in the forest at Kpokasa, it was the leaders of Dangogo, indeed Gaama Dyankuso himself, who granted them permission. Soon, however, divination revealed that the Watambii had made evil *obias* there—protective charms that killed offenders rather than just making them sick—and someone had died as a result. The *gaama* made them leave the area and relocate their gardens just behind their village. After the site had undergone purificatory rituals to erase the damage, young men from Dangogo, including Agbago and Kala, cleared new garden sites nearby for their elderly mother Boo, Boo's daughter Nai, Nai's daughter Dyamati, Agbago's young wife Apumba, and several others. The area was left abandoned at various points, but in the early 1960s Dyamati's daughters (Naina, Akobo, and Beki) returned, together with Abatili's wife Ina.

A few years later, divination found that Kpokasa was still contaminated by the earlier misdeed and needed to be treated again with purificatory rites to remove the pollution. Akobo's husband, Aviate, was a specialist in the necessary *obia*—what leaves and barks and other ingredients to use, exactly how to bathe people—and agreed to supervise, while teaching it to Abatili, his classificatory nephew. Both of them arrived upriver several days early, Aviate to prepare the leaves and other paraphernalia, and Abatili to assist. Naina, Akobo, Beki, and Abatili's pregnant wife Emma were also there with their children, taking care of their gardens and cooking for the men. And Naina's son Amombebuka had come to hunt in preparation for the event. On the day of the ritual his brother Dosili brought the rest of the participants in the *gaama*'s official motor canoe—Apumba and Gadya (the *gaama*'s wives who had worked at Kpokasa many years earlier), Nai, Kala and his wife and her granddaughter, and Rich. The *gaama* couldn't come because of the arthritis that he suffered in his knees, and Sally remained in Dangogo since she was in menstrual seclusion and banned from traveling in a boat with men. Abatili's wife Ina also stayed behind since her period was due; she joined Sally in the hut the next day. Nai, who had not been to Kpokasa for many years and was bursting with excitement about returning to a place that held such warm memories, did a little dance of joy as soon as she stepped from the canoe.

It being the rainy season, the path through the forest was badly flooded, at one point reaching Dosili's waist, so Kala and Rich cut an alternative path with their machetes and helped the older women through the dense foliage. When the group reached the camp, they passed under the palm-leaf structure that marked its entrance and found Aviate putting the finishing touches on the ingredients for the ritual washing. There were baskets filled with mixtures of leaves and barks and kaolin, others with broken pieces of rice stalks, sugarcane, corn cobs, and calabashes. There were small bundles of red and black feathers, rice stalks, and other plants, and a sardine tin holding three tiny sacks and several eggs. Another sardine tin held water, kaolin, and a thin strip of white cloth. There was an old basketry sieve, a winnowing tray on which a large X had been traced with kaolin, a calabash bowl, and buckets upon buckets of water. In the middle a banana leaf had been laid out with a white cloth spread on top of it.

Within an hour of the group's arrival everything is ready for the ritual. Dosili and Abatili present some cloth and rum, and Aviate dribbles a libation on the ground, addressing a long list of individual ancestors for some ten minutes. Aviate and Abatili then perform the ritual exchange representing payment for the *obia*: "Madyomina!" "Ka!" "Madyomina!" "Ka!" "Payment on the ground!" (Abatili puts down the first of the small green *madyomina* sticks he's cut and announces, "A big jug of rum!") Then: "Madyomina!" "Ka!" "Madyomina!" "Ka!" (He puts down the second stick and declares, "100 lengths of cloth!") Finally, "Madyomina!" "Ka!" (The third stick goes down: "12 bottles of beer"!)

With preliminaries taken care of, the ablutions begin. Aviate leads Nai onto the cloth, has her sit down with legs outstretched, and administers the first washing, taking care to explain each step to Abatili. He rubs some of the solutions down her body from head to foot, first on the left, and then on the right—once, twice, three times. He ties the strip of white cloth in a slipknot and passes it down her body in the same configuration, with the knot untied and retied after each application. He squeezes solutions from the three tiny sacks into her eyes, one by one. He takes an egg and passes it down her body three times, touching it to the cloth after each pass. He then dips the feather bundles, one in each hand, into the water in the sardine tin and uses them to sprinkle her from head to toe, both sides at the same time. This too is done three times. Finally, he takes water in the calabash and pours it through the sieve (which Abatili is holding above her head and shaking vigorously) as she rubs it all over her body. This final washing is repeated a half dozen times.

Abatili then takes over, washing members of the matrilineage first, lineage wives and their children next. Dosili washes Abatili and Abatili ends the sequence by washing Aviate. After a half-hour of rest, second washings were offered and all partook, eager to benefit from its restorative powers. Eventually the water was used up, and women set off to the creek to replenish it for yet more washings of Nai, Kala, and a few others.

By nightfall, everyone has canoed back to the village. It has been an especially strenuous outing for Nai, but she is thrilled to have been able to return to the site of such precious memories. Yes, garden camps are the site of hard physical work, but they're also an immensely welcome respite from the social tensions of life in the village, and women take every opportunity to spend time there—as much as 75 percent of their days during the heavy agricultural months. Since developing the back pain that left her dependent on a walking stick (though she still made an impressive figure wielding an axe to split wood for cooking fires), Nai had repeatedly requested permission from Gaantata to return to Kpokasa, but he had always said no, and her greatest (oft-expressed) complaint about old age was being condemned to a sedentary life in Dangogo, missing out on the joys of her upriver garden camp. When Sally emerged from the menstrual hut, Nai gave her an impassioned report of the visit, telling her how each person had embraced her warmly and how she'd been led around to see each structure and each garden. It had been a shaking experience, bringing back memories of all the different things she'd done there and reminding her, she said, of how old and useless she'd become.

Three months later, in the heart of the dry season, we had a chance to taste the life that Nai so missed, spending a week in Kpokasa at a time when garden sites were being selected and the process of clearing them was beginning. No outboard motor this time . . . together with Dosili, we paddled a canoe, one of several that were traveling in tandem to take small groups of kin from Dangogo to various upriver camps, staying close enough to each other to allow for relaxed banter during the four-hour trip. One person or another would break into song as they paddled, and birds called from the treetops.

When we arrive, Naina, Akobo, Beki, and Abatili's wife Ina are already there with their children. Soon we hear a machete knocking on a tree to announce another arrival, and Takite, a nephew of Nai's from the other side of Dangogo, shows up with his wife and child to help with the selection of sites. They're greeted warmly and persuaded to spend the night. A few days later Abatili and Dosili will return the favor, meeting Takite in his camp to provide similar support.

The harvesting of rice that was planted four months earlier is going on at the same time that new gardens are being staked out for the coming season. And women are using machetes to cut wood from the burned trees, later splitting it roughly and tying the pieces in a bundle to take back to the village, where they'll split it further and use it for their cooking fires.[1] Except on Wednesday, a "taboo" day for certain activities in that particular stretch of forest, the women spend roughly 7:00 AM to 3:00 PM cutting rice, then return to the central clearing and take on other labor-intensive tasks. Sally sets out to help with the rice harvest but effects a prudent retreat around noon to avoid collapsing in the equatorial sun. Even on Wednesday there's a whole range of tasks that keep the women busy—threshing the rice to remove the stems (though hulling it with

FIGURE 10.1. Tianen spinning cotton from her garden.
Photo: S. Price.

mortar and pestle is prohibited on Wednesdays), breaking palm nuts with rocks for hours at a time to make cooking oil, drugging the creek for fish, digging up root crops, spinning cotton to make calfbands, and more.

One day we join Naina, Akobo, and the children, as they drug the creek for fish. They begin by cutting 3-foot branches of the *uwiindeku* plant,[2] complete with leaves and berries, which they bring back to the central area, chop into small pieces, mash with a large mortar and pestle, and load into baskets. At the stream, Naina first makes a prayer for a successful catch, and they begin rubbing the mush (with the same motion that they use for laundering clothes), releasing it into the current, which stains the water a dark green. The two women wield machetes to chop fish and the children use their bare hands, snatching up the fish as they jump wildly in and out of the water. After an hour they've caught only five really big fish, which is a bit disappointing, but Naina is pleased that once she's smoked them, she'll have some to bring on her upcoming trip to her husband's village.

FIGURE 10.2. Pete ("Peh-tay") making calfbands
with an umbrella spoke. Photo: S. Price.

Sally spends a full day interviewing Akobo on the history of each
woman's gardens (paying her, since it prevents her from attending to
her own work). She also elicits who cleared what gardens for whom each
year in Kpokasa from 1962 through 1967, learns about how women assess
the advantages and disadvantages of working gardens that have been
cleared in virgin forest versus secondary growth, and discusses what de-
termines whether they replant a rice garden for a second harvest. She
makes a map of the central area with its eight palm-leaf structures (two
of which have fallen into ruin) and the plants growing around them,
such as cotton, hot peppers, okra, bananas, pineapples, and sugarcane.

By the time the interview's over, she has elicited more than fifty
named varieties of rice, and mapped one of Akobo's gardens which includes twenty-eight of them, with partially burned fallen trees marking
the boundaries. Why take the trouble to plant so many different types
in one small clearing in the forest? she asks. After all, the rice will all
look the same once it's in the cooking pot. But Akobo makes clear that,

in addition to the ecological insurance they provide in terms of differential vulnerability to disease and pests, planting the various red and white varieties is more enjoyable than sticking to one variety . . . the patchwork garden gives personal pleasure to what would otherwise be a tedious, physically exhausting aspect of her life.

Sally's also mapped the crops in other Kpokasa gardens and learned about more than a dozen types each of okra, taro, yams, cassava, and bananas. Only one variety of tobacco, but she muses that if Akonda or another tobacco addict were present, she could certainly discover a few more.

Meanwhile, Rich has gone off with the men to scout out sites for the next set of gardens. Using newly sharpened machetes to clear the way, they explore the surrounding forest, looking for sites that have the right slope, exposure, and drainage. But they're particularly on the lookout for large boulders and two sacred trees, *kankantii* and *katu*, both giants of the forest.[3] All three of these are preferred abodes of Apukus (forest spirits) and if they get singed when fields are burned, they become *kunus* and possess people. Likewise, the men must avoid termite hills, which are the abode of redoubtable spirits called *akataasi*—though, unlike Apukus, these latter may be neutralized with a widely-known *obia* as long as the rite is performed before burning. (That *obia*, which Rich heard Asipei teaching Akobo one day, consists of mashing the leaves of five named plants in a mortar, adding stagnant water from a rotted tree trunk, and sprinkling the mixture all over the termite nest.)

Abatili finds a likely site in an area of secondary growth—it had been farmed some twenty years before—and cuts a couple of forked poles, slices off a palm frond to suspend across them, and says we'll check in the morning to see whether the "god-who-has-the-place" has given permission to cut the garden.[4] Once Dosili, Amombebuka, and Takite have finished selecting their sites, everyone heads back to the camp. It's been several hours of tramping around in the forest and Rich's feet are scratched and bleeding.

Meanwhile, Abatili's daughter Dyam, as the oldest girl, has been put in charge of watching over the younger ones in the camp's central area. In the morning she heats water, adds medicinal leaves, and bathes herself and the others. Then she and Poi play at snakegod possession, calling out *hoi hoi!* and *hue hue!*, and rolling around wildly on the ground. By the time the men return for the evening, Poi has pre-

FIGURE 10.3. Dyam babysitting at Kpokasa. Photo: R. Price.

pared a meal of wet sand and brings it to Rich. The next day she comes back to her "husband's village," bearing a tiny bundle of firewood tied with a rag. This time she has a calabash tied onto her belly to show that she's pregnant. The "food" she's prepared is accompanied by a broken tin lamp and some dishes—a coconut shell, a sardine tin, a piece of a broken plate—each carefully topped with some kind of cover, as well as a calabash handwashing bowl. Rich thanks her with a piece of cloth, and Dyam goes wild with excitement, taking it to Beki to show her the present. Tumbui then brings a play meal to Rich. She tries to take the broken spoon that was included in Poi's offerings, but Dyam reminds her that she mustn't touch anything that belongs to her co-wife. Poi begins to fight with Tumbui, but Dyam reminds them that they're in their husband's village, where they should always be on their best behavior. These little girls are practicing for roles that they'll soon be assuming in earnest.[5]

Once all the adults are back from the forest and the gardens, the women, who have bathed in the stream, heat water that they've brought back in buckets, and pour each man a basin-full to wash in. Then it's time to relax, with meals taken more informally than in the village, women and men eating separately, but within hearing of each other. There's opportunity for talk of the day's activities, reflections of every sort, and ample gossip about goings-on back in the villages and on the coast. (Naina: So-and-so's husband just returned from the coast, so she'll certainly be celebrating this week! Akobo: But isn't he the one with the short penis? And Beki jokes that if she were still married to her first husband, he would probably be teaching her to eat "Lower-River style"—within view of men.) Abatili turns on his tape recorder and the children need no encouragement to jump up and begin a spirited bout of tyeke (secular) dancing.

On Sunday the men begin to clear the underbrush in the sites that the gods have approved, women do some rice cutting and weeding. Back at the camp, young girls carefully examine the bodies of the men, looking for ticks—it turns out they're much easier to see on white skin. In late afternoon, we all depart downriver.

The next week Rich returns with the men, who will continue to clear the underbrush for the next five or six days. They pull on long work pants over their breechcloths (to protect against ticks) and, holding a forked stick in the left hand and a machete in the right, they stop frequently to sharpen the blade with a file. It's an uncomfortable job, with wasps and other flying insects buzzing around their heads in the heat, and an ever-present danger of scorpions and snakes. Once finished, they leave the brush to dry and settle for a week, before the task of felling the trees can commence.

Tree felling for a garden is a big deal. Abatili invites Dosili, Amombebuka, and Takite to join him the next Monday. But first he'll go hunting for a day, to have food to serve while they're working. Rich is delighted when Abatili invites him to come along. Although he'd never shot a gun before coming to Saamaka, hunting has become a real pleasure. (Rich hunted or fished almost every late afternoon for an hour or two throughout our stay in Dangogo.)[6] As they walk stealthily through the high forest, Abatili asks Rich from time to time whether he doesn't smell howler monkeys or, later, deer. They examine tracks of wild boar, agouti, paca, and armadillos that had come to drink at a stream. They see broken branches where a tapir had passed. They wade through

FIGURE 10.4. Tree felling. Willem van de Poll, *Suriname: Een photo-reportage van land en volk* (The Hague: W. Van Hoeve, 1959), 83.

FIGURE 10.5. Beki, Ina, Dyam, and others working the earth
at Kpokasa. Photo: R. Price.

swollen streams and walk up and down a series of hills—the forest is
rarely flat. They pass by a tremendous variety of tall trees, some cor-
rugated, others smooth, others spiky, as well as a variety of vines, thick
and thin, white and pitch black, soft and stone hard. They shoot a
couple of toucans high up in the branches. From time to time, Abatili
calls out to different animals, sometimes using a leaf to help make the
appropriate sounds—an agouti comes running once, and later a curas-
sow (a large bird that walks on the forest floor). He shoots both. (Another time, when hunting with Rich, Abatili severed a five-foot-long
poisonous snake with a slash of his machete, with the front end wrig-

gling its way off into the forest. And, on their best day, they came back with the news that they'd shot four white-lipped peccaries and would need help, the next day, to carry them back to Dangogo.)

On Monday the men arrived at Kpokasa to fell the trees, in some cases standing on a scaffold built of poles to raise them above the buttresses, and swinging their axes at opposite sides. Before beginning, as they had for clearing the brush, they said a brief prayer asking for protection from the god-who-has-the-place. Abatili, a master of tree-felling songs, sang to the forest spirits while they worked.[7] As each tall tree fell, it brought with it a tangled mess of vines, large branches, and smaller trees, and the men would race to get as far away as they could. (In his youth, Agbago had accidently killed a brother when felling trees in Guyane and years later Kala had almost suffered the same fate when a tree fell on him, smashing his leg.) The five men worked steadily, pausing only to drink from a calabash, counting each tree downed as a small triumph, and finishing off the new garden for Abatili's wife in a single long day.

A few days later, Rich joined Abatili, Dosili, Amombebuka, Takite, and a handful of men from Asindoopo who trekked behind that village to fell trees for the gardens of Gadya and Apumba, two of the *gaama's* wives— this is a communal responsibility and was carried out with strong camaraderie and joking and with women providing a festive post-work meal.

Three weeks later, the dry season was already at its height and the sun had been beating down relentlessly. Abatili, in consultation with others in Dangogo, decided it was time to burn the fields, and invited Rich to come along with him and his wife Ina. He chose a relatively windless day, said a brief prayer to the ancestors and the gods of the place, and with Ina's help, set several fires along the windward edge of the area that was to become the garden. By nightfall it was clear that the burn had been successful, and they returned to the camp to sleep. The next morning, they inspected the blackened, still smoking field, almost inch by inch, to see if they might have created a *kunu* by burning a boa constrictor that carried a Vodu god. They found a couple of charred armadillos and an agouti that had been caught by the flames, but there was no sign of the sacred snakes, so they breathed a collective sigh of relief. Once the rains came again, it would be time to think about getting the new field ready to plant, mainly women's work—first gathering the remaining charred branches and burning them in heaps, and then getting out the short-handled hoes to begin working the earth before sowing the seeds.

CHAPTER 11

....

At the Ancestor Shrine

Dangogo had three ancestor shrines on our side of the river, one for each of the matrilineages. Bongootu Pau, named for the founder of Dangogo who built it around 1870, and located just in front of Gaan-tata's house where much of the village's ritual activity took place, was the most important one. A day rarely went by without one or more groups of men pouring libations of water and rum while speaking to the ancestors there. Once we saw the head of a tapir kept overnight in the shrine, then cooked by the village women and feasted on, accompanied by cassava cakes by the whole village sitting on stools around the shrine—what was left was then laid out on a banana leaf for the ancestors.

Early April 1968. Almost all our neighbors are sick, apparently with the flu (or might it be malaria?). Seena and other children are crying and running fevers. Naina says she would go to Dyuumu, but she's heard that a new injection has arrived by plane and that it would kill the first person who tried it—so far, no one has. Takite comes over from the other side of the river and makes an *obia*—various crushed leaves and warm water in clay pots—for Dyam and Beki, and says he'll do another the next day for Seena and Akobo. Nai asks Kasindo to call Naina's Papagadu (snakegod) to find out what's causing all the sickness, but he says, "There's sickness everywhere these days" and declines.

Nai then summons Tita, a lineage niece who lives across the river, to come so that her Apuku (forest spirit) can be asked what's making everyone sick. Sally's sitting with Nai when Tita arrives. Her notes describe how Nai takes some kaolin and a calabash of water and prays to the god, whose name is Tyipoko. When it comes, it chants "What's going on? How are you?" and then declares that all the sickness is from a kunu that's trying to kill everyone. "It's Ma Faansina! Asipei needs to be the one to say the prayers. Otherwise, you'll all die." And it asks Nai for some rum. Nai offers a small bottle of rum and Tita (possessed by Tyipoko) rubs some all over her body, drinking the rest. She rubs a hand from her eyes to one side, repeats the gesture ten times, and stands up. Nai asks Tyipoko, "Have you left?" A few minutes later, after Nai ushers Sally and Tita out the door, they go to Beki's house where Asipei will do the prayers. Tita asks, "What are we going to pray about?"

Beki is lying in her hammock, as a group gathers at her doorstep— Nai, Tita, Asipei, Akobo, Naina, Kasindo, ourselves, and five others. Asipei addresses the ancestors, calling specifically on eight or nine to come to his aid in asking Faansina to desist, to stop making people sick. He says that he doesn't really know how to pray—but that they do, which is why he is asking for their help. He tells how Kala met his wife Faansina (the sister of Gaama Agbago's Ndyuka wife, Peepina) downriver, how he brought her to Dangogo where everyone lived well with her, and how soon after he brought her back home she died and quickly became a kunu. "How Kala lived with her, exactly what he did with her, only the Great God knows," says Asipei. And then he threatens Faansina, saying that the son she had with Kala has by now had three daughters, and that if she kills someone here, that person will surely go and kill those grandchildren of hers. So, in her own interest, she had better desist. And he promises a fuller prayer the next day, at Bongootu Pau.

Tita tells Nai that this very kunu (Ma Faansina) had tried to kill her years earlier but that an operation in the city saved her life. And she reminds everyone that a couple of months earlier, when Abatili was very sick, Gaantata found that Ma Faansina was causing it, that everyone on this side of the river should wash in Dungulali-Obia, and that the gaama should offer special prayers at the ancestor shrine in Asindoopo to beg the Ma Faansina kunu. But none of that had been done.

The next morning, a large group gathers at Bongootu Pau as Asipei begins dribbling water from a calabash and addressing the ancestors.

Tata Bongooto, my grandfather Bityenfou [who succeeded Bongootu on the captain's stool], we give you water. Gaama Atudendu,

FIGURE 11.1. Asipei praying at Bongootu Pau. Photo: R. Price.

Gaama Dyankuso, we give you water. My uncle Konuwomi [a Dangogo captain], we give you water. We give you water. We give you water! Plead with the woman for us, plead with her for us. Beg her to leave the family alone. As Kala himself so often says, "When a man takes a woman in his family, he [Kala] doesn't joke around with him." No one should start joking around with him about it. Because you're not the one who gave her to him. Well, when a woman comes to her husband's village, she won't bring bad behavior, she won't try to beat you. She'll just come to your village and live well.

Well, then, that woman came to her husband, who was from the lineage of Adisi [Kala's and Nai's matrilineage]. Well then, after a while, he took her and brought her back to her people. Well, when he brought her back, then suddenly she died, and she became a kunu! She became a kunu!

Well, that's why we're calling on you, asking you to plead with the woman for us. Plead with her in the nighttime, plead with her in the daytime. Take her and put her on your lap. Help us plead with her however you can, we beg you. [Spectators clap rhythmically, intoning the ritual "Great thanks."]

We beg you, ancestors. We're pleading with you here, we're begging you from the bottom of our hearts. Well, old ones, we don't know what to say to make her [the kunu] respond, so that's why I am calling you, the old people, to go to the Mama. Well, go talk to her, take her on your lap. Well, beg her for us, tell her that we know that she's right, we understand her motives. Because the thing the man [Kala] did with her, we don't know what it was. Not at all! Well, when she left, we and she had never quarreled, we had never fought. We thought that we and she had lived sweetly together. But whatever may have happened between husband and wife, it certainly didn't please the ancestors.

When Mama left, she died suddenly! Once dead and buried she whooshed up, came straight for the lineage of Tata Bongootu [Kala's lineage]. Well, now, you, the old men who were in the family, that's why I'm calling on you, to go to the Ndyuka gods [since Bongootu often visited Ndyuka territory and Faansina was a Ndyuka]. Well go, sit yourselves down, plead with the Mama for us! Say, "She is justified, she is right." Please, thank you, we beg you! [Spectators clap and intone thanks.]

Well, Ma Faansina, you see how you came to Saamaka? Kala brought you here, we celebrated, we were happy. We lived sweetly in those days. But now things have changed. Not one man or woman quarreled with you. Not a single one! Well Mama, it's certainly a shame. Ah, how we lived sweetly! But we can't know what you and the man did when we weren't there. Well, Mama, well that's why we've come to plead with you. I call you to plead with you. I call you to ask you to let them be. Mama, I call you. I call you. We lived sweetly together, that's why I call you. I call you to beg you. The family you see here is my family. Well, they brought me into this world—well, aren't they my family? They're my family! Well, that's why we call you. We call you to tell you, "Don't look at how long the liana is." If you cut it too long, you won't be able to carry the load. [When you gather firewood and cut an overly long liana to wrap it in, the wood will be too heavy to carry—i.e., don't bite off more than you can chew, don't do more killing than you can handle.] Well now a "death club." . . . Your husband Kala said that if you saw a club right down the middle until it's cleanly cut, *kelekele keleke*, well, you'll throw it, *viii*, into the air, and it will split in half, *kele*! One side will hit the person who caused the *kunu*, the other side will hit the other person. You are in the right! That's the way a death club works. Well then Mama, you'll kill the lineage here till the lineage is wiped out. But then Mayoto, your own son with Kala, will be as good as dead too! Ma Faansina? I'm talking to you now! Well, Mayoto will be as good as dead. Well those children here [the ones the *kunu* is threatening to kill] (you understand Saamakatongo perfectly well, because you lived here) those children here will whoosh up, will go straight for Mayoto's daughters, go kill them *fia*! Mama, living people won't be left on the face of the earth! Mama, that's no good. Well, that's why we come to you at the ancestor shrine, come plead with you, to say you are right, you are a hundred, hundred, a thousand, thousand times right. Please, thank you, we beg you. [Clapping and general thanks.]

The sick people here, let them get up from their hammocks, but they mustn't get up only to be stricken again. Not at all! Think of Mayoto! Well, because you must think of him at a time when there's so much evil on the face of the earth. Well, once you kill people until you see dead people whoosh up *vuuu*, making right for the throats of those kids [of Mayoto], Mama, that's no good! Well then, you see we've come to the ancestor shrine to tell you that you're right, to say "Ma, you're justified, a thousand thousand, a hundred hundred times!" That's what we've come to beg you, to say please, please leave these children alone. [General thanks, clapping.]

Nai adds, addressing Faansina, "You are right! Now, let off!" Asipei puts down the calabash from which he's been pouring water as he prayed and takes up a bottle of rum, which he begins to dribble to the ancestors.

Well, you folks in the land of the gods [the land of the dead], here we are, calling on you. Father Bongooto, my grandfather Bityenfou, take

rum. Gaama Atudendu, Gaama Dyankuso, take rum. My uncle Makoya, take rum. Father Kwenkwen, Mandea, take rum! My uncle
Gaduansu, take rum. Well this rum that I'm offering to you here, Asimadyo, Baamuko, Asapampia, Kositan, Gide, take rum. Father Saaye,
Potyi, take rum. Take rum, go counsel with the woman, counsel with
her, tell her she is right. Well, because if she weren't justified, she
wouldn't have come and grabbed people here. So she must be right.
Well, admit that she's justified, tell her she's right. Tell her to please
leave off—she is right.

Well, now that we've come to pray to you at the shrine here, we
give you rum. We ask you to stick with the task of pleading with her,
truly. Make the family awake again. Please, we beg you. [General
clapping and thanks. Nai interjects: "The earth is shaking!"]

Father Bongootu, the earth is shaking. My uncle Gaama Atudendu, the earth is shaking. Well you said, when there's a famine, if
a person, a child, has their mother and father in the land of the dead,
you had better not take your eyes off that child because, if you do,
he'll get sick, the famine will get him. Well, now, don't you see? It's
famine time here on earth. Don't you see how big it is? It's big!
Uncle Gaama, the famine is big! Well now, it's come at us broadside,
it's almost all over, it looks like we'll die! Well the thing you said . . .
Well, as you are over there now [in the land of the dead], you must
not take your eyes off us. Beg the kunu for us, please. We beg you!
[General clapping and thanks.]

The next day, a small flotilla of canoes paddles down to Dyuumu where
the Dutch missionary doctor announces that everyone has tested
positive for malaria.[1] On their return to the village, Doote asks, "Did he
give you medicine?" Beki says, "No. Only pills."

When Nai becomes ill several days later, Asipei comes to pray in
her house, in the presence of Konoi, speaking once again directly to
Faansina, this time in a very conversational tone, almost as if she is
sitting there with him. The following day, we hear Akobo and Naina
cursing Kala (who's off in Guyane) for the way he treats his wives, causing all these problems. That evening, Assistant Captain Apaasu prays at
Nai's doorstep to Faansina. In the course of his prayer, he admits that
he hasn't "gone ashore" (referring to a proverb that says, "the person
who's ashore is the one who knows what the dog is hunting")—he has

no idea what Kala did to incite Faansina's rage. And then Apaasu, a powerful Komanti-man (the medium of a warrior-spirit), makes an *obia* for Nai. The ingredients must be crushed in a mortar by a virgin, so Seena is handed the pestle and she sets to work. Then he cuts a stick at the edge of the forest, splits one end, places a calabash in it, and forces the apparatus into the earth next to Nai's door, pouring in the crushed leaves. He sprinkles liquid from the calabash onto Konoi and other bystanders, including us, and then washes Nai and ties a white fabric charm, filled with Komanti ingredients, on her wrist. Naina performs the *madyomina* exchange with Apaasu, giving him four *malembelembe* sticks, four eggs, and some pounded rice.

Within a few days, everyone, including Nai, seems to have recovered and life returns to normal with Beki and her sisters going to Kpokasa to prepare their gardens for rice planting.

....

Bongootu Pau served as the locus for a great many problems, including one that was brought up with special frequency during our stay in Dangogo—the complicated pregnancies of Dyeni, Dosili's youngest wife. Three weeks after our arrival, Rich's fieldnotes describe an early morning ceremony for her, with Dosili and a dozen others present. Doote spoke to the ancestors, pouring libations of water and rum, and praying that Dyeni bring forth to the lineage "both men and women." He mentioned that her first pregnancy had ended in a stillborn child and that she had miscarried not long before. And then he invited Captain Aseni, Dyeni's father, to pray, as he continued to pour libations. At the ceremony Dyeni was wearing an *obia* necklace that included brightly colored parrot feathers and a cowrie shell, which she told us had just been given to her at Nai's house.

The next month, Dyeni suffered from an unusually heavy menstrual period and when it was over Kala took her and Nai to Bongootu Pau for more prayers to the ancestors. A few days later, she told Nai that a ceremony was planned for her but that it had to wait until they could find two cocks, one white and one black—Nai lamented that her chickens only produced white ones.

Dosili complained to Nai that people were always planning ceremonies for Dyeni without telling him. He'd heard that Doote was taking her into the forest Tuesday and would finish a ceremony the next day in honor of a forest spirit named Gangu, which one of the cocks had revealed as the cause of Dyeni's troubles. Over the next few weeks, there were various ceremonies to calm that forest spirit's heart, and Dosili paid the specialist who conducted them a bottle of rum and three lengths of cloth. A few days later, Dosili went to the sacred village of Daume to get an *obia* for Dyeni's illness. He had also been cutting a garden for her, and had taken her on a nighttime fishing trip where he shot seven fish with a bow and arrows.

He was also treating her to frequent nights together, despite having recently taken a new wife (whom he called, affectionately, "Ass-to-her-knees") and keeping up the pace of his notorious extra-marital dalliances. (He complained to Rich that a married woman in Dangogo that he'd been sleeping with was going to tell her husband and that he also felt trapped by a fantastically hot woman in Bendekonde who was pregnant from a close kinsman but planned to claim the child was Dosili's.) Dyeni told Nai that if she were strong enough, she'd beat Dosili for all his nighttime wanderings—"He never sleeps at night, he just runs after women!" (With half the men from the village off working at the French missile base for months or years at a time, an unusually large number of women—many of them married—were available, and Dosili, Abatili, and their age mates were taking full advantage.)

Meanwhile, Nai and her friends gossiped at her doorstep about the inappropriateness of the Dosili-Dyeni marriage—Dyeni's mother Titii had bloodied Dyeni's head by hitting her with a heavy stick to try to stop the marriage in the first place, and Dosili had simply taken her without her family's permission. The backstory is a little complicated. Dyeni's father's father, Captain Gide of Dangogo, had a wife from Akisiamau (Titii's village) who lived badly with him, which caused conflict between Dosili's (and Gide's) lineage in Dangogo and Dyeni's in Akisiamau. The finding that Gide was Dyeni's *neseki* (spiritual genitor) was generally interpreted as a hostile act, a way of punishing her lineage because of his wife's bad living. (For Saamakas, the physiological conception of every human requires three contributors—not only a father and mother, but also a *neseki*, a spiritual genitor or "namesake." The first time a baby falls ill, specialists perform divination to discover its namesake so that the proper rituals can be performed to restore the baby to health. It usually turns out to be a recently deceased relative.)

When we return in 1968, Dyeni says she's finally pregnant again, having missed two periods, and she's having belly pains. At his weekly consultation, Gaantata tells Dosili to bring a large bottle of beer for her to wash in the next week plus six small bottles, three lengths of cloth, and a length of white cloth as payment. Dosili also asks Captain Faansisonu's help with a small ceremony to take care of a curse (*siba*) that someone directed at Dyeni, which divination had found was causing her distress. Meanwhile, Dosili tells Dyeni she has to go for a consultation at Dyuumu, but she refuses. "If you die," he says angrily, "it won't be my fault." But the next day, he takes her to the clinic where the doctor draws a blood sample and begins a gynecological exam, at which she jumps up and escapes to the canoe. (Back in the village, the women who hear about it agree that she's not so sick that he had to "stick his hand in.") At Gaantata's next consultation, he washes Dyeni in the beer Dosili provided and the payment is given. And the following week across the river, Mamagadu washes Dyeni to try to cure her belly pains.

There's considerable controversy about how to handle Dyeni's ongoing ills. Nai summons Titii, and goes over the many different divination findings and cures that have already been tried. But the main discussion is whether Dyeni should be allowed to take the missionary plane to the hospital in the city for tests and treatment, as the doctor recommends. Nai and Dosili are for it, Titii against. The fear is that "her womb will be closed" at the hospital. There are numerous informal meetings. And most agree it should be left in the hands of the gods. Dosili finally gets all to agree for him to take Dyeni to Dyumuu to urinate into a bottle just before the plane takes off for the city so doctors at the urban hospital can do tests and send back medicine to treat her. But Gaantata tells everyone that the important thing is for the *gaama* himself to come to Bongootu Pau in Dangogo to pray directly to Captain Gide, to ask him to stop troubling her.

When the *gaama* arrives, a large crowd is waiting outside the ancestor shrine. Seated on his special stool, he begins speaking (with Asipei supplying responses):

Before we get started (that's right), I sent word up here (that's true), to say that the woman here (right) . . . if I'd have known there was this problem I'd have come up here a long time ago (yes). . . . So, the woman is ill (exactly). Till she can hardly stand on her feet (yes).

She seems to be dying (yes). . . . So, that's why I sent word to you (right) to say I'm going to come up and address the ancestors (exactly).

Well, divination has told us that our captain is involved (that's right). . . . He came to the woman, he became her *neseki*. . . . Let's say you have some lousy ripe seeds and you plant them (all right). And all you can harvest is enough for a single meal (that's all). That's the sort of *neseki* he became (yes). He gave her just a little bit (right). He wanted to hurt her (he did). So I'm going to call on my brothers in the land of the dead (yes), those I was close to (yes), to help me tell the captain to desist (that's right).

And, after asking Captain Aseni (Dyeni's father) to pray first, which he does for five minutes or so, the *gaama* enters into a meandering prayer that lasts a good hour, drawing on his unmatched knowledge of the ancestors' esoteric names (often the lengthy drum names that called them to council meetings) and proverbs in esoteric languages. He first calls on his immediate predecessor, Gaama Atudendu, using a proverb in seagod (Wenti) language, then several eighteenth-century men from his clan. Then leading women from the nineteenth century. Then the "twelve clans" that escaped to the forest and made the Saamaka people. Then back to a large number of eighteenth-century founders, calling their convoluted praise names. (He invokes Gaama Gbagidi, for example, as "Avo Gbagidi Gwago, Sembe kuma miseemu, Yewo watalo, Sada kuma Legwa.") To each, he says he is offering water and begging for help. *Gaamas*, captains, assistant captains, famous men and women of the past are all invoked by the scores, some with personal reminiscences or mention of their feats, citing reasons why they should stand and help. At one point, he says he's praying on behalf of white people, black people, and Amerindians—for everyone on the face of the earth—and he prays for a couple of minutes in esoteric language (some Komanti, some "First-Time language") completely unintelligible to almost everyone present.
Eventually, he comes to Dyeni's problems.

Ancestors, you must stand up now and listen to what a living person is telling you. You see this girl here? We did some harm to the person who's her *neseki* when he walked this earth. Later on, he became this girl's *neseki*. Right now, it looks like she may die. Dyuumu says they could take her away to the city. They'd fly her off, cure her as best they could, and fly her back. Well, the cures we knew, they don't seem to be with us anymore, do they? So, I've started to work with whitefolks' cures. It does the trick, doesn't it? We haven't given in to the whitefolks in other ways. We're still ourselves. But whatever's killing the girl, whether it's water gods, forest gods, something new . . . or an ancestor. Grandfather Doon [another name for Bongootu], you're over there, you must listen to what I'm saying. I'm pouring a libation for the girl. . . . Well her *neseki*—it's true he was treated badly here on earth. But now he must take this water, wash all over in it. We're making offerings, let him help the girl live. Ancestors, Death mustn't kill her! Everyone must die but it's not right that she dies now. In the name of the seagods, Mama Lolu Faasina-ibo [apparently a seagod], in the name of all the gods, I'm pouring libations.

Look at the man [Captain Aseni, who's pouring the libations] here. This is the only girlchild he's had. She learned how to cook and now she's big enough to bring him food to eat. But now she's dying. Let her live! I'm pouring libations to ask you to beg her *neseki* to desist and let her live for as many years as the Great God intended people to live. I clap my hands in your honor.

After considerably more prayer and erudite rhetoric, Agbago returns once more to the matter at hand, still addressing a panoply of ancestors by name:

There's a girl here who's pregnant, her day isn't far off. . . . We bring her to the doctor. When the doctor helps, we're in his hands. Doctors are human beings too. She gives birth and the doctor is happy. That's the outcome I ask the ancestors for. . . . Let them cure the girl, let her stand up. Let her come back to us. Let's call out *madyomina*! Because do you imagine that the water that I've offered here today comes for free?

Assistant Captains Kasindo and Aduengi then perform the *madyomina* exchange, with the latter saying they'll offer one hundred lengths of cloth to the *gaama*. Agbago says he'd like a cloth to be raised right then and there to Bongootu and he names some of the other sites at which he'll raise a cloth to thank the ancestors for listening to his pleas.

Before the *gaama* leaves, he sits, chatting, at Nai's doorstep. Aduengi, who is Gide's grandson (and therefore enjoys a ritualized joking relationship with him), says, "If I could only get my hands on Gide, I'd knock him POW!, right in his face, then knock him again, until he left poor little Dyeni alone."

During the final five months of Dyeni's pregnancy, our notes record numerous interventions of gods and *obias* as well as visits to Dyuumu. Soon after the *gaama's* prayer, she goes to Dyuumu with a fever but back in the village throws away the anti-malaria pills the doctor gave her, saying she doesn't believe in them. Three days later, on Gaantata's orders, she is taken to Akisiamau where the avenging spirit of her lineage (an anaconda god) is called to be informed of her pregnancy and spoken to for divination. The god says that she needs to be washed in certain leaves in Dangogo and under no circumstances should she take the plane to the city, where they would end her ability to bear children. Meanwhile, Dosili has spoken with the doctor who says she needs to take the plane that week, but Titii adamantly refuses. There is much discussion about what to do throughout the village. Nai and Beki want Dyeni to consult the seagod of a woman named Akonomisi.

In June, Gaantata is informed that "something is swelling Dyeni's belly but we don't think it's a child." The oracle reassures them and says it's a normal pregnancy and that it will come to term. In August, Gaantata washes Dyeni in beer. Mamagadu is also performing rites for her across the river. Doote performs an anti-sorcery rite for her on rocks in the middle of the river, washing her with a mixture of leaves from a large clay pot and sacrificing a cock.

At the end of August, Dosili takes Dyeni to Dyuumu, since her belly is hurting badly. Before they leave, Naina instructs her not to drink any water offered by the nurses and to refuse to bathe in any of the hospital's water. Instead she should have a Saamaka woman who lives nearby heat river water and bring it to her to drink and bathe in. The next week, Dyeni is back in the village. We see her carrying a bucket of water from the river and splitting logs with a large axe. There's a small ceremony for her at the doorstep of the Tone shrine, with Nai in attendance. And then on September 27, Dyeni gives birth to a girl at Dyuumu. Nai dances *bandammba*, "shaking her thing" in unbounded delight. Later she goes to tell Gaantata the happy news, and there are ceremonies across the river to inform Mamagadu. The afterbirth has already been brought upriver

FIGURE 11.2. Dyeni's newborn daughter has just been "brought outside." Mamagadu is being asked about further rituals and thanked for her help during the pregnancy. Seated in the background, from left to right, are Doote, Dosili, and Apaasu. Photo: S. Price.

and buried near Dyeni's house across the river, where she'll arrive with the baby later in the day, and women are tying hammocks in her house so they can stay with her for the first few days. (Nai has expressed concern that she not roll over the infant and crush it in the hammock.) Some are sewing little newborn-style caps, and others are bringing firewood to assure that warm water will always be available for bathing.

A week after the birth, villagers gather across the river for the ceremony to "bring the baby out" (*puu a doo*), introducing her to the village. Pomala has mashed up *sangaafu* and *malembelembe* leaves, mixed them with kaolin and water, and poured them into a clay pot. He sprinkles it all around the interior of the house, purifying it so that men can enter without weakening the power of their *obias*. With a ball of kaolin, Aduengi has traced a line from the house to a circle on the earth, about ten feet from the doorstep, and placed a stool in the center, facing east. Simoni, a friend of Dyeni's, goes inside and wraps the baby in one of Dosili's breechcloths and a length of new cloth. Holding the newborn, she puts her right foot out the door, takes it back, and does the same with her left foot, finally stepping out into the sunlight, right foot first, and bringing the baby to Dyeni, who's sitting on the stool. Aduengi sticks his finger in the pot and gives the baby a bit of the solution to suck, then washes mother and child with the mixture. Next he grabs the baby and, careening around wildly, touches her to the inside back beam of the house, knocking down some calabashes and pots with a clatter, touching her to the ground outside and the side of the roof, and then knocking over a winnowing tray—all in the traditional demonstration designed to encourage the child to be lively and mischievous, as children are meant to be. Then he ties a palm-frond necklace on mother and child, praying to their "souls" to keep them healthy. Dosili presents his gifts—several cloths and a carved comb—and Mamagadu is brought out from her sanctuary to be thanked for all her help throughout the very trying pregnancy.

CHAPTER 12

....

The Cock's Balls

Hitching a ride with a Sunday fisherman from the Afobaka dam to Paramaribo in 1968, we began to satisfy our curiosity about chickens' testicles. Mr. Tjen a Djie ("just call me Kennedy"), a Chinese Surinamer who crooned Nat King Cole songs as he drove his Chevy pickup, turned out to be an industrial-scale capon producer. "Only one-percent have black balls at six weeks—that's when I cut them off. They grow much bigger as the cocks get older and stay whiter during breeding season." He never asked us why we wanted to know.

In Saamaka, cocks offer a privileged way to consult the invisibles, just as they do in societies throughout West and Central Africa and the Black Americas. Indeed, white cocks provide one of the most common forms of divination, and we'd seen many sets of cocks' balls scrutinized in Dangogo—at the ancestor shrine, at shrines for the gods, in front of Gaantata's house, and at the Dungulali shrine. The bird would be asked to speak—that is, to allow the gods or ancestors to speak through it—before men would split its belly and examine the testicles. If they were white, the gods (or ancestors) were pleased, and the tiny seeds would be placed on a sacred leaf at the shrine. If they were mottled or dark, there was a problem.

We first saw chicken divination just a few weeks into our stay, when Alogo, a woman Sally's age who often visited Nai, suffered her second stillbirth. It was clear to all that something had to be done—a cock might hold the answer. As it happened, the chicken refused to speak and during the next few weeks Gaantata, Mamagadu, and other gods were consulted, all without a clear response. After a time, rumors began arriving from Guyane, first by tape cassettes accompanying returning men, sent by kinsmen at the missile base, then by returning lineage men themselves. They said that Alogo's husband, Dantabai, had adultered with Godofutu, her mother's sister—a major scandal. In an unusual gesture, Alogo's lineage permitted her to visit Kourou, accompanied by one of her brothers. And soon, both Alogo and Dantabai returned to Dangogo, announcing that he was ready to "go to *kangaa*" to prove his innocence. The ultimate Saamaka lie detector, this ordeal had a long history. In the eighteenth century, a German missionary living in a Saamaka village wrote:

> If a crime has been committed . . . and there is a suspect, the person is taken to this type of Obiaman for the Kangra ordeal to be administered. The accused must kneel, and the sorcerer conjures him in the presence of the gods. He then takes several taro leaves and burns them, reducing them to ashes. With these ashes, he coats the tongue of the suspect, and takes a feather, which is as thin as possible, from the outermost tip of a hen's wing, and he thrusts it through the ashes-coated tongue. If the feather passes through without difficulty and without crumpling, then the person is held to be fully innocent. But if the feather breaks, there is no doubt of his guilt.[1]

Today, the *kangaa* ordeal, which remains the final arbiter of guilt or innocence in Saamaka, is in the sole hands of the Abaisa clan in the village of Masiakiiki. We were told that if the person's tongue swelled up and choked him, they were guilty, if the medicated feather simply passed through, they were innocent.[2] In Alogo's case, the trial was never performed. She became pregnant just before her husband's appointment at the ordeal, and *kangaa* has a prohibition on dealing with a man whose wife is pregnant. The couple traveled back to Guyane, Alogo had her child, and we heard nothing more of it during our stay.

But before long, sometime after the big *obia* washing at Kpokasa that we participated in (see chapter 10, "Upriver"), Beki's kids keep having fevers, and people decide to speak to the ancestors through a cock. On the eve of the sacrifice, Doote and Tando come over and pour libations at Nai's doorstep, announcing the upcoming consultation to the ancestors. At dawn, we all go to the Bongootu Pau ancestor shrine, bringing a white cock from Nai's chicken house. Tando pours libations as first Doote and then Asipei pray, calling on their ancestors to help make the chicken speak. Tando pours some water over the cock's head, gives it a final sip down its beak, and then lifts the chicken by the back of the neck. Doote asks, "Will you speak with us?" The chicken flaps and squawks, signaling Yes. Doote continues, asking whether it's Tone who's causing the illness. When the chicken remains silent he asks the same question four more times, using different wording each time, giving the chicken plenty of time to reply, but it doesn't budge. Doote asks whether it's "one of those many gods that Saamakas have," and the chicken flaps weakly. So he continues, "Is it a Papagadu?" No. Asipei asks Doote to see if it's something that someone said, and Doote complies. The chicken is silent. Tando tells Doote to ask if it's an Apuku. The chicken enthusiastically flaps Yes. Before they can get a good answer to which forest spirit is responsible, the chicken suddenly expires. Doote remarks that he's long suspected an old Apuku that was involved in a long-ago incident at Kpokasa. "Maybe," he says, "that's what's causing the trouble. We'll need to do more divination." Tando grabs his machete, splits the cock's beak—something only men with Komanti spirits do—and holds the cock's head down so a few drops of blood fall in front of the shrine's wooden statue. Then he quickly slits the belly and shows Doote that the testicles are pure white. The men sing, "weti fou kokoo, weti fou kokoo," the white fowl's testicles, the white cock's balls.

Later that morning, sitting around waiting for Gaantata to be consulted, Doote repeats that he knows which Apuku is involved. Evil was done long ago at a boulder near the path to Kpokasa. Gaama Atudendu told him about it and said it had never been properly taken care of. Asipei says he's heard the same thing, and Konoi, just joining them, volunteers, "There's a stone in the forest there that's already killed two people." Everyone agrees that the ceremony that had been performed, in the presence of Nai and Kala, had not been enough to solve the problem. The forest at Kpokasa, in particular the Apuku who lives in that stone, still needs to have its heart cooled.

CHAPTER 13

....

Nai's Rivergod

Melville and Frances Herskovits, visiting Dahomey, West Africa, in 1931, were told that the priests of the ancient river cult had, long before, rebelled against a new ruling dynasty and been sold into slavery. "Nothing of their cult is said to be known today in Dahomey, and the old gods they worshiped are left to trouble the Dahomeans. . . . Sometimes, it is said, they hear drums beating from the river bottom, and sacrifices are given to the rivers, although the proper invocations to appease the gods are no longer known."[1]

In the 1970s, once Rich had been authorized to study First-Time (see chapter 23, "Returns"), he learned of a spiritually dangerous incident that occurred during the eighteenth-century Saamaka wars against the whites. The protagonist was Gweyunga, an African-born runaway slave and priest of the river goddess known as Tone.[2] As the colonial army tried to forge a broad creek, Gweyunga, who had the power to "bring down the rains," sank the whites in their tracks, and large numbers of them drowned. Even earlier in Saamaka history, another African-born runaway, Kwemayon—also remembered as a priest of Tone—sang to Gansa, the goddess of the Suriname River, *Gansa, mi yanvalo, mi yanvalo nawe*, and then descended into the river, sleeping underwater at the foot of the falls.

Because she was born with a caul, Nai was a Tone-child, a special being sent by the river goddess.[3] Tone gods control the rains but also bring their adepts wealth and babies. Their rites include special drum rhythms, songs, and dances, and they have their own sacred leaves and speak their own language.[4] During our time in Dangogo,

Nai participated in rites for Tone held in the village of Malobi, several hours downstream, where many of the descendants of Gweyunga live. Once, when Kala returned from such a rite, we overheard his excited report to Nai. "The riverbank was filled with people, you could hardly find a place to stand. I saw Galimo swim out to the middle of the river and go under . . . and stay. Looked like he'd drowned. Was I scared!" Nai exclaimed "Baad!" "But after a while," Kala continued, "he emerged serenely. He wasn't even panting, and when he swam ashore, he said he'd seen Gansa and that she was getting herself ready to come ashore. Asensi [head priest of Tone] carried Gansa ashore in a calabash, and the crowd whooped and hollered as he placed her in her clay pot in the Tone shrine."

Nai was not only a Tone child by virtue of her birth. She was also conceived by a Tone spirit, binding her doubly to these river deities. Nai's identification with her namesake (neseki)—a Tone child called Ma Tobosi—was complete, giving Nai a spiritual role at the very heart of her lineage. For this namesake was not only, like Nai herself, born a Tone. She was also the great avenging spirit (kunu) of Nai's lineage.[5]

Ma Tobosi's story begins with a man named Zogia, Nai's maternal great-grandfather, who, people say, was as fierce and abrasive as Kala and often squabbled with his family.[6] After spending some time in Matawai territory, Zogia traveled to the Tapanahoni River to visit a Ndyuka friend he'd met on the coast. One day, he and his friend went fishing. Seated at the prow, Zogia was told to steady the canoe by holding on to a branch protruding from the bank while his friend fished from the rear. But as a large fish tugged at the man's line, the branch snapped, the craft rushed downstream, and the Ndyuka somehow managed to leap onto a boulder, just before the canoe crashed over Gaanolo Falls, the largest on the river. Zogia had time only to call out to the river-god, Tone, to save him. The Ndyuka hurried back to the village to get help and the rescuers eventually found Zogia downstream, lying unconscious on a sandbank. After treating his wounds for some days, the Ndyukas consulted Gaantata, who said that in return for sparing Zogia's life, the rivergod required a payment of 12 fowl's eggs, 12 calabash spoons, 12 calabash bowls, 12 balls of kaolin, 12 lengths of cloth, 12 bottles of rum, and 12 bottles of beer. A delegation of Ndyukas accompanied Zogia back to Dangogo to announce the payment. However, his sisters, brothers, and other family members refused, saying that this was his responsibility. As a result of the non-payment, it was not long before Tone punished Zogia with a virulent case of leprosy.

But even then the payment wasn't finished. Before long, the river-god sent Zogia's lineage a Tone-child, Ma Tobosi, born with teeth jutting forward, no upper lip, and no vulva. Tone priests from Malobi who were summoned to treat her made the necessary changes so she could urinate. She grew into adolescence and, after being treated many times by the Tone priests, lived for a while with a man from the village of Akisiamau. When her younger sister, who was normal, slept with her husband, Ma Tobosi gathered up her Tone pot together with her other Tone paraphernalia, threw them all in the river, and killed herself, becoming the most powerful avenging spirit of her matrilineage.[7] Shortly thereafter, she was discovered to be Nai's namesake.[8]

Years later, Zogia, now with advanced leprosy, was setting fishtraps (which he did with great difficulty, using his elbows and teeth as he had no fingers), and caught a large carnivorous fish. A woman from Akisiamau, who saw him with it, told him she would sleep with him if he gave it to her. That evening he dressed in his best—it had been a long time since he'd had a woman. He knocked and entered but she had tied a string around the door to her hammock room and, lacking fingers, he was unable to undo it. The next day she said casually that it had been a mistake and that he should return that evening, but when he knocked, he found no one home—she was sleeping in another house. He swore revenge and when he died, became an avenging spirit for her matrilineage. That created a special relationship between Akisiamau and Dangogo, requiring them to pray and make offerings together from time to time in order to quiet the spirit's wrath.

What this means is that Nai's forebear Zogia is ultimately responsible for the creation of two avenging spirits—the one he cast upon Akisiamau because the woman tricked him, and the much more powerful one that Ma Tobosi created by committing suicide. Often, when Nai was involved in rituals for Ma Tobosi—at once her namesake and the great avenging spirit of her lineage—people from Akisiamau would join forces with those from Dangogo in trying to cool the spirit's heart.

Dangogo's shrine to Tone was made years before for Nai. Under the stewardship of the Tone priests from Malobi, who came to maintain it periodically, it housed not only an altar for the rivergod herself but also the clay pots or dishes in which most of the snakegods (Vodu)

FIGURE 13.1 AND 13.2.
Two views of Dangogo's Tone shrine.
Photos: R. Price.

of the village resided. Our own first washing with Tone leaves, inside that shrine, came early in our stay, at Nai's behest. Once Gaantata had spelled out the various flags that needed to be raised and the bottles of rum that needed to be offered at ancestor shrines, she made a point of telling Kala several times of the importance, when that was all over, of letting Tone know about our stay and asking the protection of the river goddess. Many times during our stay, we witnessed ritual washings in Nai's presence of pregnant women and couples seeking fertility. Sometimes Gaantata would find that the cause of an illness or mishap (once, the sinking of a freight canoe loaded with cement for the mission hospital) was caused by inattention to Tone, and prescribe reparative rituals. During our time in Dangogo, a day rarely passed without Nai's involvement, via her ties to Tone, in a ritual of some sort, often in the Tone shrine. As Asipei told Rich one day, alluding to a young couple who had been unable to conceive a child, "after they came to Nai and she prayed to Tone for them, Kiya [the wife] didn't once go back to the *faagi*. Nai is a god!" And Nai herself took pride in her special Tone powers. One day in 1968 Sally mentioned to her that it was about her time of the month. Nai: "*Kambo!* Don't go anymore! *Pai! Pai!* [Give birth! Give birth!] I was [spiritually] conceived by a Tone god, and if I say that to a woman, she will get pregnant. . . . Tone will bring her a child."

....

CHAPTER 14

Agbago's Seagod

One morning Nai announced to us that it must have been Todye, Agbago's famous seagod, who was responsible for bringing us to Saamaka. We'd heard certain things about this Wenti-god in the course of attending prayers and divination sessions—that when he possessed Agbago ("came into his head" is the Saamaka expression) he spoke French Creole; that before Agbago's arthritis had ruined his knees, Todye would stride around while speaking, never once sitting down; that he could read palms, foretelling the future; and that, like other seagods, he had the power to bring his master money, whitefolks' goods, and children. Indeed, Todye was widely credited with facilitating the creep into modernity that had been taking place since Agbago took the chiefly stool, with *bakaas* and their goods and institutions increasingly penetrating Saamaka life. Todye had been with Agbago for more than a half century.

Saamakas' relationships with Wentis date back to the very end of the nineteenth century, when Kodyi, a man who was working on the lower Saramacca River near the coast, was possessed by a Wenti named Wananzai. That one soon brought others. Tata Yembuamba, from the undersea city of Oloni, possessed Pobosi and was the first Wenti to show himself in Saamaka territory. And Tuli, who possessed Dyameleti, ritually prepared hundreds of early twentieth-century Saamaka men to go to the coast to earn money. Men who had seen Tuli in their youth described to us how he would dive into the river and come up hours later wearing a beautiful necklace and holding a perfectly dry flower in his hand; he would ask a bystander to take two bottles to the river and to fill them up, and when people back in the village tasted them one was filled with rum and the other with sugarcane syrup.

But it was when Kodyi and other Saamakas first came to the Oyapock River, on the Guyane-Brazil border, as canoemen in the gold rush around 1900, that they realized they had truly arrived in the heart of Wenti country. Kodyi's god Wananzai would dive into the river in the morning and come back in the evening with remarkable tales of the underwater world, and he brought back other Wentis who possessed other Saamakas. By 1905, a man from Dangogo named Asimadyo had brought his sisters' sons Agbago, Gasiton, Kositan, and Gide to Kodyi's recently founded village of Tampaki, on the Oyapock. Soon Agbago got possessed by Todye, and his brother Kositan by Zaime. A Wenti named Asantea even possessed a Creole woman who was married to a Saamaka.

It turns out that, like humans, Wentis have both personal differences from one individual to the next and many things in common. Pretty much everything that Saamakas know about Wentis was learned from people in possession, through whom the gods recounted aspects of their normally invisible lives. The folks at Tampaki, for example, learned from Wananzai, Todye, and the other Wentis that under the water at Gaama Lajan (which might be translated as "The Mother of All Money")—a rock formation several kilometers below Tampaki on the French side of the river—was what might best be described as the Central Bank of the World. There, Wenti maidens—not unlike Wagner's Rhine Maidens Woglinde, Wellgunde, and Flosshilde—stand watch over barrels and barrels of golden money, which they sometimes roll out into the sun to dry, singing beautiful songs all the while. They also learned that Wenti villages are "almost like a school," with lots of children running all around, and that if asked appropriately, Wentis take delight in placing a baby into a human woman's womb. They learned that Wentis have strong affinities with whitefolks. They learned that Wentis abhor death and blood, do not like rum or other strong drink, sun or heat, and do not mix with anything evil. Rather, they love white, bright, shiny, clean things, anything sugary or bubbly, and all things cool from the sea. Most important, they learned that Wentis bring humans good things—in particular, money, whitefolks' goods, and babies.

In short, Saamakas came to understand that Wentis are in many ways like especially generous people, except that they live underwater. Their home territory is the sea, where they have numerous towns and cities, often at the base of mountains that rise steeply from the waters.[1] But they also travel up rivers and sometimes live for a time at the foot of a rapids. And when they feel like it, they come ashore and mingle with humans, unnoticed, which they very much enjoy. They also serve as messengers. One day, returning from a visit to her husband's village, Naina told Nai and Kala excitedly about an experience she'd had on her way downstream. A hand had suddenly reached out of the water, grabbed the gunwale of her canoe, and placed a beer bottle in it. She was terribly scared. As soon as she arrived in the village, her husband's people performed divination and found that it wasn't anything evil but rather that a man in Guyane, who'd heard that she'd recently been possessed for the first time by a snakegod, was sending her a present.

Todye had four siblings, who also possessed Saamakas—Tata Yembuamba (who led his medium Pobosi to become the official guide for an ill-fated early twentieth-century expedition into the Suriname interior), and three beautiful Wenti women, Korantina, Amentina, and Yowentina (whom we learned much about years later in Guyane). The parents of this sibling set, Digbeonsu of Oloni ("a name to be very careful with— she is the sea," we were told) and her husband Adyeunsu are also active today.

Unfortunately, we never had a chance to speak with Todye. But there was another Wenti with whom we often interacted. Sally's friend Akonomisi, who was married to Kasindo, one of the assistant headmen of Dangogo, was the medium of Sido, a Wenti who helped out with several pregnancies and births during our stay. (He actually presided over three births in a single day in 1968, rushing from one house to another.) Sido had an unusual origin. Some years earlier, an eight-year-old sister's son of Akonomisi named Sido had drowned while accompanying his grandfather on a trip to Paramaribo. Buried in the riverbank, he was borne away by Wentis and eventually sent back by them to possess Akonomisi. Whenever he appeared, he spoke Sranantongo, the language of the coast, but (for reasons unknown to us) with a marked Javanese accent. He took the guise of a benevolent, elderly visitor from the city who found Saamaka customs quaint and provided welcome entertainment as well as a great deal of help, especially with problems of pregnancy and birth. (He was also Dangogo's reigning expert for anything concerning snakegods and was frequently summoned to deal with these matters.) After word got out in the village that Sido had possessed

Akonomisi, the mother of a sick child would bring the child to her, with offerings of cloth and sugarcane syrup, in the hope that Sido would provide a cure. Men might bring soft drinks or a sea shell to ask what day they should undertake a trip. Sally once wrote down a song that was making the rounds at all-night "plays," which alluded to the range of Sido's influence.[2]

Mi duumi tee mi weki
Mi ta luku so sembe tee mi lafu
Mundu a sondi ta du
Fa a mbei pe pe sembe
So a mbei pe pe hati.

[I sleep till I awake
I look at a certain person till I break out laughing
There are [amazing] things about this world,
Just the way it makes all sorts of people,
It also makes all sorts of temperaments.]

Everyone knew the backstory to this song, which was composed by a woman named Akelele in the wake of a conjugal dispute. She'd been having trouble with a co-wife and told her husband she was leaving him. He'd sought out Sido to help him keep her. Sido said he'd need some urine from when she was menstruating to do the job. She refused for a long time to provide it, but eventually agreed and gave him the requested liquid, which Sido used to bring them back together. But now, after continuing problems with her co-wife, Akelele wants it undone. She wants to leave her husband once and for all, but cannot—Sido's *obia* has bound her to him. By now, the husband would like her to leave, too, but feels helpless. So the two of them go to Sido. And he says what's done is done—deal with it.

With time, as we listened to Saamakas talk about the *gaama*'s Wenti, we learned about the many ways that Todye had shaped Agbago's life, helping him build reasonably harmonious relations with whitefolks, assuring his success in a broad range of economic and political endeavors, and even bringing him two children with a wife who "could no longer have children." We were told that Mama Boi (a.k.a. Wilhelmina), from the downriver village of Santigoon, was bearing Agbago sons but no daughters. So he made an *obia* to cause her to bear daughters (to assure that her lineage would grow), but it backfired and put an end to her fertility. She was incensed and accused him of witchcraft, saying she would much rather bear sons than no children at all. It was then that Todye took over, and Boi once again began to menstruate. At dawn on the day she was to emerge from the menstrual hut for the first time, Todye appeared to the villagers and told them to come to the landing place. There, he said, he would present a baby named Daute, whom he had carried from the undersea Wenti village of Oloni, and place him in Boi's belly.[3] And some months later Daute was born and later spent most of his life on the coast, close to his relatives in Oloni. We met him but once, in Paramaribo.

We also heard stories about Todye's more mundane exploits. Our friend Asipei described how the gaama and Headcaptain Faansisonu had been called to the city for some government business and were getting bored just waiting around. Faansisonu called Todye and asked him to find him some day work so he could earn a little money. Three days later a bakaa showed up where they were living and asked Agbago if he could suggest a reliable employee for a job he had. The gaama introduced Faansisonu. The bakaa asked how much of an advance against wages he wanted. Faansisonu, afraid of incurring a large debt, said "50 guilders," which the bakaa quickly handed over, saying he'd be back soon to take him to work. The gaama turned to his friend: "You really blew it! You should have asked for more." They never saw that bakaa again. ("Of course it was Todye himself!" Asipei remarked.)

Todye's encouragement to increase relations with whitefolks sometimes put the gaama at odds with his own people. In the early 1960s, there was much controversy about whether to permit the Moravians to build a hospital at Dyuumu and a landing strip across the river close to the sacred site of Tuliobuka, where the Pikilio and Gaanlio meet. But the gaama approved the project and at its inauguration, he named the building Hospitaal Jaja Dande, after his Matyau-clan ancestor who had permitted the eighteenth-century Moravians to teach the Bible to Alabi, an early gaama.[4]

On Agbago's return from the Netherlands in 1968, he held a large-scale meeting with all the captains and assistant captains in an attempt to persuade parents to send their children to school. Since the eighteenth-century peace negotiations, when Saamakas made schools one of their first demands, there had always been ambivalence. The

Moravians who ran the initial school in the 1770s did their best to prevent their few pupils from maintaining central aspects of their culture. The schools set up by that same church in the 1960s, such as the one several boys from Dangogo attended at Dyuumu, also required them to take on a "Christian" name (e.g., Isadore, George, Herman), to wear pants instead of breechcloths, and to abandon participation in "heathen" rites such as ancestral feasts. They also encouraged baptism. The *gaama*, under Todye's influence, was now arguing that schooling was needed for modern life, and that any school was better than none. "Without school," he asserted, "we remain slaves!" And he added, "When I was in Queen Wilhelmina's country [older Saamakas' way of referring to the motherland ruled at the time by Juliana], I even saw women doctors! Girls must go to school too." Headcaptain Faansisonu cleared his throat and replied on behalf of the others, saying, "Each family has its own ways and the ones I know don't want their girls to be 'spoiled' like those in Botopasi [a Christian village]. I beg the *gaama*'s pardon for saying this, but no real Saamakas want their girls to go to school." He then named a dozen villages that wanted schools for boys, but only if they were secular government schools.

In Dangogo, parents were divided. Women wanted their sons' help in preparing their gardens for planting and for other chores and often saw no benefits from the schooling that deprived them of it. Kala once lectured the schoolteacher at Dyuumu: "It's fine to teach the boys reading and writing but I absolutely forbid you to ruin them by teaching them Christianity!" While Faansisonu's sons were faithful pupils at Dyuumu, Beki's son Elima generally played hooky out of fear of being beaten by the teacher. And more than once, after persuading Nai to give him fifty cents to buy pencils at the Dyuumu store, he bought candy instead. Todye, who was often blamed for the Afobaka dam and other disasters of modernity, was, in the opinion of most of our neighbors, once again going too far. People even joked, "The *gaama*'s becoming a *bakaa*!"

....

CHAPTER 15

Kala's Snakegod

Wearing Lukunya's special breechcloth and his cape with the little brass bell, Kala began a violent series of chest heaves, as if he was going to vomit. His shoulders moved rhythmically and we heard deep animal-like grunting, "Hu-hu-hu-hu!" The god began to speak in a language that sounded "African" to us: "I'm off to Alada!"[1]

We'd been waiting in Kala's house for nearly an hour, along with Nai, Anaweli, and Maame, as attempts were made to coax Lukunya to come and possess Kala. Two snakegod specialists—Akonomisi's husband, Kasindo, and her Wenti-god, Sido—had placed special palm fronds on a table and lain various Papagadu leaves along its eastern edge. Kasindo had traced a rectangle of kaolin on the floor around it, and Anaweli had stood a bottle of beer in a large white china bowl on the table. Kasindo had opened it, sprinkled in some kaolin so that the bottle fizzed over into the bowl, added some creek water, and floated a parrot feather on the foaming surface. Sido and Kasindo had sung several melodic Papagadu songs, mixing Saamaka words with those particular to snakegods. And Sido had prayed to Lukunya to join us, saying that if we'd done something wrong, we apologized and promised to make it right. Meanwhile, Kasindo began pouring the solution over Kala's head and body, and rubbing it in. It was then that the god arrived.

Lukunya said little that the two of us could understand, but amidst the hu-hu-hus he indicated his desire for a separate calabash to be washed in. Speaking in a mixture of Saamaka and Sranantongo (the language of the coast), he called Kasindo and Sido, and then Nai and ourselves, and anointed each person with water from the calabash, announcing

FIGURE 15.1. Akonomisi in her rice field. Photo: R. Price.

that it was Gaama Atudendu (Agbago's predecessor) who had brought the two white people to Dangogo. Lukunya poured the kaolin water over himself several times. As people outside heard the commotion, they came to receive the ablutions as well: Tando prayed, while being washed, that the god would bring him "Money! Not work, money!" Sido said that the god might stay with us for the rest of the afternoon, and we all made our way to Gaantata's shrine, for the bi-weekly oracle consultation, Lukunya tagging along.

Once we settle in, various problems are brought to Gaantata for consideration—illnesses, pregnancies, marital discord, rites for a man about to leave for work at the missile base in Guyane—but suddenly Lukunya greets the oracle and Gaantata says he has something to tell him: before Kala leaves for his long-planned trip to the coast the *agida* drum (sacred to Papagadus) must be played at the shrine next to Tone's (a long-abandoned shrine to the anaconda god belonging to a man who'd once held Kala's captain's staff). The man who's interrogating reminds everyone that Kala's god is the "heaviest" of all Papagadus in Dangogo. Faansisonu takes a bottle of beer he'd brought for another purpose and hands it to Lukunya, who then wanders back toward Kala's house.

A week later, as a group is sitting around in front of the Tone shrine, waiting for a ceremony to begin, Kala suddenly announces to Akonomisi (or was it her Wenti-god Sido?) and Kasindo that he wants to reveal some things about his god that they might not know. First, it has had eight previous *basi* (priests)—Sido makes nine. In his village over to the east, Lukunya is like a schoolmaster. That's why, like Gaantata, he has a bell, which he rings at eight o'clock in the morning to call the other snakegods to come to school. Anyone who says his god is harming someone in Dangogo is lying—Lukunya never does harm to anyone here. In a long story we didn't fully understand, Kala describes how the god had once set out to kill a human child but stopped at the last moment and then renounced killing forever after.

Lukunya was hardly a typical Papagadu. During our time in Dangogo, nineteen women, but only two men, had one. Papagadus are generally seen as a women's thing, closely associated with their gardens, and the great drum that speaks to them in ceremonies is "dressed" with a woman's skirt. Little girls often played at Papagadu possession, dancing with arms undulating as they called out in stuttering cadences. Papagadus love to get "dressed up" and show off their looks. They favor sparkly things and are said to "own" both kaolin and gold—people must make a ritual payment to them before extracting either from the earth.

There are three kinds of snakegods, the most common of the Saamaka avenging spirits:[2] Papagadus (also called Vodu or Daguwe),[3] who live in boa constrictors; Watawenus, who live in anacondas; and Gaan-sembe-u-matu ("big person of the forest"), aka Gaan-Vodu, who are said to live in the largest of terrestrial constrictors. The snakes are envisioned as carrying the gods in the same way that a canoe carries a person.

According to herpetologists, boa constrictors (*Boa constrictor constrictor*) are the largest and most common terrestrial constrictors in Suriname,[4] so the Gaan-sembe-u-matu, which Saamakas say is virtually never seen alive, must simply be an unusually large boa constrictor. After all, a snakegod's identity is only determined when it possesses a person—that's when people find out what language it speaks, what songs it sings, what leaves it wants for its ritual washings, and what drums it likes to hear. Years after our stay in Saamaka, the tutelary spirit of our Saamaka friend Tooy ("Toy") spoke with us on the subject:

I'll bet you don't know how a Papagadu says its praise-name. It says, "I'm Adji-kodo-gidi-unzu-moyon. If the wind blows, I coil up, if the wind doesn't blow, I coil up." But this isn't just any Papagadu! It's the one that lives underneath the earth—The Great Papagadu, The Earth Mother, The Big-One-of-the-Forest, it's all black without any stripes! And it's got the head of an agouti! If you come upon it, you've seen the face of Evil. You'll die.

In any case, as a Papagadu, Kala's god Lukunya belongs to the most common kind of Saamaka possession gods. The ceremonies at which they're summoned to dance are led by the largest of Saamaka drums, the *agida*, played with a stick and a hand, as the drummer straddles the drum, which is lying on its side. We have always viewed Papagadu ceremonies as the most beautiful and graceful of all Saamaka rituals (see chapter 17, "Playing for the Gods").

The journey of a Papagadu from the time it rides its boa constrictor "canoe" in the forest to its final consecration, when it can speak through its medium in the village, takes several years, many ceremonies, and a good deal of money. When the skeleton or blackened corpse of a boa constrictor is discovered in a recently burned garden, Papagadu priests are summoned to bear it to the edge of the forest and bury it under *obia* leaves in a shallow, temporary grave. They also conduct divination with a cock to make sure that the god is a Papagadu, not a Gaan-sembe-u-matu. The next step occurs several months (sometimes years) later, when the priests construct a two-foot-long coffin made of *sangaafu* reeds in the village, and bring it to the garden as they sing Papagadu songs. There they unearth the remains, place them in the coffin, and after tying it onto a plank of wood, raise it on the heads of two bearers for interrogation: "Is it time to bring it to the village? Do any other rites need to be done?" If all is well, they ritually clean the area so women can again garden in it, and bring the coffin back to the village for a week of Papagadu dances, songs, and other ceremonies. The *agida* drum is played each evening, many of the village Papagadus come in possession to dance, and cries of "Vodu-e!" and "Dagowe-e!" ring out at all hours. During the day, boys rush around the village carrying the coffin on a plank in mock divination—the idea is to have fun, to honor the god with celebration. The priests then bury the coffin in the riverbank or next to a forest path, as onlookers sing melodic Vodu songs. At the

FIGURE 15.2. Elima (right) and Tando's son
Suyeti on the doorstep of our house,
eating oranges after having peeled them to
make masks. Photo: R. Price.

time of our stay, the priests were paid fifty to a hundred guilders (equal
to fifty to one hundred lengths of cloth) for their services.

Children participated in all these events, readying themselves for
full participation. Girls mastered the sinuous moves of a dancing Papagadu by the time they were five and frequently simulated possession.
And we once saw Elima carefully treating a small lizard that he'd killed
with his slingshot to all the ritual attention he'd seen being given to boa
constrictors—constructing a miniature coffin from pieces of wood and
reeds, carefully burying the lizard in it, and placing a palm-leaf structure on the top of the grave.

Sometimes a Papagadu possesses a person even before the snake's
remains have been buried in the village. Other gods wait for years. And

when the medium of a Papagadu dies, the god may or may not return to possess a descendant.

Kala's absence from Saamaka during much of our stay meant that we had relatively few encounters with Lukunya. But we were present at many events for the Papagadu that possessed Nai's granddaughter Naina.

Some thirty years earlier, Naina's mother, Dyamati, had burned a boa constrictor in her garden. The man who performed the requisite rites after the snake was found was paid 12 lengths of cloth, 1 hammock, 1 hammock sheet, 3 liters of rum, 12 metal spoons, 12 calabash bowls, 12 pottery bowls, and tobacco. Yet the god never possessed anyone. Now Naina was showing signs of upcoming possession, trembling whenever a rite was held for the snakegods. When Gaantata was consulted, he said they should ask Sido's assistance in "making the god" so they could communicate with it.

Once again, Sido and Kasindo were in charge, orchestrating (with Kala's help) the complicated ceremony, which involved kaolin, parrot feathers, beer, and large quantities of Papagadu leaves. Eventually Naina was possessed, but the spirit refused to speak. Kasindo led it to the river and tried to wash off the various deaths it had caused over the years—including three children of Naina's sister Beki, for which the god presumably felt ashamed. But nothing worked and they ended the session. The next day was more successful. The god came quickly and this time began speaking in Saamakatongo with Papagadu grunts and stuttering mixed in, revealing that her name was Ndovie. She told the names of her mother and father and surprised everyone by declaring that she was a new god sent by Nai's Tone *kunu*, not the one that had lived in the snake Dyamati burned. She asked them to buy various accessories for her in the city—a little silver bell, a cowrie shell, and a white porcelain bowl.

Ndovie quickly became a valued part of the neighborhood. A few weeks after her first appearance, she was called again in order to set a date for the final rites in which her porcelain bowl would be placed in the Tone shrine with those of the other Papagadus of the village—no specific date was set but they said they'd do it eventually. But she dealt with an array of other issues as well. She warned Naina's brother Abatili to be careful because of the jealousy over his job as the *gaama's* senior boatman; she told Naina's sister Beki to wash her son Elima in a certain leaf solution if she ever wanted him to end his unruly ways. She told Naina's son Amombebuka that his "namesake" was unhappy and that he needed to pour libations to him. Beki's namesake was also angry, Ndovie explained, which is what had caused her recent toothache—she should make a trip to her father's village where the namesake had lived. Naina's son Dosili asked Ndovie why a large fish he had on the line the day before got away and was told that Konoi's anaconda god did it— he should ask Konoi to do mafiakata divination to learn more. Kasindo complained to Ndovie about how difficult one of his children was to bring up, and the god's reply was a curt "deal with it."

Ndovie explained that she had twelve children so they should be careful when they burned their gardens in the coming days. Also: "A white man has come to live with us so we must be watchful of him and he must be watchful of us."

Throughout this séance, the god rocked back and forth from the waist, rubbing her hands over a ball of kaolin and giving each person some to do the same. She already seemed completely at home. When at last she was ready to leave, she leaned over forward and let out three little screams. After half a minute Akonomisi asked, "Naina, are you awake now?" (the equivalent of "Good morning"), to which Naina answered, "Yes, thanks."

The first appearance of a Papagadu is often quite violent, unlike Ndovie's easy arrival and willingness to speak. We've seen women, driven by the drumming, rolling wildly on the ground, frothing at the mouth, skirts up over their chests, while other women try to quiet them and protect their modesty. As the agida plays and other snakegods dance, the newly possessed person can take hours to calm down, as Papagadu priests wash her with sacred leaves and kaolin. On another day, the god may be summoned and its eyes ritually opened by squeezing in drops from medicinal plants, and prayed to speak. If it talks in a language that Saamakas have difficulty understanding, it is treated with special rites until at last it is able to tell its name and why it came.

Papagadus are only one kind of kunu—spirits that seek vengeance on the lineage of someone who has offended them. (When a Saamaka suffers paralysis, the diagnosis is almost always the wrath of a Papagadu.) Other snakegods, forest spirits (Apuku), and deceased humans can also seek vengeance for wrongs done to them. The advantage for the community of having such a spirit possess someone is that it enables communication. When sickness or some other misfortune strikes, they can call it and find out how to cool its heart—if only temporarily.

In addition to boa constrictors, which we saw from time to time (while Rich was hunting in the forest or when Sally was on the path to the river), the most common constrictors we saw were anacondas, which frequented the edge of the river, especially upstream from Dangogo. We were told that outboard motors—their noise and petroleum waste—had much diminished their presence, but we still saw them a number of times.

Papagadu are never killed except by accident, when fields are burned prior to planting. Whenever they're seen in villages or garden camps, they're gently urged away with poles or other incentives, since no one wants to create a kunu. One day, Nai showed Sally the hole next to her chicken house where a boa constrictor had spent much of the previous year, sticking its head out from time to time. Apaasu had first prayed to it to leave and when that didn't work had poured gasoline down the hole, forcing the snake to take up residence elsewhere.

In contrast, the anacondas carrying Watawenu gods are deliberately killed when they endanger someone—or, often, when they attack a man's hunting dog. There was a young anaconda that spent several months in the reeds near one of Dangogo's river paths during our stay—people simply gave it a wide berth as they walked past.

Asipei told us how one of Gaama Atudendu's wives was attacked and almost pulled under at the Asindoopo landing place by an anaconda, which wrapped itself around her. She was saved when some men managed to saw through its body and free her. More recently, at the same spot, Assistant Captain Apaasu of Dangogo was attacked as he debarked from his canoe. He slashed at the snake with his machete, but it struck his boat instead, and the snake slithered away. He called out to it, "If you're a man who wears a breechcloth, be here tomorrow morning to settle this affair! And if you're a woman who wears a skirt, come meet me here tomorrow morning!" He went ashore and slept. The next morning, no one would lend him a gun, fearing that they would be implicated if a kunu was created. So he took a bow and arrow and went to his canoe. Soon, the snake appeared. He complimented it, "If you're a man, you're a real man. And if you're a woman, you're a real woman!" Then, as the snake opened its mouth, he shot the arrow right down its gullet. The snake slid back into the river and Apaasu returned home.

Akonda was the only person in Dangogo who was possessed by a Watawenu during our stay, but we saw the god only once and briefly, singing sweet, melodic songs. A small lineage-segment across the river had a Watawenu as its great kunu, and we were told that this god had been responsible for the deaths of all of Baala and Aduengi's ten siblings. But, otherwise, we heard relatively little about these gods during our time in Saamaka, and it was only forty years later, when we got to know Tooy in Cayenne, that the full world of these gods—their songs, their language, their lore—was revealed to us.[5]

Near the end of our stay, when Kala was still in Guyane delivering Maame back to her lineage kin, Nai told Naina that she dreamed she saw him, possessed by Lukunya. He walked up the river path and sprinkled kaolin near her house, then stopped and cried out in his special language at Beki's doorstep. Kabuesi was running behind the god yelling "Father Vodu's come!" but Nai reprimanded her, saying, "Let's listen to what the god has come to tell us." And there the dream suddenly ended. Nai and Naina first speculated that something had happened to Kala, that perhaps Lukunya had done him harm. But later they decided the dream meant that Kala would return to Saamaka that year to cut gardens for the women, at long last.

CHAPTER 16

....

A Touch of Madness

In 1963–1964, Rich participated in a Paris seminar with the famous ethnopsychiatrist Georges Devereux, who taught that while mental illness was universal, the ways it manifested itself (as well, obviously, as the ways it was treated) varied from one culture to the next. In Saamaka, we heard a number of stories about people whose "head was spoiled," who'd become "crazy." And we had a chance to witness one case up close—one that probably would have been diagnosed as schizophrenia in Western medicine—over the course of more than a year.

During our first four months in Dangogo, Akonda's daughter Afude, in her twenties, often visited Nai to chat, with her mother's propensity to steal tobacco the most frequent topic of conversation. Married to Gonima from Asindoopo, who had cleared gardens for her and her mother in Mama Creek, she was an active participant in the round of village life, one day making calfbands with a group of women, another having her Papagadu speak through her at a ceremony, another planting peanuts in her garden, another bringing Nai a present of a cassava cake from the *gaama*'s wife Gadya. And then one day Akonda rushed to Nai, announcing that her daughter had had a fit: "Her head's gone crazy!" Nai told Akonda to tell her brothers Kasindo and Binotu to go across the river and ask Doote to raise Gaantata to find out what was wrong. Akonda explained that they'd already gone downstream to seek help at another oracle but had returned empty-handed. "Get them over to Doote," Nai urged.

The next morning, August 19, Kala, Doote, Asipei, and several other men pour libations and say prayers at the ancestor shrine maintained for Gaantata in the forest glen before moving to the doorstep of Gaantata's shrine. The oracle refuses to walk, despite their pleas. They tell Gaantata they'll return in the afternoon, and when they do, Kala prays for Afude at Bongootu Pau, informing Bongootu himself that Afude's condition is serious but not hopeless—she just needs his help. He recalls how a village elder who is now on the coast once cured someone with this very same illness.

Later in the day, Akonomisi sits down with Nai and says Akonda is responsible for her daughter's fits. "Afude is the one who brings Akonda rice from her garden and tobacco too. Akonda never gets enough. . . . But look at her belly! Think of how she stuffs herself!" Akonomisi continues, "One day I saw Afude return from the garden without rice, since she'd been giving her mother so much. Akonda was furious, saying 'I'm going to teach you. I'm the one who gave birth to you!'" Nai holds her head in her hands and shakes her head. "Just think, I was the one who carried water to Akonda the day she gave birth to Afude."

August 23. Binotu reports to Nai that he's gone to the village of Kampu to get leaves to make an *obia* for Afude. There's a woman there right now with the same illness—the *obia* includes something that they'll drip into Afude's eyes. The next morning Akonda comes to tell Nai that the leaves have arrived from Kampu and that they'll raise Gaantata to ask him about supervising the cure.

August 24. Gaantata conducts a washing of Afude's whole lineage-segment—twelve men and twenty-six women are involved. After almost an hour of washing them one by one, Gaantata summons Afude. Kala pulls her over to Gaantata but she resists. Faansisonu and Kasindo, both close relatives, help get her to the oracle, where the ablutions are finally performed.

August 27. Kala, Doote, and Nai discuss Afude's problems at Nai's doorstep. Doote reports that he "killed a cock," performing the attendant divination, the day before. It indicated that *siba*—sorcery-via-words—in the lineage-segment was the cause. They all agree that people in that lineage-segment don't get on well with each other and the possibility of *siba* seems real. Nai brings up one case they all appear to know about. One of Kasindo's wives noticed that a path through her rice garden had been trampled all the way to her tobacco plants, so she followed it and found Akonda standing there. They fought and Akonda ended up with a broken finger that to this day still can't be straightened.

Akonda then pronounced a curse that killed the woman. Kala brings up a second case, also known to all. Akonda once stole some tobacco from the garden of a sister-in-law in Daume. Again, they fought, and Akonda pronounced a curse that caused the death of her child. Nai, Kala, and Doote agree that it's these cases of *siba* that are killing Afude.

August 28. Kasindo, as Afude's mother's brother, is leading the quest for a cure. He travels to Afude's father's village, Bofokule, to ask their lineage to help him pour a libation to ask the aid of their ancestors. While there, a canoe carrying the hair-and-nail packet of a man who had died on the coast passed the village on its way upstream and Kasindo hailed it and had them come ashore so that divination could be performed with these relics, asking those in the land of the dead what was causing Afude's illness. The surprising answer was that she had singed a Papagadu when she burned her garden that year. When Kasindo reported the news back in Dangogo (Nai was told "it's a slithering-on-the-ground thing"), his brother Binotu went to a man in Akisiamau who accompanied him to Afude's garden and performed the necessary rites to cool the snakegod's heart. Later that day Kasindo remarked to Rich that *kunus* (in this case the Papagadu) love to confuse people in order to make finding a cure as difficult as possible. "It's always a *kunu* that makes you 'find' so many different causes for any illness, that makes you pay so many payments. But no matter how many causes are supposedly 'found,' there's a single origin—the *kunu*. And once a person is finally cured, you don't even know for sure which of the many cures you tried was the one to fix it—the *kunu* makes it that way on purpose."

September 1. Afude ran off into the forest yesterday and wasn't found and brought back till nightfall.

September 2. Kasindo paddles to the village of Afude's *neseki* (spiritual genitor) for libations. Since the libations in Dangogo didn't seem to be working, they thought this might work better. In the late afternoon, Kala tells Nai that Afude just woke up, after sleeping all day.

September 3. Kala goes across the river to interrogate Mamagadu about Afude. The oracle outlines the payments she must receive to intervene in the cure and asks that Afude be brought over from Wednesday till Sunday to sleep near her shrine, where she'll perform the rite in a week. She also says that on Wednesday, when Afude arrives, they should have someone perform *mafiakata* (the divination in which a person "knocks their hands") and that she'll communicate further instructions through that medium.

Later that day, Doote informs Gaantata that they've sought the help of Mamagadu. "When someone [whatever is trying to kill her] is strong, you can't fight him by yourself. So we beg that you not be offended and we ask your forgiveness for having sought additional help." Gaantata agrees that Mamagadu's assistance is agreeable to him. Doote asks Asipei's son Pagai if they have done divination by carrying Afude's *akaa* (soul) yet. He says yes and that it said the cause of illness was *siba* within the lineage-segment. And they had already poured libations for that.

Rich visits Faansisonu's neighborhood and finds Kasindo playing the role of watchman for Afude, following her when she runs off and bringing her back to her house.

September 4. Konoi, terribly indignant, reports to Nai that Akonda went across the river to try to get some tobacco and that meanwhile Afude, left all alone on her doorstep, pulled off all her clothes and was sitting in front of the house stark naked. She adds that Akonda keeps two cups of tobacco going at once, and it still isn't enough for her. Later in the day, Kala tells Nai that Afude will soon be better. "Since they 'found' that it was her *neseki* that was sickening her, and have poured libations, she's quieted down a lot." Meanwhile, we see that Kasindo is spending a lot of time going around the edge of the village gathering medicinal leaves for Afude's various cures.

September 5. Tianen visits Nai and says that the only person who's responsible for Afude's illness is her mother. "She's a thief, a beggar, she simply can't get enough tobacco. Did you know that Afude has started taking tobacco? She puts it in her mouth—I don't know what exactly she does with it!"

September 14. It's the day for Mamagadu's rite for Afude. About fifteen people gather before the oracle's shrine. Mamagadu is raised on the heads of two men and she quickly leads off a couple of other elders to gather leaves, directing them at which ones to pick, as they walk around the village. Then she calls for Afude, who is sitting on a nearby doorstep, to come forward. When she shakes her head, refusing, Faansisonu and Kasindo drag her over. But soon she tries to wander off, looking distracted. She looks miserable, as usual these days. When Akonda, standing nearby, yells at her to obey, she cries out, "Leave me alone, for once!" Faansisonu finally grabs her and stands right behind her, hands wrapped firmly around her torso. She wriggles around and her clothes keep coming undone. A woman named Sakuima keeps trying to cover her up but she resists. They threaten her saying that if she doesn't behave Fosumii or Kala will come and they have big sticks and machetes all ready. Once in a while someone calls out to an imaginary Fosumii or Kala in another neighborhood telling him that Afude is being bad. (This is exactly the way they frighten kids.) Mamagadu said that they needed a *biyongo* (a special, extra ingredient or two) and took her priest Tioye aside to tell him about it in private. He went to his house and came back with a white kerchief wrapped around some leaves and a parrot feather. Afude was sat down at the nearby ancestor shrine. Mamagadu told Doote to tie her head with a white kerchief and place the *obia* packet on top. She was passive as Doote, under instruction from the oracle, washed her with a bottle of beer and kaolin that Kasindo had brought with him. Mamagadu said that Afude must sleep on the oracle's side of the river for some days and Aduengi offered her a house. They led her over to it but she soon began wandering around. Akonda was put in charge of bringing her back and keeping her there.

Toward evening, Kala returns with a delegation from the village of Pempe, where a madman has set fire to twenty-three houses. There's discussion of how whitefolks do it right by putting madmen in a special house by themselves, where they can't harm others. Everyone is worried that Afude could do something like that in Dangogo.

September 17. Kala angrily tells Kasindo that Gaantata is not the one responsible for Afude's madness. "He told me this personally the other day, when we raised him. Nor is it Mamagadu. Nor the big *kunu* of the lineage-segment. It's only one thing: Akonda's *siba!*" Kala insists that Gaantata and Mamagadu have agreed to try to help, but that the real problem is the things that Akonda said that causes deaths in the family. If, says Kala, Kasindo wants to seek other cures, all he has to do is ask Gaantata's permission first.

September 18. Kasindo catches Afude after she escapes into the forest. Later she begins to load up a basket and says she's "going downriver." Akonda seems quite depressed and doesn't interfere with her daughter's activities.

September 20. Afude's husband visits and sleeps with her on Mamagadu's side of the river. Akonda visits Nai and complains that Afude tries to untie the *obia* packet that Mamagadu made for her and once even tried to take someone's canoe and come across to the other side of the river, where she normally lives.

Akobo advises Kasindo to seek additional help for Afude from the Dombi clan, way downstream, who have a powerful *obia* that cures mental illness. He replies that he'd go to them only if Gaantata and Mamagadu instruct him to.

Later in the day, Sally sees Afude visiting at Akonomisi's house and finds her looking better than she has in months.

September 21. Asipei tells Kasindo he knows a man from Botopasi who can cure Afude's illness but only if she were having really violent fits. He won't treat people who aren't ripping off their clothes and running all around.

Akonda visits Nai and tells her that Afude is being impossible. Akonda says that Afude spent most of the day crying.

September 22. In the morning, Asipei remarks to Nai that "Afude's co-wife is beyond the pale, she's hardly a human!" Nai: "Well, shouldn't we be doing something [ritual] about that?" Asipei: "We should be try-ing everything possible!" Asipei recalls that his father died of this same illness. The first time, Gaantata cured him but it recurred when he was working in Guyane. When they brought him back, he stopped having fits, but he withdrew into himself and hardly spoke more than a couple of words a day until he died.

Later in the day, Nai, very agitated, joins other villagers searching for Afude, who has disappeared. After a half hour, she's found and led back to her house, where she sits on her doorstep quietly singing Apuku songs to herself. She keeps jiggling one foot. People gather around and exclaim "Afude!" "The world is coming to an end!" Suddenly, she begins to cry and rolls onto the ground, face down, bawling like a baby. They sit her down and tell her to be quiet. But she suddenly jumps up, grabs a machete, and strides toward the forest saying she's going to make a garden. One of her aunts runs after her and firmly leads her back. Nai begins weeping, almost uncontrollably but eventually quiets down, crying into a kerchief. Kasindo says there should be a village-wide meeting. This is a problem he can no longer handle himself.

September 24. After hearing twelve unrelated cases lasting a couple of hours, Gaantata says he'll take on Afude's illness and wants her brought to him, which Agumii (her classificatory grandmother) man-ages to do. He orders her and the others in her family to wash in a special square marked out with kaolin near the path to the river. Akonda, Afude, Agumii, Kasindo, Binotu, Faansisonu, and a number of others pour calabash-fulls of the leaf mixture over themselves. Afude is sat down (with difficulty—she resists but Faansisonu does it by force) on a white cloth that Doote has spread out on top of some medicinal leaves, following Gaantata's instructions, facing east. Doote opens a bottle of beer (the top falls "open," which is good) and washes her in it, again at Gaantata's instructions. And then twelve different small bottles of leaf-solutions are taken from Gaantata's shrine (they had been prepared over the previous days) and each is poured and rubbed over Afude. As he washes her, Doote repeats, "We're not the ones who are washing Afude, it's Gaantata who's washing her." Then despite her protests, Afude is led under Gaantata, into and then out of his shrine. Gaantata instructs Doote how to bundle up the leaves she's been sitting on and where to dispose of them and everyone waits for him to complete the task, alone with the oracle.

Later in the day, Kasindo seeks out Doote to bring some men to raise Gaantata once more, since he'd forgotten to ask whether he would be permitted to seek a cure for Afude elsewhere. We're not present at this ceremony but are told afterward that the oracle gave his approval.

October 3. Divination across the river finds that Afude's illness is caused by an Apuku, not by sorcery. Afude's garden was cut between two *katu* trees and one of them seems to have been singed when she burned the field prior to planting. But her co-wife may also, somehow, be involved.

October 9. New divination (we're not sure what kind) is performed to find the cause of Afude's illness. It says that, contrary to some previous findings, her co-wife is not involved. This is purely an Apuku matter, which fits the diagnosis that Akonda had called on a forest spirit to do evil deeds.

October 10. Sally reports that she could hardly sleep all night in the *faagi* because Afude, her only partner there, sang to herself all night long.

October 25. Afude's case is again brought to Gaantata who says that an Apuku is the cause. People discuss the different cures they've tried: washing in the glen, washing at Bongootu Pau, washing at Mamagadu. Each time, Apukus ruined the cure. Gaantata prescribes another washing at Bongootu Pau. If that doesn't work, they'll need to try Mamagadu again. And if that doesn't work, they'll need to try something completely different.

October 31. Afude visits Nai and they have a long and normal conversation. Afude talks frankly about her illness. Nai later tells Kasindo that Afude is getting much better and will soon be completely cured.

November 3. Akonda tells Nai that they'll be washing Afude at Mamagadu the following Friday.

November 5. Nai tells Doote that Akonda took some kaolin and went to a *katu*, or a silk-cotton tree—"one of those trees that forest spirits like"—in the forest at Mama Creek and paid the Apuku to kill Afude. Doote says that it must have been more than simply telling the god to do it. Every kind of divination they've consulted shows it was *siba* conducted in the forest, he says. Kasindo, sitting with them, says he'll never cut another garden anywhere near Akonda's, since she's already killed a wife of his with *siba*. Doote says that the several deaths Akonda has caused by *siba*, including her own mother's, are all coming home to roost now. She's far from free of them yet.

[A week later we leave for stocktaking in the United States. Our notes about Afude pick up in March 1968.]

March 15. Going hunting behind the village with Elima tagging along, Rich sees a strip of cloth on a two-foot-high pole next to a fire fan similarly suspended at the foot of a particularly wrinkled tree. Elima says it's from an *obia* made by Doote for Afude in our absence.

March 20. Afude and Akonda are preparing their garden for planting rice.

April 13. Gaantata is asked if he can now complete Afude's cure, since she seems so much better. He says to ask again on another day.

April 20. Apenti, Faansisonu's older brother and the doyen of the lineage-segment, asks Gaantata to tell them what more to do for Afude. He says he'll teach them some medicinal leaves. Forest leaves? they ask. Yes. From a large tree? No. Those smaller leaves we use to make *obias*? No. Twenty different plants are then mentioned with five getting a yes. Then they ask if whitefolks' things are needed, such as a white cloth, a cowrie shell, or a bottle of beer, and they're told yes. They agree that only one of the leaves will be hard to find, and discuss where it might grow. And, with Gaantata, they agree on a day for further consultation.

May 18. Akonda's brother Pande reports that a woman in Asindoopo dreamed evil about her. An unnamed person had made an evil *obia* against Gonima, Afude's husband, in the garden where Akonda and

Afude worked at Mama Creek. But since Gonima never goes there, the *obia*, which had to do with an Apuku (forest spirit), jumped on Afude and sickened her instead. Akonda is very upset by this news.

June 6. Gaantata is raised and is ready for Afude's final cure, which was postponed because of deaths in the village and other more pressing problems. Kasindo has now gathered the necessary leaves three times because they've rotted during the earlier postponements. Gaantata orders Kasindo to mash the five kinds of leaves in a mortar, which he does. They'll need a gourd, not a calabash, for the washing, says Gaantata. They find one in Akonda's house and bring it. Afude is then washed, brought into and then out of the shrine, and Doote warns Akonda, with Gaantata nodding his approval, that if there's any further *siba* in the family, the *obia* will not work. Akonda is indignant, expressing her innocence, but Doote, with Gaantata's approval, is insistent.

In various fieldnote entries after this, we find that Afude is acting completely normal—doing chores, drugging streams for fish, harvesting lots of rice, helping prepare an ancestral feast along with other women, helping braid palm fronds for a new roof, and so forth.

October 9. Afude visits Nai for a long session of discussing her mother's propensity for stealing. It's almost the same conversation as the ones she used to have with Nai eighteen months earlier, before her illness began. It seems the multiple cures had finally worked.

....

CHAPTER 17

Playing for the Gods

One evening when we're sitting on our doorstep, we hear drumming across the river. Kala says, excitedly, "They're playing Papagadu! You can go, if you want." Sally pulls on a fresh wrap-skirt and Rich a patchwork cape and we paddle across. Then, along the parallel paths (one for men, one for women) to the "other" part of Dangogo, where we can hear Doote, Apaasu, and Captain Aseni praying in the snakegod shrine. In front of it, Dyeni, Baala's daughter Faanselia, and some other young women are dancing and laughing, pretending to be possessed. The Papagadu drums are in full voice—Pomala on his feet, bending over the great *agida* lying on its side, making it speak with his left hand and a thick drumstick, and Aduengi and Baala, sitting on stools, one playing the *tumau-apintii* with his two hands, and the other beating the *kwedik-wedi* with two thin sticks.

The men standing around say that the *agida* isn't loud enough and decide to tighten its head before the next day's ceremonies. Pomala calls out to the women to dance more energetically, so their gods will come. The women call back that the drums aren't playing forcefully enough yet. More women arrive, some calling out "Vodu-ee!" Aduengi and Baala spring up from their drums occasionally and *tyeke* handsomely, their tall, thin frames lending particular grace to their moves. Their mother, Yegi, looks like she might be possessed but her god doesn't quite come and the women who've moved in to support her back off. Tita dances around in mock possession, sprinkling earth into people's hands, as if it were kaolin and calling out "huehuehue!" As the drumming grows louder and quicker, women dance over and fan the drummers with a cloth or give them a congratulatory hug. Yegi's god finally arrives, as does Tita's and then Faanselia's. Women come with the special clothes of each god and help them dress. (Papagadus not only love to dance—they love to show off and look pretty.) Before long, heavy rain stops the play.

A few weeks later, in the same place, we're all back for more. This time, we spend the whole day across the river. Gaantata has said that the Papagadu shrine needs to be cleaned up. And Kala has been insisting that Tita's particularly fierce snakegod, Alewa, who has had its own house/shrine since her mother first caused the *kunu* during the burning of a garden, should be put into the Papagadu house across the river with the other six snakegods. Now the day has arrived for this rite. Early in the morning, Nai accompanies us as we paddle across, then walks with Sally down the women's path while Rich takes the other one into the village.

Outside the Papagadu shrine, we are offered stools. We can hear songs and prayers inside. Near the doorway, men are crushing leaves in a mortar. Women, off to the side, are sifting kaolin. Other men emerge from the house carrying seven sacred vessels, one for each of the gods, and set them on *sangaafu* leaves behind it. The priest, who's come from Akisiamau to supervise the rite, pulls an old cowrie shell from the darkened leaves in each bowl and spreads the leaves on the ground along the back wall of the house. As Papagadu songs are sung (beginning, as always, with "Yanvalu"), the priest paints the vessels—three Chinese porcelain bowls, one soup tureen, and three black clay pots—with a solution of white kaolin water. He asks which vessel belongs to which god and then decides that the one belonging to Godofutu's god should be cleaned out and retired, noting that this god already has a vessel in the Tone house across the river and "one god should not have two vessels." He sets the other vessels out in the sun to dry and then paints the tops of the feet of each person present, including us, white with the kaolin liquid.

The "river washing" is next, as the priest paints kaolin on each person's shoulders and his female assistant smears some mudlike paste on their chest and back. Tita, whose god is the focus of these ceremonies, leads the procession to the rapids, where everyone bathes as the water is beaten vigorously with branches and everyone shouts "Vodu-ee, Dagowe-ee!" The priest, standing on the bank, prays loudly for "children, money, and food" as he tosses large chunks of kaolin into mid-stream.[1] Aduengi, splashing around in the rapids, ostentatiously feigns possession and makes the appropriate sounds—it is a joyous, raucous event. Tita is possessed by Alewa, arching her back as people hold her horizontal in the water while others beat the river with their branches and cries of *Vodu-ee!* ring out. Kesegogo, seeing her mother possessed, runs out to her and is violently possessed herself. Women drag the two of them to the shallows where, before long, they quiet down.

Gradually, everyone gathers once again before the snakegod shrine. The priest brings the six remaining vessels back into the house where, amidst more singing and the shaking of calabash rattles, he loads them with mashed-up leaves, kaolin, cowrie shells, and parrot feathers. Meanwhile, people take brushes of unspun cotton on a stick and red dye made from roucou plants to paint seven white strips of cloth with wavy snakelike lines—some have snake heads as well. These little flags are then erected, one for each god, in front of the vessels, held up by sticks made from palm fronds.

Teenage boys begin playing the drums, later joined by Pomala, Aduengi, and Baala, and women begin to dance. While sweet Vodu songs are being sung inside the shrine, the drums are playing independently outside. Women call out "Vodu-ee!" A cock is brought into the house, sprinkled with kaolin water, and interrogated by Doote and Apaasu about whether the ceremony has been conducted properly thus far. Despite their persistence, the cock is largely unresponsive, and it expires without providing a good answer. However, the testicles, shown around to all the men, are white, so they decide things couldn't be all that bad. The cock's head is cut off with a knife and the carcass held over each vessel, so that blood can pump into them. The ritual exchange of *madyomina* is quickly taken care of and a second cock called for, with the same results as the first. The priest, after questioning Doote, finds out that no one had gone to the ancestor shrine to alert Tita's deceased mother, the person who had originally burned Alewa, the god for whom this ceremony is being conducted. That's why the cocks have been uncooperative. The second cock's white testicles are lain, along with those of the first, on *malembelembe* leaves on the altar. And Aduengi traces a sacred space with kaolin on the ground in front of the shrine, where the two cocks will be cooked for the afternoon's food offering.

At noon we leave, cross the river, eat lunch, and scribble some notes. When we return two hours later, Nai tells us that in our absence there was some drumming and that Alewa had come to dance.

People are taking turns washing themselves, using calabash bowls to scoop the leaf solution from seven large clay pots that had been set up in front of the shrine. As they pour the liquid over themselves, they ask Alewa for "children, money, and food"—some of the men pray in addition for "women." Meanwhile, village women arrive with the ceremonial foods they've been cooking in two open-sided cookhouses and people are invited to "burn their hands" with peanut rice and game or fish. Later, everyone is given a sweet cashew-nut mixture, a special offering for Papagadus, in their cupped hands, as a song about it is sung. The mixture is also spread on the altar for the gods to share. Some people take a calabash ladleful of the liquid that everyone has been washing with and drink it after mixing in some sugar to cut the bitterness. Eventually, all are given a full plate of ceremonial food to share with the gods. Nai decides she's tired and asks a grandson to ferry her back across the river and help her up the steep path to her hammock.

When darkness falls, the priests are still singing and the rattles still shaking inside the Papagadu shrine but young men have begun to play the snakegod drums outside. When the real drummers arrive—Pomala on the *agida*, Gaduansu on the *tumau*, Baala on the *kwedikwedi*—women begin to dance, first feigning possession as others shout "Vodu-ee!" As the gods arrive, one after another, each is taken off to be dressed in its special clothes before returning to the dance area.

Suddenly, Kesegogo spasms and collapses, falling and then rolling around on the ground. She looks like she's swimming the crawl on the sandy earth. Women pour water from one of the clay pots on her, making a large puddle of mud with Kesegogo writhing around in the middle, vomiting several times. They lift her and take her off, trying to put a pair of men's underpants on her for modesty, but she keeps exposing herself as she rolls around. Kesegogo already has a Papagadu, so this kind of "wild" possession means a new snakegod is trying to "come into her head." From time to time men apply juice squeezed from leaves on her eyes, mouth, toes, and belly. As soon as she tries to stand up, she loses her balance, arching her upper body, throwing back her arms with hands bent backward. Several times, she charges at the *agida* player, falling onto his bent-over back with her breasts all over him. She runs repeatedly at the Papagadu shrine, one time smashing into it hard, almost cracking her ribs. People seem amused at her behavior, entertained.

Baala's wife Ayampa loses control and begins to roll around on the ground. People tell Baala to take her to her hammock, which he does. After a while, Yegi, who's been supporting Kesegogo, begins trembling and soon her god has taken over. The two gods hold hands, facing each other, making Papagadu sounds. They go into the shrine and after a while Yegi emerges, herself again, and sits down on a stool. But Kesegogo comes out and starts to roll around on the ground once more.

Before midnight, the drummers say they've had enough. Women should take Kesegogo to her hammock—she's done enough for one night. But Tita quickly gets possessed by Alewa and dances, balancing a bowl of kaolin water on her head, before the drummers. She comes to herself after a few minutes of graceful, controlled dancing and the evening's play breaks up. Everyone agrees that it's been particularly sweet.

The next morning, the Papagadu ceremonies continue. When we arrive across the river, we hear Apaasu praying inside the snakegod shrine, addressing the ancestors: "Gaduansu and Makoya knew twelve leaves to use for these gods but those of us who are left today know only one. So please help us to do what's needed." After the libation, the payments are brought for the visiting priests—rice, new cloths, coconuts—as the *madyomina* exchange is performed. Then the men carry their stools into the Komanti (warrior-god) shrine next door, with its four-foot-tall wooden statue covered in kaolin and its various iron implements lying around, and Apaasu and Doote lead prayers to those *obias*. Soon the Papagadu play strikes up. As the drummers work, they're fanned with cloths by the women, who also wipe the sweat from their faces. Women also dance up to them with presents—rice, cassava cakes, meat, fish, and cloths. By the end, the *agida* player, who's come from Akisiamau, has a large basketful of gifts to accompany him home.

Kesegogo is washed in the same pots that had been set up the day before. Tita, Yegi, Faanselia, and others wash as well. After a while, Kesegogo collapses and begins to roll around on the ground, just like the previous night. People call out "Vodu-ee! Dagowe-ee!" For a quarter of an hour, she writhes on the ground, runs around the area, thrusts out her chest, and arches her back, arms outstretched and wrists flapping like a bird. She charges the *agida*, hugs the drummer, and strides around.

And then goes back to rolling around in the mud. The female priest from Akisiamau brings some leaves in a basket and begins mashing them in a mortar. She takes the resulting juices and pours them in a calabash over Kesegogo's head. Kesegogo continues to roll around and is by now covered with mud and sand. Godofutu and Dyeni keep close to her, pulling her skirts closed when she becomes exposed. The priest squeezes leaf juices into her eyes and some dark smears are made on her shoulders. As we watch her eyes, they're sometimes half-shut and unseeing, sometimes askew or crossed, sometimes normal. Suddenly, Alewa joins her, dancing some gifts to the drummers, very much under control, and balancing a porcelain bowl on her head. Soon Godofutu's god Politiki joins the play—saucy, smirking, making occasional Papagadu sounds. Kesegogo runs into the shrine and a crowd, including us, pushes in to see what's up. We find her new god engaged in animated conversation—in Papagadu language—with Yegi's god. They hold hands, facing each other, as on the previous night.

Meanwhile, in front of the drums, the god of a woman named Apentimuyee has come. She and Politiki hold hands and bounce-dance around the area. At the shrine, the priest calls for an egg and a parrot feather and then pierces the egg, drains it, and hands the contents to a bystander to cook for herself. He fills the shell, its crown broken off, with a leaf solution and gives it to Kesegogo to drink. Everyone is ushered out of the shrine except for a couple of women, who dress Kesegogo in Papagadu fashion—an over-the-shoulder kerchief, head tied with a white kerchief. The priest ties another white cloth around her head that reaches the ground, forming a train behind her, and sticks a parrot feather into it at the level of her forehead. She's given a whitened piece of sangaafu plant which she carries for the rest of the rite. He leads her to the agida, where she begins to dance in a very controlled manner, just like a mature Papagadu. The woman assistant leads her to step up onto an overturned mortar marked with kaolin, right in front of the agida, and supports her, holding her hand, as she dances on top. Then the god steps down, continues to dance gracefully, and begins to speak, with the characteristic stuttering of a Papagadu. "My father . . . is Wayama . . . My mother . . . is So-and-so" (we couldn't hear the name). Without disclosing her own name—which is normal the first time a god speaks—she then begins dancing with the several other snakegods that have come to join the play. There is now quite a crowd of women, all possessed, gracefully swaying their arms and executing the steps of the Papagadus, following the commands of the drums. Other women rush to fan the drummers and wipe away their sweat. Some of the gods dance up to the drummers and give them long, sweaty hugs.

At last Tita's god has been correctly housed. And a new god, Kesegogo's second Papagadu, has been made to speak and is well on the way to being fully domesticated, a part of Dangogo's panoply of snakegods.

....

This was only one of several series of Papagadu rites and plays that we participated in during our time in Dangogo. Some were larger, with a number of people from other villages. But our fieldnotes for this one effectively capture the general flavor.

For reasons we don't understand, we neglected to record notes on Apuku (forest spirit) dances, although we both recall attending several such evening ceremonies, animated by a different drum battery from Papagadu "plays," with the "long drum" or "Apuku drum" substituting for the large *agida*. While Papagadu dancing is sinuous, with arms waving gracefully, Apuku dancing is more staccato, with a good deal of one-foot hopping. Instead of cries of "Vodu-ee!" women hoot "Ooooooo" during Apuku plays. And Apuku gods are not dressed up, as Papagadus are, instead wearing normal wrap-skirts and donning a white head kerchief and a white kerchief tied around the breasts. But as in Papagadu plays, the Apuku dancers are almost all women. In Dangogo, twelve people had Apukus that occasionally possessed them— and all were women. When one of these gods was found by divination to have caused an illness it would be "called" and its wishes heard and satisfied. Sometimes, Gaantata or Mamagadu prescribed a large-scale evening ceremony, when all the Apukus would come and dance before the drummers. At times during Apuku ceremonies, calabash rattles are shaken (even more vigorously than for Papagadus) while special songs are sung. Three decades after we left Dangogo, we often saw our friend Tooy enthusiastically drumming, singing, and dancing for the Apukus in the urban setting of Cayenne.[2]

....

CHAPTER 18

A Tree Falls

In the midst of a heavy late-afternoon thunderstorm, a young woman named Kulia rushes to Nai to report that a giant tree has fallen across the upper path to the river. Others quickly gather on Nai's doorstep while Kala and Konoi brave the elements to have a look. Kala, returning, announces that no one should try to walk under it until Gaantata is consulted. There's talk that it's the kind of tree used for making coffins and that it wasn't old or rotten—very bad signs.

The next morning, Sunday, Gaantata is raised. Kala asks, "Does this mean evil for the whole village?" Gaantata says that it certainly does and indicates that he wants to walk through all of Dangogo while they ring his sacred bell. Pomala follows the bearers, solemnly ringing the bell as the oracle makes a ten-minute circuit of the village. Gaantata instructs that no one is to touch the tree or walk under it till the following Saturday, when the men should cut it in pieces. Also, that next Sunday each household must bring a bottle of beer and two lengths of white cloth, and that every village on the Pikilio must contribute four bottles of beer and a single length of white cloth. Gaantata says he will make an *obia* to purify the village on the condition that all residents who are not away working on the coast be present. Someone adds: "There will be so much beer that the smell of it will reach the coast and wash those people!" Gaantata then goes on to give counsel on other matters, including a major purification for Faansisonu's people, who have been suffering much sickness, leaving the tree *obia* till the following week.

Saturday morning, as planned, most men of the village are working on the tree, pulling off thick vines as well as a climber that they break off for later use in *obias*, and making cuts with their axes in the fallen trunk. Kala has cleaned up a small shrine that's been damaged by the fallen tree and pours a libation of rum from a champagne glass, invoking several ancestors, including Kwenkwen, who first cleared this path, and Bongootu, who founded the village. He ends with a prayer to Gaantata, informing him and the ancestors that they are cutting the tree.

In the late afternoon, Gaantata is raised by Aseni and Tando, with Kala doing the interrogating. Should they take a breather and finish cutting the tree the next morning, before consulting Gaantata again? (Yes) Does Gaantata want anything else? (Yes) For the *obia* the next day? (Yes) *Biyongo* (ritual spices or power objects, such as quartz crystals, mica, vulture bone, the claw of a giant anteater . . .)? (Yes) After Gaantata indicates that he wants some part of a tree, they ask: Bark? Leaf? Sap? Root? (All negative) Fruit? (Yes) Forest tree? (No) Village tree? (Yes) Mango? Orange? Awara palm? (All negative) Palepu palm? (Yes) "Do you need anything else?" (Yes) "From a tree?" (Yes) Kala and others name some forty trees before they hit the right one, *kapeepau* (often used for firewood), amid laughter and handclapping. "Should we make a fire with it?" (Yes) "Today?" (Yes) "Next to the fallen tree?" (No) "At the path to the river?" (No) "Inside Nai's house, for her and Konoi to burn and collect the ashes to use in tomorrow's *obia*?" (Yes) "Anything else you need?" (Yes) "Something from whitefolks' land?" (Yes) "Something that you buy?" The oracle doesn't give a direct answer so they begin naming every conceivable product bought on the coast, from matches to cowrie shells, and eventually ask if both men and women use it. (Yes) Someone suggests money itself. (Yes!) And it turns out to be copper cents. Every person in Dangogo, says Gaantata, must bring a penny the next day, in addition to the one beer and two white cloths per household.

Later, realizing that there is a shortage, Rich says he has a cache of fifty pennies and Kala takes twenty, giving two dimes in exchange.

The next morning men finish cutting the tree and removing the heavy pieces from the path with wooden levers. Several men haul away lengths of the tree to make doorsteps. Gaantata is then raised and supervises the cleanup of his sacred glen and shrine, declaring a ban on all other work in Dangogo for the whole day. He then begins what becomes a three-hour-long ceremony. First, he asks for certain *biyongo* to be brought to him—the ashes from the special fire in Nai's house, some sand from a creek, tail feathers of macaws, and broken pieces of white-folks' chalk. (Each ingredient is determined by the usual question-and-answer procedure.)

An *obia*-boat is used for the washing in the glen—a dugout shaped roughly like a short canoe, filled with beer, kaolin, and sand from the creek. Gaantata asks Faansisonu to say an opening prayer and he prays that each person who washes in the *obia* live 120 years. As the washings begin, Kala, Faansisonu, and Asipei begin making the *obia* bracelets that will be given to each participant—a white cloth wound around a bundle containing sand from the creek, the ashes from Nai's house, one copper cent, and a piece of chalk, with a macaw feather sticking out.

Nai is the first person Gaantata calls to be washed, followed by pregnant women. The washings continue in fits and starts, as Gaantata complains about how details are being carried out and supervises the corrections. Some sixty women including Sally come next, often washed three by three. A bit of the solution is put aside for three women who are too ill to get out of their hammocks for the ceremony.

The solution is renewed with new bottles of beer before the men wash. Gaantata orders the three captains to be the first. A beer bottle is opened for each, with Faansisonu's bottle cap falling "closed." Gaantata, after some discussion, tells him to pour libations to a certain *kunu* to take care of the issue. He then has the other men including Rich washed by threes, in no special order—about forty in all. When it's over, Kala and another man do the *madyomina* exchange, using green sticks as temporary symbolic payment. Gaantata is asked what to do with the leftover beers and says that the two bearers should each get one with the rest reserved for the following Sunday.

As the ceremony winds down, it becomes clear that the bracelet-making is taking too much time. When this is brought to Gaantata's attention, he says that only boys who've been given breechcloths and girls who've received the skirts of womanhood need to get them. Kala remarks that Maame is old enough to get one but Faansisonu gently kids him into admitting that if she's old enough for a bracelet, she must be old enough for her skirts of adulthood and a husband. Kala mutters "OK, OK. Forget about it." There is some confusion as people try to recuperate the pennies brought for various children's bracelets.

Before Gaantata is brought back into his shrine, Kala also makes sure to ask him about the taboos of this *obia*. The answer is that the

FIGURE 18.1. Tioye, Kasindo, and
Aduengi conducting the
ritual. Agumii is being washed.
Photo: R. Price.

obia bracelet must not be worn while the person is using soap or limes or eating pepper or in the *faagi*. And as payment for the *obia* he wants the men of the village to give twelve bottles of beer, four white cloths, and twelve aluminum spoons, and the women, twelve large carved calabashes, twelve small carved calabashes, twelve balls of kaolin, plus some rice, cassava, and peanuts.

With the bracelets still taking too long to make, Kala decrees that each man should make the ones for his own family. Men sit around for an additional hour, finishing the task. Kala makes the ones for us.

Several weeks later, Kasindo tells Rich that Gaantata himself has claimed responsibility for making the tree fall in order to protect the village from three minor *kunus* that were making their way up the path from the river to attack Faansisonu's family. All of them had been sent by the major avenging spirit of the lineage, created by a late-nineteenth-century incident in which a mentally-ill man was mistreated by their ancestors. (We knew this *kunu*, having spoken with him several times when he possessed Faansisonu's older brother, Apenti.) To stop them from reaching Faansisonu's compound, he simply dropped the tree. And with the *obia* bracelets now in place, he said, everyone should be able to breathe a bit easier.

....

Sickness

Bellyaches, fevers, back pain, snake and scorpion bites, funguses, menstrual disorders . . . physical problems were a constant part of daily life in Dangogo, and our neighbors undertook proactive efforts to deal with them virtually every day, divining for their causes, consulting oracles, praying to specific gods and ancestors, conducting ablutions with medicinal leaves or beer, summoning possession gods, and engaging in countless other forms of ritual activity as well as selective use of the mission hospital. We present, as one example, lightly rewritten extracts from our fieldnotes for the final ten days of our 1967 stay in the village, when Beki's children Poi and Bane fell ill. (Of course, much else happened on these days besides attending to these illnesses—but we do not treat those events here.)

It was the beginning of the short rainy season, and everyone in our neighborhood seemed to be suffering from fever, headache, and vomiting. Those who'd gone to Dyuumu had been told they had malalia-siki and given a pill.[1]

Friday, November 3, 1967. The village is already asleep when Poi, in her hammock in Akobo's house, begins vomiting weakly every few minutes. Nai is alerted and goes to talk to her akaa (soul), saying she mustn't be sick, she must get better. She calls on Gaantata, Mamagadu, Dungulali-Obia, the "gods of the family," and Amafu (the Komanti who possesses Assistant Captain Apaasu and whom we spoke with several times when he was called to cure someone) to help. Then she sends Amombebuka across the river to ask Konu, her classificatory niece, to conduct mafiakata divination in hopes of finding out what's trying to kill the child. Bane then begins to vomit as well. Nai addresses her mother, Boo, asking her to disclose why the kids are sick:

> Help us beg the ancestors, the great kunu, Gaama Dyankuso, Gaama Atudendu . . . to let Poi live, to let Bane live. Remember, we gave you a tremendous funeral! Agbago, Maimisi, Nana [and various others] all made it really big! We buried you with eighty cassava cakes and so many cloths! We wrapped you in the very best hammock sheet! Now I'm the only one left in Dangogo, so we need you to stand up and help us. Please help us beg Gaama Dyankuso, since you and he share the same neseki. My children are all I have left in this world. Let Beki keep having children. Let the little ones sleep and awake in the morning. Let the fever cease. Stand up in the land of the dead and pray for them! Great thanks!"

She asks Beki what god they could have treated badly lately and exclaims "My God!" several times. Amombebuka returns and reports that it's Naina's Papagadu that is causing the sickness because it hasn't yet been taken from the river and settled in its vessel in the Tone house. Naina is called and says she'll postpone the trip to her husband's village that she'd been planning in order to join him for a ritual for his neseki. They all agree that once a god has possessed someone, as Naina's Papagadu, Ndovie, had some months earlier, it should be settled into the shrine without delay. Nai says, "We'll all have to depend solely on the Great God to take care of us in the meantime." Beki is sent off to Akonomisi's house in another part of the village to ask her to arrange for the necessary ceremony. When she returns she says that Akonomisi alerted the gods to prepare for the coming ceremony. She then describes a dream she had the night before about seeing a boa constrictor at Naina's doorstep. Nai prays to Naina's Papagadu—"God, you are in the right, but please desist!"—and returns to her house to sleep.

Saturday, November 4. An hour past midnight, we're awakened by a loud commotion. Beki is knocking frantically on Nai's door, screaming "Bane is dying!" Elima, who had tied his hammock in Nai's house, is slow to open the door, so Beki gives him a beating and he screams bloody murder. Carrying Bane, Beki rushes to the doorstep of Gaantata's shrine, where she lets out loud mourning wails. People from throughout the village come running and gather at the entrance of the shrine. Akobo arrives carrying Poi, very feverish, tied onto her back.

Several people squeeze juice from medicinal leaves into Bane's eyes, and Akonomisi orders for some broth and cassava cake to be brought to feed him. Anaweli tells Binotu to find a particular leaf but he returns with the wrong one so she runs off to get it herself, then mashing it and squeezing the juice into Bane's eyes. Bane seems to have a moderate fever and vomits every time Beki gives him her breast. People can't seem to leave him alone. They keep asserting that Naina's god couldn't be causing such damage just because it hadn't yet been settled in its shrine. It has to be something else.

After fifteen minutes standing around in the chilly night air, Beki sends Amombebuka across the river to wake up the priests of Gaantata so they can raise him for a consultation. When Tando and Aseni arrive, they lift the god and Tioye begins interrogating him: Is it the family's "big kunu"? The god answers in the affirmative and says they must go to the Tone priests in the village of Malobi. Several weeks earlier Gaantata had asked them to get certain leaves in Malobi, and that had not been done. Now, they must be gotten immediately and the whole village must be washed in them. Gaantata says that's all he has to say and they retire him to his shrine. As everyone prepares to go back to their hammocks, Nai asks if Beki and Bane need to sleep in Gaantata's shrine. Captain Aseni, looking a little embarrassed, says he doesn't think so. Nai, hard of hearing, asks what Gaantata said about that. Aseni and the other men hem and haw a bit and admit that he said nothing, so everyone simply goes home. Beki, who'd already lost three infants, seems considerably relieved that she is no longer alone in dealing with the crisis.

Sunday, November 5. In the morning, almost everyone in the village comes by to ask after the children. Both of them are still vomiting but Beki says that since the (Dutch) mission doctor is (temporarily) in the city, she won't take them to Dyuumu because the (Surinamese) nurses, who have no respect for Saamakas, wouldn't see them on a Sunday (their day off). Instead they do a ritual that must be performed by a boy and a girl. Elima and Seena are told how to mark a square with kaolin on the earth in front of Akobo's house, find the proper medicinal leaves, and mash them up with water, and the mixture is used to wash Bane and Poi. People discuss asking Apaasu for an obia he knows and finding out when Akonomisi is planning to perform the next set of rituals for Naina's god. Everyone agrees that Naina's Papagadu couldn't be the ultimate cause of this but that Ma Tobosi, the great Tone *kunu* of the lineage, could well be directing it to harm the children. Nai asks Amombebuka to go across the river to let people know that the children have awakened but are still weak and to ask anyone who knows a cure to bring it over.

When the men from across the river show up, their first stop is the Tone shrine, where they say prayers for the children. Later, when they lift Gaantata for an interrogation about a long list of other problems, the god points at Bane and Poi and says that the cause of their illness is indeed Tone and that they should ask Pomala to gather Tone leaves for washing them. Doote complains to Gaantata that it's just not practical to try to get leaves from Malobi, since arrangements would have to be made a long time in advance, and he thanks the god for letting them do it locally instead. He admits that they have been remiss in not performing Tone rites adequately and asks forgiveness.

Monday, November 6. Beki and Akobo try to get Poi to take the malaria pill the doctor had prescribed several days earlier, but don't insist when she refuses. Nai tells us that the Papagadu of one of Asipei's wives had been consulted and confirmed that Tone is the one causing the children's illness. When she sees Kasindo, just back from a funeral in another village, she pleads with him to get the necessary ritual for Naina's god taken care of soon. He suggests doing it on Saturday and Sunday since a major Dungulali ceremony is planned for Friday. Beki goes across the river to see if anyone there has a medicine that might help for Poi and Bane.

In the afternoon, Pomala arrives with the Tone leaves and gives them to Beki. Beki says she'll take the kids to Dyuumu the next day, since they don't show signs of improvement, even though she was told not to come back till Thursday for the next dose of pills.

Tando comes by in the evening. Because he's a Komanti-man, his prayers will have special force. Sitting on a stool in front of our house, with Nai, Beki, and Akobo looking on, he calls on a number of ancestors, mainly people he knew, reminding each one why they should help him pray for the children's health—Kenkina, the man who left him his Komanti shrine; Gasiton, who taught him so much during cock's crow conversations; Piki Muyee, a woman who'd fed him rice crust when he was a little boy; Saaye, who had both a Wenti-god and a Komanti and can therefore surely help; and many others. When he's done praying, he takes each child on his lap and addresses their souls, ordering them to get better.

Beki also persuades Tando to kill a cock the next day to find out, once and for all, the cause of the illness, so that they can do whatever is necessary to remedy it. Beki, Nai, and Akobo discuss cock divination and agree it's the best kind—"Cocks don't lie," they say.

Tuesday, November 7. Pomala has set up a large clay pot with the Tone leaves inside a three-sided open rectangle traced with kaolin on the ground, open end to the west, so the person being washed faces the rising sun. Beki, sitting outside her house with Asipei, has prepared the payment of a pot containing several balls of kaolin. Inside are Doote, Nai, and Pomala. After praying to various ancestors, Doote comments that "when you have two things and you lose one, you still have one left. But when both of your children are sick at the same time, you'll have none left." Doote tells Beki to go to the river for a bucketful of water. As all bring their stools outside, there's discussion about how each year is different—some years bring lots of sickness, others have none. Asipei reflects that this is true as well for different months. Doote leads the whole group up to Bongootu Pau, where he begins a libation of water after explaining to Asipei that Beki had asked him to kill a cock to get to the bottom of this sickness. Doote addresses a long list of ancestors, explaining that he has something very particular he wants them to help with. Beki's children are sick and aren't getting better. He plans to kill a cock the next day. So, the ancestors should investigate what is killing the children and be ready to have the cock tell them about it. Then everyone goes back to the clay pot and washes partially—first Nai, then the children. It's still early morning and Doote says that the full washing should take place only after the sun is up.

Returning from Dyuumu later in the day, Beki and Akobo tell Nai how the doctor refuses to give the children injections—he'll only give them pills. "Why won't the doctors at least try to cure them?" In the afternoon at Bongootu pau, Doote and Asipei, in the presence of Nai and Beki, pour a libation to the ancestors to inform them that they'll kill a cock the next morning to see what's causing the illness.

Wednesday, November 8. Beki and Akobo are both feverish with malaria. Nai also has fever and bad diarrhea. The cock is killed at Bongootu Pau and indicates that an Apuku is responsible,[2] although it is indecisive about that forest spirit's identity.

Captain Aseni comes over from the other side of the river to tell Nai, who is in her hammock, that Mamagadu was raised the day before to ask about the children's illness and prescribed washing in a certain leaf mixture. Doote, who's chatting with Nai, says he once knew this mixture but has forgotten it. "If only the *gaama* were here [instead of on a visit to Holland]. He still knows it!" Tioye says he's forgotten it too. Amombebuka volunteers to go upriver to the garden camp of Faansisonu's older brother Apenti, a great Komanti specialist who is said to still know the formula. (Whenever we saw Apenti, he was accompanied by an old hunting dog named Zepelin, after the Cayenne-based German airship that once flew low over Dangogo during World War II.)

Thursday, November 9. Doote reports to Nai about the previous day's cock divination. He's been so busy with other ritual obligations since then that this is the first chance he's had to tell her. He says the cock pointed to an Apuku without saying if it was an old one or a new one. Later, he says, he took Gaantata aside in the sacred glen to ask him which Apuku it was and the god revealed that it was a new one, a forest spirit that the sisters themselves had singed in their gardens at Kpokasa. Akobo asks whether he'd explain to her exactly where Apukus live—is it only in *kankantii* and *katu* trees, or is it in other trees too?—because once she knew that, perhaps she could figure out when and where they'd wronged it. Doote names six or eight of the trees in which these spirits most frequently live, besides the two Akobo mentioned. Also in boulders and sinkholes, he adds. They agree that Apukus often wait years before striking. So Akobo tries to think of when and where it might have been. They discuss the famous stone that was singed decades earlier and that once was found responsible for killing two people. Akobo says they've always steered very clear of that one! Beki and Akobo discuss every field they've worked at Kpokasa—what trees were in it, what boulders near it—but still can't figure it out. Doote says that Gaantata wasn't specific except to say that the damage was done in the last few years. But he would try to find a certain leaf that would allow him to narrow this down. Pomala, who has joined the group, says he knows where that leaf grows near Mama Creek and will go upriver to get it for him. Doote says that when the *gaama* returns from Holland, he'll supervise a major ritual to take care of that Apuku, whoever it may be.

Friday, November 10. Kasindo wakes us at 6:00 AM to come to Nai's house where he reports that he's had a nightmare about the two of us.

He's already told Doote, he says. Nai tells Rich to look for men who can raise Gaantata immediately, and he goes across the river to talk to Doote. There he's told that the men are consulting Mamagadu, and he joins them at her shrine off to the side of the village. Eventually, he finds Doote, who says he'll deal with the dream later.

Akobo decides not to go to Dyuumu to get a second malaria pill, instead participating in the all-day Dungulali-Obia ceremony being held across the river so she can get her clay bottle refilled with Dungulali solution.

In the evening, it's finally time to begin the ceremony for the installation of Naina's Papagadu, who's been credited by some of the previous divination for causing the sickness. It's to be taken from the river and placed in its vessel in the Tone shrine. Akonomisi calls Naina into Nai's house, where she reminds her that she'll need an undecorated calabash (since if it had markings, they might communicate something that would displease the god) as well as a new white cloth to cover it. She tells Naina to wait in Nai's house the next morning until she's taken the god's *akaa* (soul) from the river and brought it to the Tone shrine. That night, Naina should sleep in Nai's house.

Saturday, November 11. When we show up at the Tone shrine early the next morning, the place is bustling with activity. Akonomisi and Kasindo are tearing up leaves and mixing them into a solution in a large clay pot. Asipei has made a palm-frond pole and stuck it in the ground, with a parrot feather and a strip of white cloth at the top. Elima is sent off to the creek to get a bucket of cool water for the pot, with the injunction not to speak to anyone on the way. Kaolin is sprinkled into the pot. Florida Water (an eau-de-cologne bought on the coast) is added to make it smell sweet. Once the drums arrive from the other side of the river, Doote sounds the *agida*, Akonomisi dons Sido's clothes, Kasindo begins shaking Sido's rattle, and all but the drummers join in a procession to the river, Kasindo carrying the flagpole, the white cloth, the calabash, some leaves, and a stick of *sangaafu* plant. At the riverbank, the flag is set in the ground pointing east. Sido and Kasindo wade in ankle deep and with the rattle still shaking, they place something on the river bottom. Women start crying out "Vodu-e!" and the *agida* can be heard in the distance, almost drowned out by the sound of the rapids.

Sido faces east and prays for the god to come ashore, as women sing Papagadu songs. After Sido retrieves what he'd placed on the riverbed, puts it in the calabash, and sprinkles in some river water, his hands begin to tremble. Women cry "Vodu-e! The god has come!" Sido places the calabash containing the god's soul on a woman's head, covers it with the white cloth and puts the flag on top with its parrot feather hanging over her face. The woman sets out up the path, lurching here and there as the god pushes her, following Kasindo who's sprinkling the path with kaolin. Sido is still at the river, throwing in chunks of kaolin. The woman with the calabash runs wildly through the village, accompanied by women yelling "Vodu-e," and eventually goes into Nai's house. There's banging inside the house for a few minutes and then we hear the characteristic hu hu hu! Ndovie emerges from the house dressed in her new clothes, her breasts and head tied with white cloths. Sprinkling kaolin all around, she shuffles and dances her way up the hill to the Tone shrine, where a crowd awaits her, shouting "Vodu-e! Dagowe-e!"

As the drums play, Naina's god begins to dance. People compliment her: "She dances well!" and "That god really suits Naina!" Other snake-gods arrive and stride around. Even the elderly Kandamma, whose Papagadu is Ndovie's father, ties her head in white and, sitting on a stool, dances the upper part of her body. Naina's god comes and sits on Kandamma's lap, then Nai's lap. Inside the Tone shrine, Ndovie is washed and anointed with more kaolin. Meanwhile, Sido takes the calabash containing Ndovie's soul and sets it in a porcelain bowl on a low shelf in the rear of the Tone shrine, alongside a number of similar bowls, each holding someone's god.

After several hours of drumming and dancing, Ndovie is the last of the Papagadus to depart. Naina grunts with pain as if waking from a bad hangover and asks Seena to bring her some clean clothes.

That evening, Akonomisi visits to say that there will be a ceremony in a little while up at her house for Naina's god, since they had "brought a god from the river" that day. She says she'll need a cock for the following day as well. And the next morning, the women should be up early to prepare the rice, the peanut sauce, and the other foods needed for the feast to be devoted to the god. (We seem to have missed that evening ceremony at Akonomisi's house, though our notes mention that we heard the *agida* playing in the distance.)

Sunday, November 12. Before dawn, Nai, Naina and her husband Pompia, Doote, Akonomisi, Kasindo, and ourselves are squeezed into the

Tone shrine where for nearly two hours different ingredients, topped by a couple of bright-colored parrot feathers, are added to Ndovie's porcelain bowl. Kasindo says they should be playing Papagadu drums outside but he couldn't find anyone to do it. Akonomisi's Wenti, Sido, possesses her, is greeted and hugged by each person, says a few words in his Javanese-accented version of Sranantongo, and directs the rest of the rite. Kasindo lifts a large cock, which he took from Nai's chicken house, by the back of its neck, right in front of the bowl on the altar. Although Sido and Doote both ask it many questions, it doesn't seem inclined to give answers. Doote finally goes next door into Gaantata's shrine and prays to that god for help in getting the cock to speak. But it expires before it says anything intelligible. Meanwhile Sido—who plays the part of a foreigner in Saamaka—says he can't be held responsible for the cock's not talking because where he comes from, they don't do this sort of divination at all. Kasindo splits open the cock's belly and examines the testicles—they're shown around to the men and they're pure white. He then lifts the cock over Naina's head, let's some blood fall onto it, and she immediately starts saying "huehuehue," as Ndovie takes over. Kasindo drips some of the cock's blood into the vessel. Pompia and Kasindo perform the madyomina with green sticks, not with the actual payment for conducting the ceremony. Then Pompia prays for the customary "children, money, food." Now that the god has been fully settled, he prays, may it stop killing and sickening and start helping them. And he invites the god to join them later in the day for a food offering.

Akobo takes the cock outside in front of the shrine and the women go to bring the various uncooked foods that will be prepared for the offering. Once it's been plucked, the cock will need to be placed on the fire by Sido and Kasindo.

Later in the morning, there's a two-hour Gaantata consultation. Seventeen issues are raised, including our imminent departure. Rich presents a bottle of beer and a white cloth to Gaantata, who thanks us and asks to have it put in his shrine. He gives his OK for the trip we've been planning to the United States and approves the day set for our departure. Just after he goes on to deal with another problem, Kasindo comes rushing in and asks Doote if he'd asked Gaantata about his bad dream concerning our departure. Doote replies that it has all been taken care of—the god has approved our trip. Gaantata, asked why the cock didn't speak that morning in the Tone house, explains that it wasn't that the ceremony hadn't been conducted correctly. Rather, it was that the payment for the rite had been made with ritual sticks rather than actual cloths and rum. Once that was done there would be no problem.

After Gaantata is put back in his shrine, people take their stools over to the Tone shrine where women have brought two large winnowing trays filled with dishes for the food offering. Inside are Kasindo, Akonomisi, Nai, Naina, Kandamma, Beki, Agumii, ourselves, and a couple of others, all on stools. Kasindo loads up a large porcelain bowl with pieces of cassava cake dipped in broth, meat from the cock, peanut rice, white rice, and game. He places a few malembelembe leaves on top and then piles still more food on top of them. Sido, who has possessed Akonomisi, directs all of this. Kasindo begins a libation of water as Sido prays and directs him to pour water over Naina's hands, then to place her hands on the loaded bowl. Sido addresses Ndovie: "Come eat the rice and peanut rice and the meat!" Naina's hands begin to tremble, as Kasindo places more malembelembe leaves around the shrine and just outside the doorway. Kasindo rubs Naina's whole body (or is it now the god's?) with food and then does the same with Poi and Bane. Sido tells each of the spectators to take a handful of the food to eat, and each does, some coming in from outside the shrine. All the chicken bones are brought back inside and placed on the altar. A calabash of water is passed and everyone is told to take a sip. Then a mixture of ground-up cashew nuts, sugar, and water is spooned onto each person's cupped hands to be licked off. Tianen, on behalf of Nai, presents a cloth of thanks to Akonomisi's soul, saying a short prayer. Pompia makes a speech of thanks to Kasindo and Akonomisi for settling his wife's god. Kasindo takes the god's necklace, which he has made over the past couple of days, and places it on Naina's neck, then removes it and asks Kandamma to hold it to see if it "swings" when interrogated. It does, which is a good omen.

People realize they've forgotten the madyomina payment, but Beki goes out and returns with a basket filled with cloths and balls of kaolin, and Pompia and Kasindo perform the spirited ritual exchange. Later in the day, Nai expresses concern that Kala's cats will eat the food left for Naina's god in the Tone shrine but others reassure her that, since the feast was for the gods, the cats won't eat it.

Before our own departure for the coast, we hold the standard family meeting with Nai, Beki, Akobo, Abatili, Dosili, and Naina.[3] We leave the key to our house's padlock—and responsibility for the house—to Beki, the key to our storage trunk—and the responsibility to air out its contents—to Akobo, Rich's gun to Dosili, and our canoe to Abatili.

At last, Ndovie is settled in as a permanent resident of Dangogo. We leave the next day, hoping that the sickness that has been plaguing the family will finally let up.

....

CHAPTER 20

Death of a Witch

Among the Ndyuka Maroons, to the east of the Saamakas, well over half of the people who died in the 1960s were found, by post-mortem divination, to have been witches. Their belongings—their estates or legacies—were confiscated and their families forced to accept the attendant shame.[1] Saamakas took a different tack, joking that if they were to divine for witches, there'd be nobody left at all. Indeed, although we heard frequent discussion of witchcraft (wisi), and though it was often "found" as the cause of an illness or death, no alleged perpetrators were ever identified—it was thought more prudent, for the good of the community, not to know. Don't ask, Don't tell.

In Dangogo, there was one exception. When we first arrived, Sindobobi had suffered a serious stroke and was confined to her house, barely able to sit up, so the first time we saw her was the day Nai brought us to her house to participate in a feast in honor of her mother. Sometime later Kala told Rich how he'd gone to Sindobobi's house and found her lying naked in her hammock on urine-soaked rags, and how he'd thrown away the rags, washed her off, and dressed her in clean clothes before leaving. Six months after that she was dead.

Several people told us how stunningly beautiful Sindobobi had been in her youth. But they also told story after story about the deaths she had caused with her evil obias. Nai contributed quite a few, describing how Sindobobi had performed a victory dance when she heard that one of her rivals in love had died suddenly, how she had accurately predicted the death of a young ex-husband of her daughter Asabosi when he went off to work in Guyane, and how she had lain a curse on one of

Dosili's wives for failing to come to her assistance in a fight she was having with another woman, causing her to die in childbirth shortly thereafter. She also told us how Sindobobi had ritually prepared a marriage basket for Asabosi with a concoction to prevent her husband from ever divorcing her, smearing it with kaolin. The only reason he survived was because he noticed the kaolin, understood that it had been ritually prepared, and refused to eat the food in the basket. Nai scoffed at Asabosi's protestations that she hadn't learned any of Sindobobi's *obias* . . . After all, she said, isn't she her mother's only daughter?

Asipei also had stories. He told us how, on a trip to the coast, he crossed paths with his son Pagai, coming back from several years of wage labor in Guyane. His one piece of fatherly advice was that, of all the women in Dangogo, the only one he should be sure to steer clear of was Asabosi. But Pagai couldn't resist her beauty and began sleeping with her. When Sindobobi found out, she said she'd kill him if he didn't formalize the relationship with her—by clearing gardens for her, building her a house, and making her a canoe. Asipei said the only reason Pagai was still alive was that his grandfather begged Sindobobi to desist and offered to pay her. She is reported to have asked, skeptically, "What will you pay?" He ran off and returned quickly with a handsome new hammock sheet. She examined it carefully and said, "Consider it finished." "She was beautiful," said Asipei, "but her heart was not clean. Sindobobi never washed in plain water, not even once in her whole life—all she ever used was *obia* baths. Whenever you walked by her house you could smell the odor of the leaves!"

People told us how Sindobobi once boasted that she was killing Sakuima, a woman who lived across the river. When Gaama Agbago heard about it he came to Dangogo specifically to beg her to desist, offering to pay her with several cloths. She took the cloths and said she'd stop, but only because the request was coming from the *gaama*.

Another time, Nai and Konoi gossiped in front of our house about the time, years before, that Sindobobi had brashly called out the *gaanne* ("true" or "secret" name) of an Apuku in Mama Creek, causing the forest spirit to kill two people who had gardens there. And they discussed the fact that her preferred *obia* included the burial of a live cock along with a brand-new cloth in order to make her own rice grow and that of others in the area wither. That *obia*, they exclaimed, requires nine jugs of water! A woman named Akibenuma had once asked Sindobobi to make the *obia* for her, but it backfired and killed her. After her death, she became a *kunu* and killed Sindobobi's innocent sister, Ansebuka. Asipei told us that one of his wives' gardens, near Akibenuma's, was also ruined by that *obia*.

....

April 29, 1968.[2] 10:00 PM. We're already in our hammock when we hear Asabosi's wails ring out, off in the part of Dangogo where she lives with her mother. Her husband Pomala, who's been sleeping across the river in the neighborhood of his own matrilineage, shows up quickly and begins making the rounds of the houses, waking people and telling them that "the old woman isn't well." By the time we've put on some clothes and made our way to Sindobobi's house, eight neighbors have already gathered and Pomala has returned across the river to alert kinsmen and ritual specialists there. Inside the house, Asabosi is calling in a plaintive voice to her mother: "Woman, Sister-in-law,[3] where have you gone? Don't you remember the garden we cleared and planted together in Mama Creek? Talk to me, Sindobobi! Come back to me, Woman, talk to me . . ." Finally emerging from the house, she makes a frenzied dash for the bush at the edge of the village, and when the women drag her back into the clearing in front of the house, her body is lacerated by thorns. As others assemble, including a number of village officials, she is held and soothed. Three men who have arrived from across the river—Takite, Apaasu, and Tioye—tie their waists with kerchiefs and carry Sindobobi feet first from the house, in her hammock as she died, and place the hammock on three banana leaves in an open cooking shed that thus becomes the funeral house. They wrap the corpse tightly in the hammock, leaving only head and feet exposed, light a kerosene lamp at her head, and then go off to the river to wash the pollution of the corpse from their hands. Meanwhile, Dosili, whose first wife (Seena's mother) was the one Sindobobi caused to die in childbirth, runs home to get his shotgun, ties its trigger guard with a fiber charm and, next to the funeral house, fires three black-powder salutes to the west.

Pomala and Dosili agree to set off at dawn to alert the village of the *gaama* and its downstream neighbors, where people will have heard the shots and will surely fear that Nai has died.

Sitting on low stools in front of the doorstep, those present are quick to find fault with the way particular people have responded. Kasindo (as assistant captain and the illicit but acknowledged lover of Sindo-bobi's niece, Kabuesi) should have come as soon as he heard the shots. Panumao (Sindobobi's twenty-seven-year-old son, a problem child who left for coastal Suriname seven years earlier and has not yet returned) is surely not even going to cry when he hears the news. And where are all the women who should have shown up? Then come hunting stories, canoeing stories, discussion of recent divorces in the area, husbands who treat their wives badly, and the progress of particular rice gardens. An hour or two past midnight, people get tired and drift off to their hammocks, including Asabosi.

Over the course of the next week, as the extensive repertoire of prep-arations for burial is undertaken, we observed much that was familiar from other funerals as well as some things that were specially tailored to Sindobobi's personal reputation. The most noticeable divergences, given Sindobobi's age, were the relatively small attendance at each public event and the relatively brief time—eight days—the corpse was kept in the village before burial.[4] But in addition, Nai's granddaughters made plans to go off for several days to their gardens upstream, and Dosili decided not to cancel a four-day trip to Paramaribo—neither of which would have been considered acceptable behavior for the death of a community member in good standing. On the other hand, the rhe-toric of mourning was one we had heard many times before.

April 30. Pomala's elderly grandmother Kandamma arrives early to address customary speeches on the doorstep of the funeral house. First to Asabosi:

> You must not kill yourself over this, Mama. Alosa [Sindobobi's mother's father] died and Sindobobi lived on. Disen [Sindobobi's mother] died and Sindobobi lived on. Now that Sindobobi has died, you must get on with life, forget your sorrow, do not kill yourself. You have Pomala; he has no god in his head like Sindobobi, but he's there for you. Hold on to him, and live. Even if everyone in the whole village died, it would be up to you to carry on, to tend to the ancestor shrine, to take care of the oracle. Stop crying for Sindobobi and start living for Aguba [a ritually heavy name for Pomala].

Then to Sindobobi: reminiscing about the days when they both had gardens along Mama Creek, she admonishes her to release Asabosi from her mourning, to allow her to cease her crying. Meanwhile, Headcaptain Faansisonu (in the absence of Kala who's gone to Guyane) lays protective leaves across the doorstep of Nai's house as well as at Dangogo's various shrines. And then Faansisonu, Apaasu, and Aduengi walk down to the landing place to cut the bottom out of Sindobobi's old canoe to form a *bungula*, a piece some six by two feet that will serve as proxy coffin at various points in the funeral rites. Once they return, they lay the *bungula* next to the corpse and go off to Bongootu Pau to alert the ancestors that there has been a death in the village, and to ask for their assistance in making the funeral a success. When the prayers are finished, they are joined by Pomala and four or five other men, who use their machetes to clear the small area near the top of the river path where Dangogo's dead are washed, dig the trapezoidal hole in which the corpse will sit, and line its bottom with split banana trunks. Because no women volunteer for the job, the same men prepare a fire on banana-trunk "hearthstones" to heat the water for washing the corpse (though all will be reminded the next week of the ideal of same-sex corpse-washers when Apaasu falls sick and divination reveals his participation in the washing as cause). As Sindobobi's own iron stewpot is placed on the fire (and as it is later removed as well), Takite and Apaasu perform a delicate ritual dance—part of funeral rites since the eighteenth-century: each holds his side of the pot with one foot and the opposite hand, while his partner does the reverse, and then they switch, and finally switch back once again (with the pot going on and off the fire three times at each end of the procedure). Takite and some other men then go back to the funeral house to place Sindobobi's corpse, still wrapped in her hammock, on the *bungula*, and return, two of them carrying it on banana-leaf head pads, to commence the washing. A lively dispute breaks out about details of the ritual (should they, for example, sing Papa songs while they pour the water into the pot?), with different men arguing for one or another procedure. Washing the dead, like other parts of funeral rites, remains a privileged occasion for heated—and much appreciated—disputation about ritual details. As a proverb notes with approval, "There are no burials without argument." Takite and Apaasu lift Sindobobi off the *bungula*, sitting her in the earthen hole, with Asopi—a former husband of Sindobobi's sister—gripping her shoulders. Two young men hold a hammock sheet up as a screen to protect the privacy of the washing, but in fact all present watch and discuss the procedure. Apaasu fills two calabashes, one from a gourd of cold river water and the other from the boiling pot, and begins pouring cold water over Sindobobi's head as Faansisonu prays, "Sindobobi, we give you cold water . . ." They wash her thoroughly in both waters, using pieces torn from a new white cloth, and then Takite takes a razor and shaves off a bit from her hairline, rubbing the shavings onto a cloth that will soon be attached to the *bungula*, allowing Sindobobi's spirit to be consulted in divination. The wooden door of Sindobobi's house has been dismantled and laid over the washing hole, and her body is sat naked on it for the dressing of the corpse. Apaasu and Takite begin with a new cotton waist string and a scanty breechcloth, then adding seven or eight layers of skirts and capes, a similar number of beaded necklaces, and silver earrings. They take care to remove the protective charm she had worn around her wrist. When a sudden rainstorm breaks, the corpse is summarily loaded onto the *bungula* and carried back to the funeral house, where several men have constructed a crude wooden bed on which it is now laid out, with the *bungula* returned empty to the washing-area. Making the standard Saamaka association between death and rain, people blame Sindobobi for the downpour.

During the storm the sons of Kabuesi (Sindobobi's mother's sister's daughter) and a couple of their lineage brothers from the village of Gaanseei come ashore, bearing planks, saws, planes, and baskets filled with new cloths. Inside the funeral house, a thick rectangle made from two hammocks and eight or ten hammock sheets, contributed by kinfolk and neighbors, has been assembled and the corpse rolled tightly in it, mummy-style, with feet and head exposed. Sindobobi's head is tied vertically and horizontally with two pieces of white cloth. Apaasu then prepares the *avo*—a ritually powerful cloth that he brushes down Sindobobi's body, head to feet, and whisks toward the west, the land of the dead. For the rest of the funeral rites, the *avo* will be left lying on the coffin at night and during periods of little activity (to keep the spirit quiet). It will be removed whenever Sindobobi is being consulted or prayed to, and while the gravediggers are at work. All those who have touched the corpse or the utensils used in the rites thus far step forward as Apaasu dribbles rum over their hands, and then passes around what is left in the bottle to drink. It is mid-afternoon, and the group disperses. At dusk, eight men assemble in front of the funeral house and, facing west, fire some forty black-powder salutes into the air. That evening, though there should have been a "play," there's only a few minutes of half-hearted drumming with people sitting around on stools chatting, before they return home to sleep, early.

May 1. By midmorning about thirty men have gathered a few yards from the corpse-washing place at the edge of the village to begin constructing Sindobobi's coffin. Already leaning against a mango tree are ten rough-hewn planks each a dozen feet long that have been contributed by visitors and kinsmen. Two were sent to Dangogo by the *gaama* himself. Asopi takes charge of the coffin's large side, Aduengi handles the rest. Tasks are quickly divided. Some men sharpen tools on whetstones, others begin sawing, others planing, and still others going ashore to measure the corpse with a special reed. (After transferring the measurement to a long stick, they quickly chop the reed to pieces and toss it into the bush.) A small table is set up near what will be the head of the coffin, and a glass and bottle of rum are placed on a tablecloth. Dosili arrives with a tape recorder and begins playing popular *seketi* songs, recorded at an all-night play a few weeks before. (Had this been a funeral for a more honored elder, men would instead have sung some Papa, the special music of death, accompanied by a hoe-blade/knife-blade gong, as the coffin-making got underway.) After the end pieces of the coffin are set on the sides and bottom, Apaasu prays as a libation of rum is poured at the head of the coffin. "Sindobobi, we give you rum. Not one of us wanted you to die! But now that you have gone, all of us want to bury you with celebration." And using a teakettle, the men pour a libation of Dutch cocoa onto some bits of cassava cake on the ground at the coffin's head. Then all present are served dry bread brought from the city and cocoa in fancy china cups.

Slowly, over many hours, the coffin takes shape, with its steep gables, complex angles, and decorative touches. Every step of its construction is surrounded with prescriptions and prohibitions. There is considerable banter while the men work, including discussion of a coffin so heavily loaded that it exploded when the corpse decomposed and swelled. By late afternoon, the men have finished their task and begun cleaning up the area. The empty coffin is then lifted onto the heads of Asopi and Aduengi, and with Apaasu serving as interrogator, Sindobobi's spirit is asked what killed her. After some inconclusive questions and answers, the bearers carry the coffin ashore to the funeral house where Sindobobi is informed that the coffin has been finished, and it is sprinkled with a mixture of kaolin and water, leaving white splotches all over it. Inside the funeral house the bottom of the coffin is lined with a number of new hammock sheets and hammocks and the body is placed on them. Then, some thirty-odd skirt-length cloths are placed on top. An extra pair of earrings is lain next to the ears, two pairs of crocheted calfbands on top of the calves. Talcum powder is sprinkled liberally over the whole, the head is covered with a cloth, and Asabosi is summoned. As all present avert their eyes, she takes Sindobobi's most intimate garment—her beaded "wrestling belt" (made for tactile pleasure during love-making)—and lays it on her waist, covering it with a cloth. Asopi and Aduengi carry the coffin back outdoors and, as a number of men knock pieces of wood against the coffin to participate symbolically, the top of the coffin is nailed shut. Then the coffin is "dressed" with fabric—a large cloth nailed on top, kerchiefs attached to the large end, and cloth straps tied all around. Then it's raised quickly, touched to the ground three times, and walked all around village, though special care is taken to avoid any houses where someone is sick. As it is placed back in the funeral house, Apaasu prays, begging Sindobobi not to take her children and other kinfolk with her to the land of the dead.

At dusk, about fifteen salutes are fired—there would have been more except there was a shortage of black powder. Asabosi and Kabuesi lend their loud wails to the noise of the gunshots. We already smell the sickly sweet odor coming from the coffin. The funeral house is filled with baskets of cloth and sheaves of rice, contributed by various kinswomen and neighbors of Sindobobi. That evening there is an enthusiastic play, with about fifty people. The young men from Gaanseei—Antonisi, Kasolu, and Sineli—start things off with *seketi* singing accompanied by drums. Soon a line of Dangogo women are clapping their hands rhythmically and singing their own *seketi* songs. As more people arrive, the two groups join forces and various men— Takite, Aduengi, and the Gaanseei contingent—take turns jumping into the center of the crowd to sing and dance *tyeke*—head and torso immobile, as arms, legs, and feet move in flashes of brilliance. Asabosi often dances along with the men. Other women hoot appreciatively and run up to the male dancers to wipe the sweat from their faces with a cloth.

Kasolu starts one solo quietly, standing in place. Then, as drums join in and women begin clapping rhythmically, he very deliberately arranges his cape and breechcloth and—still singing—begins to *tyeke*. As he dances, he pulls from under his cape an oriental fan and slowly

FIGURE 20.1. Kasolu and Antonisi dancing *tyeke* at Sindobobi's funeral. Photo: R. Price.

opens it wide. The women go wild. Aduengi calls out, supportively, "Not every Chinese store in the city sells those!" Women run up to embrace and congratulate Kasolu. The dancing continues. Before midnight people disperse, exhausted but exhilarated.

May 2. Early morning, a group of men gather before the funeral house to discuss the progress of the rites. Assistant Captain Apaasu makes a formal speech about how a death entails three major responsibilities: washing the corpse, making the coffin, and digging the grave. He has personally supervised the first two. Now let the young men take over with the third. But of course he stands ready, once it's time to conduct the burial, to preside at the graveside as well. Apaasu then suggests they raise the *bungula* in divination. Asopi picks up the front and

FIGURE 20.2. Asabosi dancing *tyeke* in Dangogo. Photo: R. Price.

Aduengi the rear as he speaks to Sindobobi, staring directly at the piece of wood with its cloth-and-hair attachment. After pleading with Sindobobi to leave Asabosi unharmed, Apaasu interrogates, inconclusively, about the cause of death. (Sindobobi's spirit moves the *bungula* forward to indicate a yes, slightly backward to indicate a no.) Then he asks Sindobobi whether the gravediggers can safely begin their task today and whether there is anyone present who, for one or another reason, should not go to the ritually dangerous cemetery. With Sindobobi's approval, the next stage of the funeral can commence.

Within an hour or two, a dozen young men from Dangogo and neighboring villages have tied their heads with red kerchiefs, twisted to a point in front, fixed fiber charms around their waists, and begun gathering near the funeral house. These gravediggers (baakuma) will rule the village with an iron hand for the remainder of the funeral rites. Soon they set out to begin their ritually dangerous job, carrying Sindobobi's paddle, a live black hen, and three cassava cakes, plus other food and cooking utensils and their gravedigging tools. As they stride through the village toward the landing place for the trip to the cemetery, they blow wildly on a bugle (which would have been a wooden horn earlier in the century) and make a great deal of noise. Any canoe that has the misfortune to cross the gravediggers on the river will be required to pay a fine—a small bottle of rum, a chicken, the person's hat, or whatever the boisterous gravediggers wish to exact.

When they arrive at the cemetery, less than an hour away by paddle, the oldest among them pours a libation to announce to the ancestors why they have come, and who they are going to bury. After clearing a gravesite in the virgin forest, they mark off the grave-space, using a length of reed with which they have measured the coffin, and which they quickly destroy after use. Kabuesi's thirteen-year-old son, Lodi—participating for the first time as a gravedigger—kills the hen and cooks it with the same stewpot and calabashes that had been used to wash the dead. The gravediggers will eat with heavy doses of hot pepper—a strict taboo of the dead, and therefore a reassuring protection that they are eating alone. The digging is strenuous and teams of young men move in and out of the growing hole every few minutes, rubbing their bodies with earth to prevent sweat from falling into the grave.

In late afternoon, with their preliminary task complete, the gravediggers head toward the landing place, making sure not to look back. They board their canoe and paddle upstream to the village, many sporting a chicken feather in their hair to show what they feasted on. They signal their arrival at the landing place by loud, prolonged hooting.

At the funeral house, they raise the bungula for divination, with Aduengi carrying the front and Lodi the rear. Men address Sindobobi informally, asking if the site they have picked for her grave pleases her (yes) and telling her that all went well at the cemetery. They also ask her what is making Apaasu (who has come down with a fever) sick. Sindobobi's snakegod? (no) Her forest spirit? (yes) So word is sent across the river, where Apaasu lives, to tell people to pray at the forest-spirit shrine there. The *bungula* is set down, and Aduengi approaches the coffin, speaking directly to Sindobobi and offering a libation of rum: "Sindobobi, we give you rum. Don't be angry with us. Stop making people sick. Pray to the *kunu* on our behalf instead. Help those of us who are left to live." Later that evening, the gravediggers light a fire in front of the funeral house, which will be kept going for days. The visitors from Gaanseei play drums and sing *seketi*, local women clap hands and sing, and a dozen or so men sit around playing checkers. Some of the gravediggers tie their hammocks in the funeral house, above Sindobobi's coffin.

May 3. Early in the morning, the gravediggers stroll around the village in small groups, blowing their bugle and pulling coconuts and other fruit off peoples' trees. They raise the *bungula* to report that they are going to the cemetery again and to ask Sindobobi to see that they return safe and sound. They ask whether the rash of sickness in the village will pass soon and beg her to help the sick recover. The gravediggers cook and eat a meal, using food commandeered from villagers, before setting out hooting loudly and beating a drum, for their canoe. They again carry a live hen but this time it is joined by a cock for their midday meal in the cemetery. In late afternoon, they return to Dangogo still hooting and blowing their bugle. After joking about the weight of the coffin, they instead raise the *bungula* again for a brief report and interrogation. Aduengi offers a rum libation at the head of the coffin. And in the evening there is a small play that never really gets off the ground. Several local youths challenge gravediggers from Gaanseei at wrestling and get badly beaten. Kabuesi (whose sons are the victors) notes that Dangogo boys learn to wrestle on the sand by the river but at Gaanseei (which doesn't have a sandy landing place) boys learn to wrestle on the hard ground.

May 4. Gravediggers "terrorize" the village with their licentious and outlandish behavior, to which everyone must submit without complaint. Some strap on wooden penises and go in search of teenage girls to startle. Others appropriate fruits and cooked foods, without so much as asking, from people's houses. Still others catch villagers' chickens and bring them to the funeral house for later consumption. It is the final day of gravedigging, and before leaving the cemetery the men must "sweep their bodies," with their leader dusting them twice down and once up with handfuls of fowl feathers, as they face east at the edge of the grave. "The evil must go to the ground, the good to the heavens." On their return to the village, they discuss which two are strong enough to raise the coffin in divination. The large structure is quite a sight propelling its bearers around the village. But Sindobobi refuses to "talk" and the coffin is lowered back into its place in the funeral house. They try again with the *bungula* and this time, Sindobobi responds. Tioye reports that they went to the cemetery and returned without any special problems, finished their work, sang some Papa, and ate a meal. Then he asks Sindobobi, playfully, if she's ready to go [to be buried], and she says yes. "Right now?" "Yes." "Let's go then!" he teases her. But Aduengi interrupts the conversation: "We're not really ready yet. Let's wait till the proper day." Does Sindobobi have anything to tell them? She indicates that she does but that she wants to do it in private, and she points to three men who take the *bungula* off to the side of the village, where she expresses her wish that Asabosi "leave the evil things" they did together so she can live. The carriers put the *bungula* back in the funeral house. Asabosi wails loudly throughout, as Kabuesi tells her to stop—but then she, too, breaks down. Comforting the mourners, other women comment that when the coffin is there, it helps some, but that once it's taken away for burial, there's nothing but emptiness. The women discuss why the coffin and *bungula* haven't been more communicative. Perhaps, they speculate, it's because Sindobobi had had a stroke—so how could she be expected to talk to them now? Asipei suggests that there's a better reason: because she "lived so badly" Gaantata is keeping her mute as punishment. In the evening, further gravedigger shenanigans and some desultory men's *seketi* singing. Kandamma comes over from across the river and sleeps at Nai's. Nai tells her, "Sleeping here means you're helping to bury her"—you've made the appropriate gesture.

May 5. In the morning, everyone who has had anything to do with the funeral to date "has their belly tied"—a protection against the deceased taking others with her. One of the men takes a new cloth from the baskets laden with gift cloths contributed by visitors and kin, and wraps it around the person's belly, saying (to the person's *akaa* ["soul"]), "You see? I'm tying your belly. You must live!" In front of the funeral house, village women gather to pound rice in large mortars, hooting in unison when they feel enthusiastic. It is the whole community's responsibility to keep the gravediggers supplied with food.

Gaama Agbago, who has come to Dangogo for a Gaantata rite, is invited by the gravediggers to "moisten his head" with one of the pots of aromatic leaves they've prepared there. "For that woman? I think I'll pass," he says, walking back to his canoe.

In late morning, the gravediggers raise the bungula so that Sindobobi can distribute her material and spiritual belongings. She first indicates that Asabosi can continue to use their joint garden at Mama Creek, since she doesn't see any evil lurking there. She leaves her "small things"— her pots and other utensils, her stools, her paddles, her clothes—to Asabosi to distribute as she sees fit. She tells Kabuesi to leave off her "evil ways" or she'll find trouble. And she indicates that Aluntago, another relative, will soon meet trouble—but she won't tell what, or how to avoid it. When we walk by the funeral house, we notice that the large calabash that has been placed under the coffin is two-thirds full with body fluids, stained blue by the many layers of cloth they have passed through. In the afternoon, there is a fifteen-minute interrogation of the bungula, trying to persuade Sindobobi to talk about various problems—sickness, social behavior, what the future may hold—but Sindobobi remains virtually unresponsive, despite Apaasu's strongly worded dressing-down for not being more cooperative. In late afternoon, a motor canoe filled with men arrives from Akisiamau carrying a large dance-drum, and Dangogo women rush down to the landing place, hooting in appreciation. Just after dark, gravediggers and other men gather before the funeral house and shoot some seventy-five salutes, as Asabosi and other women shriek out mourning wails. Later in the evening, people gather for what should be an all-night play with Papa music between midnight and dawn, but heavy rains send the hundred or so participants scurrying for their hammocks after only an hour or two of singing, dancing, and drumming, and because of Sindobobi's reputation, people decide not to play Papa formally at all.

May 6. Burial day. In the late morning, four of the gravediggers visit the cemetery to see that the grave remains in good shape (that it has not caved in from rain and that there is no water in the grave itself). By early afternoon, the gravediggers take the coffin out of the funeral house, touch it three times to the ground, and carry it around the village, stopping at each of the village ancestor shrines, before returning it to the house. It is then taken out of the funeral house, put back in, and taken out three times, and set down outside for the final rites of separation. As drums play, three men circle the coffin, sprinkling kaolin on the ground around it. Two branches of *sangaafu* plant, whitened with kaolin on one end, are held over the coffin and slashed in two with a machete. A woman from Gaanseei who has been washed in snakegod leaves holds one of the whitened ends and faces east, back to the coffin, as Faansisonu says, "Sindobobi, we separate you from your snakegod," and as Apaasu slashes the branch in two, the woman hurries off with the whitened end. Another woman then does the same for Sindobobi's forest spirit. The *bungula*, now filled with the detritus of death—sweepings from the funeral house floor and the two brimming calabashes of body-drippings—is carried, preceding the head-borne coffin, down the river path. Suddenly Asabosi, who had been wailing on a stool in front of the funeral house, comes charging down the path, trying to grab at the coffin. Men pull her away and Apaasu gives her a severe tongue lashing, commanding her to remain with the living. Against her protestations, she is dragged ashore. The procession continues, but before reaching the riverbank, there is a final separation, from the village itself. Faansieti, a woman who happens to be standing close, is told to hold the whitened end of a *sangaafu* branch and, once it is slashed, carries it quickly ashore. She cries as the final prayers of separation are spoken. When the coffin is loaded into a canoe, many women lament, with wet eyes, "Mama Creek is finished!" or "Sindobobi-ee!" A gun is fired in the air as parting salute, while about fifteen men in four canoes set out to accompany the coffin to the cemetery. The village is quiet and sad. People disperse, but will gather again that evening in front of the now-empty funeral house to tell tales in honor of Sindobobi, who now lies in her final resting place.

Later that afternoon, we hear Nai gossiping with a granddaughter who's visiting from across the river. "When the gravediggers tried to carry in the coffin, it wouldn't budge," she reports, clearly amused. "The dead people in the cemetery didn't want to share it with Sindobobi. It took Faansisonu's full power of persuasion before they finally gave in and accepted her as one of their own."

When we arrived in front of the funeral house an hour or two after dark, there were already some forty people sitting around, men on folding chairs, women on low stools, with two kerosene pressure lamps illuminating the scene. The visitors from Gaanseei—Kabuesi's three sons and their cousin—sat near the center; Kabuesi was near Asabosi, with her son Safeli, on her lap. Kandamma, with a cloth modestly spread over her knees, sat nearby, along with several younger people from across the river and a couple of small children. Sindobobi's close neighbors—Konoi, Abatili, Ayetimi, Akobo and her sisters, and Asipei (who made a practice of listening but never speaking at tale-telling sessions)—were there. Pomala and Dosili sat off to one side, and various village officials were also in attendance—Faansisonu, Kasindo, Takite, Aduengi, and Apaasu. Riddling had already been completed, a couple of tales had been told, and people were chatting, waiting for the next one to begin. We were struck by the general conviviality and lack of interpersonal tension of the sort that often obtained between many of the participants. As we sat down, cradling our Uher reel-to-reel tape recorder, Kabuesi (who had adopted a playful joking relationship with Rich) called out, "Husband, turn it on quick, Mma [Kandamma] is beginning!"[5]

The old woman—her considerable bulk settled on her finely carved round stool, walking stick lying next to her on the ground—begins her tale about a path into the forest down which first a person and then a hunting dog had disappeared, prompting the dog's owner to consult a ritual specialist. Kasolu interrupts her in mid-sentence to announce that he had been there at that very moment and had seen a man's wife going off to make love with a howler monkey. When he finishes recounting what then happened, and singing the song the husband had used to entrap his simian rival, he tells Kandamma to go on with her story. She has just related the advice of the obia-man—that only Needle could kill the devil who had eaten the dog—and told how the man forged a horn in preparation for his encounter, when Akobo breaks in to say that she had been there and saw two children disobeying their mother by going off in search of Fire. She sings the accompanying song and then tells Kandamma to pick up her tale again. Kandamma tells of the man's triumph over the devil by his magical horn and needle and ends by interpreting her tale, almost macaronically, by reference to the idea of reincarnation.

Following several compliments on the tale's sweetness, and a few false starts at pronouncing the Mato / Tongoni exchanges that signal the beginning of a tale, Kasolu launches into a long account of the marriages of Elephant, Eagle, and Cayman—disguised as handsome young suitors—to three human sisters, and their younger brother's quest to rescue them. The complex tale is interrupted six times: Antonisi performs a song and dance mimicking Dog and Goat chasing after a beautiful woman; Kandamma draws on Jaguar's familiar trick of feigning death to entrap other animals; Asabosi contributes the song of the woman who never got tired of singing and dancing; Kandamma describes how a boy tricked the devil through song; Asabosi tells how Anasi (the spider man) summoned the Tone god from the river; and Akobo recounts Anasi's efforts to hold his lover's name in mind on his long journey to her village. Kasolu's tale finally ends, after a cameo appearance by Anasi, with the boy slaying a twelve-headed monster and freeing the world from evil.

Kandamma then begins a tale about how a scrawny little kid sets out to confront a gluttonous devil who has been eating other small boys sent out to chase birds from gardens. She is interrupted by Antonisi, with the story and song of how Hummingbird stole Jaguar's drum, and by Kasolu, who sings the song of Shit dancing at an all-night play. Kandamma concludes with a detailed account of how, by feeding the devil from magical plates until he drops, the kid makes it possible for all of us to have gardens without fear. As so often, her extensive knowledge of folktale esoterica lends special texture to the tale, as she specifies, for example, which sounds were made by the devil's upper teeth and which by his lower teeth, as he chomped on his fatal feast.

Kasolu then tells a tale that takes place on the plantation of a white king/wage-labor boss. There are two interruptions about birds flying up to Great God, one by Antonisi in which two birds dance for the deity, and another by Kandamma in which Hummingbird sets out to learn the name of a mysterious fruit. Kasolu's tale, which contains deep moral significance regarding Saamakas' stance toward whitefolks' oppression, climaxes in a riotous scene in which a bold young boy manages to cuckold the white man who until then had never felt pain.

Kasolu, getting up a head of steam, interrupts the animated rehash of his just-completed tale by calling out *Mato!* once again, this time with a tale about the unlikely pair of Goat and Jaguar. Kandamma interrupts it with a complicated story about a boy who succeeds in bringing the *deindein* drum back from the land of the devils, and Kasolu's tale ends with defenseless Goat triumphing over powerful Jaguar, by means of a magic charm given him by Buzzard.

Kandamma recounts a tale about a boy who sets off to ask Great God to solve problems—for him, his brothers, and various people he meets along the way. After people voice repeated complaints that no one is relieving Kandamma's story with an interruptive tale, Asabosi finally breaks in with one about the man who rid the forest of a devil named Asinaloonpu. Kandamma's story ends with an ungrateful brother being swallowed by a hungry anaconda.

As people begin to get restless and talk about going home to their hammocks, Kandamma protests that as far as she's concerned she's ready to tell tales till the sun comes up, and Kasolu keeps the evening alive by starting one about the boy who goes off to the land of the devils to bring back the *apintii* (talking) drum for his mother's funeral. Interruptions are provided by Asabosi, who sings the drum's song; by Akobo, who mimes Anasi singing about his courtship of a beautiful woman; and by Kandamma, who tells and sings the story of Father Gidigidi Zaabwongolo—the man who bore all the sicknesses of the world until Anasi inadvertently brought them back to where we all live. The boy, after crossing three seas on the backs of three caimans, is almost eaten by a boisterous band of devils but manages in the end to escape, turn the devils into boulders in the river, and play the drum at the head of his mother's coffin.

As one man gets up to leave and others begin to follow, Kandamma and Kasolu reiterate their eagerness to continue. She says, "We could keep telling them for three whole days without ever repeating one," and he volunteers "if people wanted to, I'd be happy to keep going till dawn." But the gathering breaks up and the evening of tale-telling is over.

The next day, men go hunting for the ancestral feast to be held the day after that. On the day of the feast, the gravediggers purify themselves and their tools with fire, and that evening tales are again told. At the final libations of the funeral, on May 9, people decide that the village of Gaanseei should hold a "second feast" in honor of Sindobobi within a week or two, and tentative plans are made to hold the "second funeral" at a later date in Dangogo, perhaps combined with the identical rites due to her sister, Ansebuka, who had died earlier that year. The host villagers present the gravediggers with cloths and other presents to thank them for their help, and the gravediggers offer the close kin of Sindobobi presents of their own. The funeral—truncated because of Sindobobi's reputation—had nevertheless transpired properly. She had been buried, even if somewhat grudgingly, "with celebration."

CHAPTER 21

....

Chasing Ghosts

Several weeks after Sindobobi's burial, Nai suggests that it's time for Ansebuka's *limba uwii*, the "second funeral" that will usher her into the land of the ancestors, where she can be prayed to and spoken with at the ancestor shrine. The complex rites are important in order to free the village of the ghosts of recently deceased villagers, and one possibility is to combine the rites for Ansebuka with those for her recently buried sister Sindobobi.

Doote supervises as two planks, each bearing a set of hair clippings wrapped in cloth, are raised in divination, leading to a decision to hold the rites jointly. By early June the date is set and kinsmen return from Guyane, where they have been working. Second funerals are the largest of all Saamaka gatherings—more festive even than funerals—and hundreds of visitors will crowd into Dangogo. A group of men go far upriver for several days of hunting and fishing, making sure to capture some turtles for the ancestral feasts.

On the day of the hair burial, conducted informally by three men near the landing place to the cemetery, the whole village is cleansed, first physically, by women with hoes and brooms, then ritually, by teenage boys purifying each house by sprinkling a sacred solution in a clay pot. New palm-frond gateways are erected on each path into the village, piles of sugarcane are cut up and boiled in giant pots before being poured into a canoe-shaped vessel, and a variety of festive dishes that are only made for second funerals are prepared—they'll be offered, with a piece of cassava bread, to every visitor later in the evening.

In the course of the afternoon, Dangogo is filled with visitors who have pulled up their canoes on river rocks just downstream in order to change into their finest clothes and apply perfume before continuing to the village landing places. Everyone wears calfbands, which are de rigueur for second funerals. Women have elaborate hairdos and many wear stacks of anklets made with aluminum taken from the inside of telephone cables by men working for Alcoa—these are painful, rubbing the skin raw, but are much appreciated aesthetically.[1] Men carry carefully folded umbrellas and sport felt hats, often with a feather. The smell of men's cologne is everywhere. There must be several hundred visitors in all.

Just after sunset, in front of Ansebuka's house of mourning, which doubles in this case for Sindobobi as well, Nai and many other villagers gather as Doote, Faansisonu, Apaasu, and Tando lead prayers to the ancestors, with libations first of water, then lightly fermented cane juice, and finally rum. They use two vessels for each libation, since there are two deaths involved. Ansebuka's grandsons, who've returned from the French missile base for the occasion, discharge shotgun salutes toward the west. A fire of special wood is lit before the door of the house and will be kept burning till the next morning. The visiting Papa players drum exuberantly for ten minutes or so. And then people drift off to socialize and await the night's events. Ansebuka's daughter Kabuesi and Sindobobi's daughter Asabosi, as well as Akobo, Naina, and other women, fan out through the village, bringing bowls of the special dishes to all the visitors.

Around nine, in front of the house of mourning, young women begin singing seketi, accompanied by handclapping. Before long, men set up some drums, the crowd gathers, and dancing begins. Men wearing special dance aprons over their breechcloths perform tyeke dancing, with dramatic sudden stops and starts that reflect perfect muscular control. Apaasu calls out, in town-crier fashion, admonishing everyone to step up the tempo: "We held a major series of libations, inviting all the ancestors to come join us. So now let's celebrate! Let's show them a thing or two!" The drumming picks up and the dancing continues. After a while two poles are brought out and held parallel to the ground by two men. The crowd parts, and Aduengi jumps onto the poles, one foot on each. Singing "alesingo!" to the crowd's handclapping and chorus of "alesingo-go-go," he scissors his legs as the men move the poles swiftly in and out, dancing his torso with consummate grace. As the crowd presses noisily forward, Apaasu, who holds a paddle symbolizing his authority in the event, pushes people back and tries to maintain order. Abatili, Dosili, and a few friends who've been dancing retire to a house to change their clothes, emerging in slacks and a colored T-shirt topped by an embroidered Saamaka neckerchief. They bring out a city drum set and, for the next hour or two the village is treated to *kaseko* singing and dancing, the calypsolike music of Paramaribo. After midnight, people gradually disperse to their hammocks, with visitors tying their hammocks in the houses of friends or relatives.

Around 3:00 AM, the Papa players, their heads tied with kerchiefs, install themselves inside the house of mourning, whose front wall was removed during Ansebuka's funeral rites. They have the long Papa drum, the *deindein* that keeps the rhythm, and a metal gong. As they sing and drum, they drink a good deal of rum and fermented cane juice and snort tobacco. By dawn they've become loud and argumentative but their playing is still strong and spirited. The soloist dances in place, almost shadowboxing, as he clenches his fists and punches out his words. After a chorus, a second soloist takes over and then a third. They sing and drum to the dead in esoteric Papa language, recounting First-Time battles, telling stories and parables, urging the two dead women to come back as *neseki* rather than avenging spirits. From time to time they demand food or drink.[2] Periodically during the night, men fire off gunshot salutes toward the west.

Meanwhile, four mortars and pestles have been set up in a nearby open shed, and women, their heads tied with white kerchiefs, have spent the night hulling rice, as Nai and Konoi, sitting on stools, look on. Two women to a mortar, they work energetically, knowing that they must finish before the "play" is brought outside after dawn.

As soon as the first rays of the sun touch the earth, the Papa drummers bring out the play, adding the *apintii* drum that handles the *adyo* rhythms to their battery for the *adyo paaya* (ghost chasing), the crowning event of the ceremony. The singers and dancers rub some crushed kaolin in between the first two toes on each of their feet and each ties his waist with a skirt-cloth. A crowd begins to gather before the house of mourning.

Kabuesi brings out seven baskets and sets one in front of each of the Papa men. During the next hour, women arrive to fill them with "payments" for the play—cassava cakes (both normal round ones and special oval ones reserved for this ritual), coconuts, lengths of cloth; peanuts, sheaves of unhulled rice; bananas, small bottles of palm oil, and dried fish.

As the *adyo* rhythms grow more heated, women pour shots of rum into the open mouths of the drummers, fanning them with cloths from time to time. Gods begin to join the play—three snakegods, two forest spirits, and three ghost spirits. Soon, four youths appear, wearing only jockey shorts but with their faces painted red, white, and black and run around the area, twisting burning sticks from the fire in their hands. Six masked dancers join them, their bodies covered from head to toe, giving them a truly frightening look as they dash at people, threatening them. Some of them have homemade wooden masks with jaguar-skin beards and agouti-hair mustaches, while others wear city-bought substitutes, including a rubber one of Richard Nixon. As they dance, they gesture lasciviously at teenage girls, brandishing stick-phalluses, and children run away screaming.

One of the youths with painted faces grabs a gun and fires a salute. Others smash the back of the house of mourning and run right through it. They stalk the masked dancers, as if they're hunting them, and then run around the village grabbing detritus—broken baskets or umbrellas, fallen palm fronds, old kerosene cans—and deposit them in the dance area. The drummers strike up Komanti rhythms, and when Tando's *obia* suddenly arrives, the masked dancers run off, fearing he might rip off their disguises. He crouches, jaguarlike, as Apaasu's Komanti joins him. They grab glowing coals and chomp on them. Apaasu's *obia* finds a thorny branch and hugs it to his chest until bystanders pull it away. Tando's takes eggs that are brought to him and announces whether they're cooked or raw by feeling them. Both *obias* grab chairs and fling them around. They throw burning fire sticks into the crowd. Then they break a bottle and chew on the pieces of glass as they rush around wildly, with spectators hustling to get out of the way of these warrior spirits. At one point, Apaasu's *obia* grabs the machete Rich is holding and runs around the village slashing in the air at people and property—eventually, men take it from him. Tando's *obia* crouches, slinks around like a jungle cat and eventually lies down, as if he's sleeping it off. Three of the youths with painted faces take up bunches of bananas and run around slicing off pieces with machetes. They grab sugarcane chaff from the cane boat

FIGURE 21.1. Masked dancers chasing ghosts in the village of Godo. Photo: Silvia W. de Groot.

and throw it in the air. Women possessed by snakegods and forest spirits strew unhulled rice, broken calabash fruits, and cassava flour on the ground, then sprinkle rum all over. Finally, the *adyo* drums play "saka saka go la-me," telling the two ghosts (and any other evil that may be lurking) to depart the land of the living forever. At last, the ghosts have been chased.

As spectators begin to leave the dance area, three women pick up brooms, knock them three times on the earth, and sweep up the garbage, each eventually loading it onto a large dustbin made from a maripa palm and carrying it on their left shoulder to be dumped on the forest path. The *adyo* players go to the fire that's been burning all night, separate it into three, and arrange the sticks parallel to one another with the burning end toward the east. Then a man extinguishes the fires with water, as all those present cover their eyes. Another man pours libations in front of each extinguished fire—water, then cane juice, then rum—inviting the ancestors to join them at the afternoon's feast. Three turtles are butchered with the meat placed back in their shells and left, for the time being, before each fire. Everyone who has participated walks down to the river and bathes.

That afternoon, there's a feast for the ancestors, after which the village gradually empties out. (We overhear Kasindo quipping irreverently, "Saamakas sure are dumb. In the morning they chase the dead and then in the afternoon they plead with them to return to share a meal. How could our ancestors have thought that one up?") A week later, there's another afternoon and evening of dancing and drumming, and it's finally time to "throw the play in the water"—the official end of a second funeral. In the afternoon, before the house of mourning, there's dancing of all sorts. Ansebuka's grandsons pass out small gifts (matchboxes and aluminum spoons) and toss chunks of soap in the air for women and children to grab. Firecrackers are set off and gun salutes shot. A table is covered with a cloth, and dried bread, hot cocoa, soft drinks, and rum are served. The celebrants then go around the village, stopping at eight houses, including Nai's and ours, where they dance and sing and drum, expecting small gifts and drinks at each.

Just before sundown, the fifty or so participants carry the drums to the river, where the drummers load them into a canoe and paddle out to midstream. Amidst hallooing and shouting, they sink their boat, letting the drums float out, then shoot the *deindein* drum with a black powder "blank," bail out the boat, bathe themselves and the drums, and swim it all back to shore. Children aren't allowed at this final rite, as the dead might try to carry them away with them. Once everyone returns to the village, no one can to go to the river until the following day.

....

CHAPTER 22

Death of a Child

Kabuesi had already suffered through more than her fair share of mourning when her last child died in Sally's arms.

"Buesi," in her early fifties, had a full personal history à la Saamaka, having been married to five men and given birth to twelve children, of whom five survived past infancy. When we arrived in Dangogo she was married to Asensi, the priest of Dangogo's important Tone cult, who lived downriver in the village of Malobi (and also had a house even farther downriver in Duwata). They had met in Dangogo when he came to construct and consecrate the Tone house for Nai, and they returned together to Malobi, where their son Safeli was soon born. Later, when she fell ill, Asensi brought her back to Dangogo, but while there he caught a fever. With time it got worse and in the spring of 1967 it was threatening to kill him.

One day we heard Buesi spilling her heart out to Nai, telling her how badly Asensi had treated her, but how, in spite of everything, she would never leave him. If Malobi weren't so far away, she would of course go to take care of him. She told Nai she had a dream about people in the land of the dead, and then burst into tears. Nai took her hand and spoke softly, as if to a child: "Believe me, I know what it's like to have a husband die. Stop crying, stop crying."

A week later, we noticed Amombebuka whispering to Naina and her sisters. Next he came to tell us: When he was in Asindoopo earlier that day he saw three men who had come upstream from Malobi by paddle to break the news of Asensi's death. By custom, the men of the dead man's lineage are responsible for grabbing the wife and holding her as they break the news, since she'll become hysterical and try to run off into the bush. If she's in her garden camp, the men of her own village will first take charge of bringing her back to hear the news. They'll lie to her, saying only that her husband isn't doing too well and would like to see her. She'll suspect that he has died, but they'll deny it. Only when they're back in the village, with everyone present and preparations made for a protective *obia* for her, will the death be announced.

That evening men from both sides of Dangogo congregated around Nai's doorstep and discussed what to do. Two of the younger men were told to go upriver at daybreak and tell Buesi that Asensi isn't doing too well. The older men said that if she insisted on knowing whether he was dead, they might as well say yes, since everyone knows how ill he's been. But after the older men leave, Nai, who often served as the guardian of traditional protocol, told them that it was important to deny Asensi's death until Buesi came back to the village and could hear it from his relatives.

The conversation then turned to reminiscences about Asensi . . . how when he came to take Buesi as his wife, Naina had helped unpack the wedding gifts from his suitcase, how they had offered him Abatili's house for the night and tied the hammock there, and how generous he had been with the presents he brought—plates, buckets, and so much more. Everyone was careful to avoid mentioning the gossip that's been circulating lately, that while Buesi's husband was dying downriver, she was carrying on an affair with Akonomisi's husband Kasindo. Rather, they focused on practical decisions that needed to be made. Who would take care of harvesting her rice when it came ripe? And what should be done with Safeli? Clearly, Buesi wouldn't be able to keep him while she's saddled with mourning prohibitions. And her mother Ansebuka, one of the oldest people in the village, was too frail to look after him. Maybe one of Buesi's grown sons could take him. Leaving the question unresolved, the conversation turned to other matters.

By the time we'd returned to Dangogo in 1968, we'd grown quite fond of Safeli (Saamakas' pronunciation of the French Creole word for "chauffeur"), a sweet child who liked to play in the space between Nai's house and our own, driving pretend canoes through little puddles, showing off with a toy hunting gun over his shoulder, and occasionally coming into our house to pose the kinds of "why?" questions that three-year-olds tend to ask. We knew that he'd been diagnosed at the

FIGURE 22.1. Safeli. Photo: R. Price.

clinic with sickle cell anemia, and that his diminished immunity to infection had been producing a series of ailments, from a swollen arm to back pain and frequent fevers. They would first be treated in Dangogo with obias prescribed in divinatory consultations of one sort or another. But Buesi also paddled down to the clinic run by Moravian missionaries in Dyuumu more frequently than most of the people we knew.

Her opinion of the Dutch doctor was, nevertheless, no more positive than those of our other neighbors. The fact that people went to the clinic for every sort of ailment (except gunshot wounds and broken bones, for which Saamaka cures have inspired the great admiration of medical experts) in no way implied that they trusted the staff there or felt grateful to them. We once heard Buesi complaining to Nai that she'd gone to Dyuumu with diarrhea and they gave her the yellow pills, which have always been used for fever, and another time she went with fever and they gave her the black pills, which of course are for diarrhea. And in any case, anyone knows that pills don't work as well as injections.

People went to Dyuumu for many different reasons. Several men had found paid day labor there, working on the grounds. Women sometimes sold food (an oatmeal tin of peanut paste, for example, earned one guilder). Boys (at least some of them) attended school. Young men played soccer. And people went to visit relatives who were in hospital beds. It was not rare for Akonda to steal oranges from trees in Dangogo and take them to Dyuumu to exchange for tobacco. (She did this at considerable supernatural risk, since most fruit trees were protected by visible kandu—charms made up of a tiny broom and feather or a gourd or a miniature bow-and-arrow designed, when violated, to cause illnesses varying from male impotence to female incontinence.) People occasionally speculated about an apron girl or married woman using a trip to the clinic as a pretext, and then going across the river to the (usually empty) landing strip for sex with a lover. And men often went to Dyuumu to sleep with the nurses from the city, who had a reputation for ease of access.

Not surprisingly, Saamakas' perspectives on Dyuumu differed from those of the doctors/nurses. When Sally, being treated for amoebic dysentery, remarked to a Saamaka woman who shared the hospital ward with her that "they sure don't know how to cook here," the woman replied, "Of course they know how to cook! But they take all the good food back to their big houses, and feed the leftover scraps to the patients."

Meanwhile, the doctors filled their official reports with allusions to the hardships they had to endure in order to conduct their work in this untamed jungle. And while Saamakas often evoked what they saw as the doctors' palatial luxury, the missionary doctors viewed themselves as making great personal sacrifices.

Our notes are filled with problems brought to Dyuumu. A baby fell out of his mother's hammock into smoldering embers and was badly burned. A woman washing at the river was stung by a ray. A large fish hook pierced a boy's shoulder by accident and needed surgery. A woman woke up one morning and found a cockroach in her ear that had to be pulled out by the doctor. A woman in the menstrual hut told Sally about seeking pills at Dyuumu to shorten her periods. And we knew quite a few people who'd had teeth pulled there (though Nai told us that when hers got bad, she'd always cut them out by herself with a knife).

Whether or not particular women should give birth at Dyuumu was often a heated debate. People took the clinic's pills when they had malarial fever, but not without a lot of complaining about how it was the *bakaas* who brought the disease in the first place, and assurances that the pills didn't work as well as the cures prescribed in consultations with Gaantata. People who'd been diagnosed at Dyuumu for high blood pressure or diabetes often didn't return because of the fear that they would be given a prohibition on salt, which they would never be able to comply with—everyone knows that human beings can't live without salt.

The former doctor at the hospital, a Dr. "Felandi" (Vlaanderen), the hospital's first physician, was used as a foil for the many perceived evils of Dyuumu. He had been universally loved, and people agreed that ever since he'd left a couple of years earlier, Dyuumu had gone downhill. Asipei told us how his replacement had beaten a woman so badly that she had to return to her village to be cured with herbal washings. Someone else reported that his aging mother was left naked on her bed. A woman announced that a new pill had arrived in Dyuumu by plane and that the first person to take it would die. It wasn't unusual for women with problem pregnancies to run away from Dyuumu because the doctor "stuck his finger in." And there was a widespread assumption that because curing was free it must be worthless—Saamaka *obias* are always paid for.

Once Buesi set off downriver to take on mourning obligations for her husband, Safeli was left in the care of a series of Dangogo women, and his cures at Dyuumu became rarer. Even Ansebuka came hobbling by Nai's house with him one day, supported by a paddle on one side and a walking stick on the other, and announced that she was going across the river to find someone to conduct divination for his fever. But Naina and Akobo, warning her that she wouldn't be strong enough to climb up the hill afterwards, told her to ask Akonda instead: "Don't worry about the payment . . . she'll accept just a piece of soap or a bit of rice." Ansebuka took Safeli's hand and turned back.

In December, Buesi, still in Duwata under heavy mourning restrictions, received word that Ansebuka was "not well." She returned to Dangogo in time to see her mother before she died and participate in her burial rites, and then returned downriver for her husband's second-funeral rites. Safeli kept going to his grandmother's house, waiting for her to return, telling people that she'd just gone to her gardens and would be back in a few days. Nai and others did their best to help him understand: " 'Buka's dead. Don't go looking for her anymore. 'Buka's dead.' " And again the next day: "Buka's dead. You and Buesi and I can stay here together. Then when I get very old you can help to bury me and carry my coffin. For now it's just the three of us." Nai also took pains to keep Buesi's spirits up: "You and I may not have the same mother and father, but we're all one people." And then, using an expression that evoked the Middle Passage: "We're all on the same ship. If you ever need something, we're here for you."

And in April death struck Buesi's family once more—Sindobobi, Ansebuka's sister's daughter, died from a stroke and was buried.

By October 1968, Buesi's mourning restrictions for Asensi have been lifted, and she's once again allowed to engage in gardening. Her camp is close enough to Dangogo so she can make day trips, leaving Safeli with one of the women who had been taking care of him during her stay in Duwata. When she returns each evening she playfully addresses him as "husband" and does a little dance of joy that makes him giggle. She tells Sally one day that everyone believes Kasindo made her pregnant with Safeli, but look at him now—he's the spitting image of Asensi.

Whenever Safeli is left with Nai he ends up spending time with us, and Buesi eventually starts leaving his food—a tin of water, a piece of cassava, sometimes a bit of smoked fish—with Sally instead of Nai. A set of twins just up the hill, playmates his age, and a little girl who brings him play meals that she's made of sand, make it easy for us to keep an eye on him and still do our work. Often he plays near Nai's chicken-house pretending to shoot the birds with a stick he carries on a string over his shoulder—as he fires his "shotgun" he says "Poko! Toko!" He boasts to us that when he grows up he'll buy an outboard motor and take it to the coast to buy a boatload of candy.

It's now the fall of our second year in Dangogo, and we've started thinking toward our departure from Saamaka. But we're still actively participating in local activities.

October 13: Dyeni has finally given birth to her first child, and arrangements are made for the baby's emergence from the birth house in a ritual supervised by Mamagadu. Sally goes across the river to participate and take photos.

October 14: We both work on notes. We hear that there's been a tree-felling accident in the garden of the *gaama*'s wife Gadya.

October 15: Rich paddles down to Dyuumu to interview a man named Peleki. Sally stays in Dangogo and conducts an interview with Asipei's wife Akundumini.

October 16: Rich attends a ceremony in which libations are poured and prayers of thanks are offered for the *gaama*'s safe return from a trip to the city. And we keep the typewriter busy with ongoing notes about everything around us.

October 17: Rich goes to the Dyuumu airstrip with several men who have agreed to play drums for his tape recorder.

October 18: Safeli, who's been left in our care while Buesi's upriver, dies suddenly after being stung by wasps.

He and the twins have knocked a wasps' nest up the hill with a stick and all three have been attacked by the swarm. The twins haven't fared too badly, but Safeli's head is swollen and disfigured from hundreds of welts, with many of the wasps stuck in his scalp. Sally's holding him and trying to soothe him as Rich attempts to extract the insects, but he's screaming at the top of his lungs. After a few minutes he falls silent. Sally continues to cradle his little body in her arms and keeps talking to him, telling him it'll soon be all right, but Nai shakes her head and addresses Sally as if to a child: "Don't talk to him anymore, Kambo. He's no longer something you should be holding. He's gone. Let me set him down." We lay him in a hammock in Nai's house and send for two men from up the hill. They listen for his breath but not wanting to pronounce his death, simply say that he's "really not well." Finally they take him in the hammock to Buesi's niece's house and send a canoe off to Asindoopo to report to the *gaama*. By that time quite a few people have gathered, and the talk is all about how to tell Buesi when she returns. No one should be at the river. The village should be quiet. When she arrives and hears what happened, Sally and three others struggle to hold her, but she nearly breaks loose. We see her teenage son Lodi off on the side, sobbing uncontrollably.

Then the speculation begins. Whatever it was that was stalking Safeli wouldn't have been able to strike when the children were at Nai's doorstep, because he would have been protected there by her Tone god. So that's why it waited till the children were up the hill at the wasps' nest. Might Ansebuka have taken him with her to the land of the dead? Maybe. Could Palaibuka (another recently deceased woman) have killed him? Certainly possible. After all, she had been a very difficult person. Pomala takes Rich aside and asks whether Buesi is still conducting an affair with Kasindo. Clearly, that could be what killed Safeli.

Meanwhile, there are tasks to take care of. All the food in Nai's house is thrown out, as are the things that Buesi had left with Sally for Safeli. After nightfall, Takite arrives from across the river carrying an old pot containing smoldering charcoal topped with a variety of Dungulali-Obia leaves, and uses it to smoke our house, using his hand to direct the smoke all around. He also gives us some orange-colored Dungulali liquid to rub all over our bodies. Dungulali specializes in keeping the living separated from the dead, so this was the first part of a complex series of rituals to assure that Safeli, who was so fond of us, would not be able to take us with him to the land of the dead.

Dungulali is an extraordinarily strong *obia*, considered a *gaan-obia*, like the magical forces to which Saamakas credit their eighteenth-century military victories over whitefolks. It's a Dangogo specialty. But unlike most of the other *gaan-obias*, which are believed to have been brought by specific ancestors from Africa, Dungulali was encountered for the first time on the Oyapock River, at the turn of the twentieth century. The man named Kodyi, who found the first seagods as well as Mamagadu, also played the central role in Saamakas' discovery of Dungulali.

Kodyi had several gods in his head, including a ghost-spirit called Akoomi, who said he came from Africa. It was Akoomi who taught him the secrets of Dungulali. Akoomi said he'd learned them from his father-in-law in the land of the dead. Akoomi told how in the land of the dead a powerful man named Pupu, the owner of Dungulali-Obia, had a beautiful daughter called Dyesu-Akobita. One day she crossed paths with Akoomi, who was on one of his frequent visits from the Oyapock, and she decided to sleep with him—the dead with the living, as Saamakas say. But other dead people intervened and bound him up preparatory to killing him, so she ran off to tell her father. Pupu prepared himself ritually, throwing his sack of Dungulali leaves and roots over his shoulder, grabbing his calabash rattle, putting his pipe in his mouth, lighting the Dungulali tobacco, and setting out on the path, very displeased. Eventually, his sack barked to warn him that he was arriving. He chased off the aggressors, found his son-in-law, untied him with Dungulali-Obia, taught him the ins and outs of its rituals, and then sent both Dyesu-Akobita and Akoomi off to the land of the living. They stayed for a time in a place on the Oyapock where Saamakas still proffer offerings.

Over a period of years, during the treatment of many cases of illness and misfortune, Kodyi learned from Akoomi the leaves, roots, and vines; the taboos, the songs, the drums, the sacrifices; and the other esoterica of the Dungulali cult, which has always specialized in separating the living from the dead. When, for example, the young Agbago (the future *gaama*) accidentally caused the death of his own brother in a tree-felling accident on the nearby Approuague River, it was Kodyi's Dungulali-Obia at Tampaki that separated him from his brother and made him whole once again. Over the years, Agbago and another brother learned the *obia* from Kodyi and, around 1915, brought it back with them to Dangogo, where they built the shrine and established the cult that, at the end of our stay, ritually separated the two of us from Safeli.

We spent the morning after Safeli's death with the Dungulali priests and a crowd of others, in front of the Dungulali shrine across the river. Men had worked feverishly the previous day to gather the necessary leaves and barks, and the shrine—really a good-sized wooden house—nearly overflowed with them. Doote, Takite, Tando, and the other men were pounding this vegetable matter in mortars, helped only by young girls since women of childbearing age are polluting to Dungulali. They sang Dungulali songs as they worked, with younger men accompanying them on drums and a special rattle—"The hole, the hole, he sees it open there. It's not my business, that" (This grave is not for me!). "Don't dig, don't dig, Dungulali. Don't dig, don't dig it, Dungulali. Evil person, don't dig, Witchman don't dig." (Don't dig me a grave.) Each of these songs against Death was followed by Dungulali's special "cheer," chanted in unison: "Dungulali-e! Path-splitting obia! Awili! Awili kandi kandi! May the path to the land of the dead remain dark! May the path to the land of the living always be light!" When the leaves were sufficiently mashed and the Dungulali liquid mixed, the men sat on stools and began passing around the Dungulali pipe, Ananagoa, filled with its special tobacco which looks like some kind of grass. As each man, including Rich, took a few puffs, the group sang, "Pipe, pipe going around . . . Ananagoa," followed by the customary cheer.

Finally, it was time for us to be ritually separated from Safeli. In front of the shrine, the priests had planted a nine-foot-tall maripa-palm frond, with a vulture feather and a piece of *sangaafu* plant (its east side whitened with kaolin, its west side blackened with soot) stuck through it. Three times, as people shouted "Dungulali-e!," the priests led us around the apparatus and passed us through it, holding the "good" end of the *sangaafu* that had been lopped off with a machete, and with which we later returned to our house. Everyone present was repeatedly bathed in Dungulali solution, after which the priests accompanied us across the river and once again smoked our house with Dungulali leaves. They told us sternly that we were to remain in our house, with the door shut, for the rest of the day.

Before we were led away from the Dungulali separation, one of the women called Rich over and said, "Make sure you don't write down any of what you saw. If you do, you'll die on the spot."[1]

The following morning, men constructed Safeli's coffin. When it was ready, Buesi brought a tray with goods to accompany the body—one of her skirts and one of Ansebuka's, some beads that had been given to her by Asensi, two pairs of shorts that Safeli wore for his trips to the Dyuumu mission, his little shoulder cape, his hammock sheet, and his tiny breechcloth. Buesi described all the signs she'd received of his impending death—hearing sounds in the forest when nothing was there, spotting a particular kind of snake—and then was led back to her house in tears. As the coffin was closed, Faansisonu prayed and addressed Safeli, pleading with him to tell what killed him so they could deal with whatever the problem was. And he begged him not to take any other little children with him to the land of the dead. When the coffin was knocked three times on the ground and then raised in divination, initial attempts to discover the cause of death failed. Libations were poured to the ancestors, and eventually Safeli said he would only answer when they brought him to the little-children's cemetery (separate from the adult cemetery on the assumption that they would be frightened by being in the midst of so many old people they don't know). By the time that happened, several days later, we had already started our downriver journey, the end of our 1968 fieldwork.

We never found out what killed him.

....

CHAPTER 23

Returns

During our final weeks in Dangogo, on more days than not, Rich paddled down to Dyuumu to spend the day with Agbago's favorite *apintii* drummer and the man most highly touted to succeed him as *gaama*. Peleki, in his mid-forties, came from Dangogo, but he'd opened a little store at the mission near the riverbank, where his offerings ranged from tins of sardines and corned beef to flashlight batteries, Quaker Oats, colored soft drinks, liter bottles of Parbo beer, kerosene, Chinese patent medicine powder, and hard candies. Rich had discovered that Peleki had a passion for First-Time history (though he considered himself a relative beginner) and little hesitation about discussing it with him. Hours went by without a client, so they had plenty of time to talk. Peleki let Rich copy a cassette tape of Agbago teaching him at cock's crow about the establishment of the land rights of clans in the eighteenth century. Whenever he wasn't sure about an incident they discussed, he'd consult his older brother Doote back in Dangogo in the evening and report to Rich the next day—never telling Doote why he wanted to know. It being so near the end of our stay, Rich couldn't help seizing the opportunity, despite the official prohibition. (As Saamakas say, "If sugar falls on your lips, you can't help but lick it up.")

Over the next five years, having become parents, we put off return trips to Suriname, but continued thinking and learning about Saamaka. Faansisonu's son Adiante, fiercely motivated to get an education and some job training, had persuaded us to bring him to the United States, and he lived with us for the better part of our first two years back.[1] We spent a year in the Netherlands working with other Suriname specialists as well as in archives and museums, and then returned to the United States, where Rich began teaching at Yale, focusing his research on the early history of Afro-Americans, in particular Maroons throughout the hemisphere.[2]

During the early 1970s, we wrote a number of articles on specific aspects of Saamaka life—emigration patterns, cicatrization, woodcarving, naming, play languages—and turned our attention to the processing of our field data, securing a grant for the transcription of our recordings that supported Adi for the first year after he moved out on his own. In 1974, we migrated from New Haven to Baltimore (as did Adi), where Rich became founding chair of the Johns Hopkins Department of Anthropology and, after inviting Sid Mintz to join him the following year, established what David Scott has called, "the premier training institution for Caribbeanist anthropologists."[3]

At the same time, Rich was thinking about trying to persuade Saamakas to lift their official prohibition so he could explore their early history in depth. On brief, several-week visits to Saamaka during the summers of 1974 and 1975, he was sufficiently encouraged to proceed and applied to the National Science Foundation for the grant that funded six months of fieldwork in 1976 and 1978. In a sense, the older Saamakas we knew best, including Agbago, had always expected him to work on First-Time someday—how else could he become a man of knowledge? Nevertheless, they wanted him to do it only when he was ready—when *they* thought he was ready—and the time finally seemed right.

By our return to Suriname in the mid-1970s, the pace of change in Upper River Saamaka villages had accelerated. Government officials or tourists dropped in and out of once-isolated villages almost on a monthly basis, film crews occasionally came and went, Saamaka men often wore long pants in the villages, people were listening to radios, and many—both men and women—were spending time on the coast. We too had changed: Rich was now a professor rather than a student, and seen by both Saamakas and other Surinamers, who'd been sent copies of his books, as an authority on Saamaka life. And Sally, much to everyone's approval, was no longer childless.

By the time we'd left Saamaka at the end of 1968, we had already been officially recognized as something close to honorary Saamakas. Gaama Agbago had marked our departure by taking our hands in his, raising and lowering them several times as he spoke for a time in the esoteric Pumbu language and then, switching to Saamaka, remarking that Sally had not committed adultery and had strictly held to the menstrual taboos, and that Rich had hunted and fished like a real man, sharing with our neighbors. We hadn't walked where we had been told not to, he said, and Rich hadn't tried to talk about subjects he wasn't supposed to.

By the time of our return in the 1970s, our earlier stay had become in some sense part of Dangogo's history, rich with (often-exaggerated) claims of the many ways that we had mastered every facet of a Saamaka lifestyle. While we had once been objects of fear and concern, we were now treated as honored guests. Here is Captain Kala, our old adversary, greeting Rich with a proverb on our return in 1978.[4]

Aso pipi mi sa dyoubi. Aso pipi mi sa dyoubi. When you first came to Saamaka, people would say, "Abatili has brought a person to me, Dangasi [another of Kala's names], and all of Saamaka will be destroyed." How come they said that? Saamaka territory has a tyina [taboo] against whitefolks. Well, they've brought him to the village they call Dangogo Hafupasi, a true slavery-time village. Outsiders do not come here! People said Abatili and I took him, brought him, put him here to kill every single living Saamaka. Then, on a day otherwise like any other, you [RP] come back, bearing all sorts of "gifts" for everyone. Aso pipi mi sa dyoubi. [He then explains the proverb:] Rice granary says that. When it's dry season and you begin to make a garden, you risk death at every turn. When you clear the underbrush, your machete can kill you, a snake can bite you, a tarantula can bite you; every sort of thing can kill you when you're clearing the underbrush! Then when you go to fell a tree, well, every single tree can kill you. The axe in your very hand can kill you. You do all those things, take all those risks, right through the time when you burn the field. And then the rice grows. You harvest it until you're all finished; you load it up in your granary. Until the granary is chock full! Then the granary says its praise name for you. Aso pipi mi sa dyoubi. Because the way you loaded up the granary until it was absolutely full, you can't possibly eat it all by yourself. When you cook it and eat it, until you can't eat more, you toss the leftovers to the fish. Let's say people come to visit you from another village. Well, you cook them some of it, even though they didn't do the work. You throw some to the chickens for them to eat. There are rats in the granary, tree squirrels too. They all eat it. It's available for everyone. *Aso pipi mi sa dyoubi.* The American came out from his country and arrived in Saamaka. People said Abatili and I put him here to destroy the world. But today: *aso pipi mi sa dyoubi.* They're all reaping the benefits. First-Time language! I, Dangasi, say so!

We missed the presence of Nai, who had departed to the land of the ancestors in 1970, but were touched to learn that it was our canoe that had been sawed off to make the *bungula* for her funeral rituals—carrying her corpse for the pre-burial interrogation to apportion her belongings and determine the cause of death, and then being placed directly on her grave. During the 1976 visit, when our two children were with us, people gave Nai's name to our daughter, assuming that she had served as a namesake for us, as she had always promised she would.[5]

In 1974, when Rich was in Saamaka briefly, and in 1975, when we were there together, we lived in our house in Dangogo. Our notes record that we found Abatili slowly recovering from a vicious beating he'd received by the lineage brothers of a man whose wife he'd slept with in a downstream village, doled out with blackjacks and a heavy plank that had split open his skull. And recently, the doctor at Dyuumu had been thrown out of Saamaka by a mob led by Kala who accused him of killing in quick succession, by injection, Akonda and two other Dangogo women—a police escort had hurried him out in a plane flown in from the city, we were told. Plans were underway for a second funeral for the three women together.

During the long summers of 1976 and 1978, we moved to Asindoopo, taking advantage of the screened-in wooden house and outhouse left to us by two women from the Summer Institute of Linguistics.[6] The change was convenient both for our ethnographic projects and, in 1976, for the practicalities of having children in the field. As many anthropologists have discovered, coming to the field with young children brings both rewards and special challenges. We were no longer marked as lamentably childless, and people in Asindoopo, both adults and children, received our six-year-old son and five-year-old daughter with real warmth, helping them to adopt Saamaka clothing (a little breechcloth for him, a beaded waist tie for her) and inviting them to join in village activities with other children. Our son's age mates in Asindoopo soon had him shooting lizards with a little slingshot and spouting words and phrases in Saamaka. At one ceremony we attended in Akisiamau, a (possessed) Komanti warrior picked him up and paraded around the village, holding him high in the air before returning him to Sally's arms. (He still remembers!) Our daughter had a less happy experience, due to a bout of intense diarrhea and vomiting early in our stay, which quickly led to life-threatening dehydration. The mission clinic at Dyuumu (which was momentarily out of intravenous solution) once again came to our rescue, radioing the capital for a two-seater plane which flew her, with Sally, to the main Moravian hospital in Paramaribo for intravenous hydration. When she was strong enough to travel, she flew back to New York with Rich (while Sally and our son returned to Saamaka) and spent the rest of the summer with her grandparents.

Living in Asindoopo was particularly useful for Rich's work on First-Time, much of which was with Peleki and Tebini, a man from the nearby village of Kampu who was considered the Saamakas' greatest living historian. With the approval of Agbago, Kala, Faansisonu, and the other Matyau clan elders who had become, in a sense, our spiritual guardians, Rich was now working with men who had known him, at least by reputation, from the previous decade. A year at the Algemeen Rijksarchief in Holland had increased his knowledge of early Saamaka history enormously, and by the summer of 1978 he was in a position to offer Saamaka historians a precious gift—important new materials about their own early past, always exchanged with the greatest delicacy.[7] Fortunately, the growth of Rich's historical knowledge coincided with a realization by some elders that if knowledge of First-Time (at least the non-ritual parts of it) wasn't written down soon it would be lost forever. In 1978, at a meeting in the *gaama*'s council house, Matyau clan leaders declared rhetorically that Rich was now a Matyau and formally asked him to be their chronicler. It was this kind of official approval, which contrasted so strikingly with the explicit prohibitions of the 1960s, that encouraged him to proceed.[8] Much of his work with Saamaka historians consisted of lengthy evening conversations, as he scribbled in notebooks and kept a tape recorder rolling.[9] He also made a number of trips, usually accompanied by Abatili and sometimes by Sally, to villages upstream and down, to expand his First-Time knowledge with elders from other clans.[10]

Meanwhile, Sally's dissertation research on art and gender followed seamlessly on her earlier fieldwork in Dangogo, since women in Asindoopo were involved in the same range of social and artistic activities. She immersed herself in the world of women in this polygynous and strongly patriarchal society, where men were the uncontested authorities in everything from politics to religious life, focusing on women's contributions to the visual and performing arts (recruiting our son to help write out notes on song lyrics during the 1976 trip).

Sometimes there were unexpected detours in the conversations about art. Asipei's wife Akundumini, now living in Asindoopo, once mentioned a white man who had come to Saamaka with his wife way back when she was an apron-girl: "We called him *Afiika fandya* ['African Fringe']," she said. And her elderly mother filled in more details: "They had a woman who cooked for them named Coba. Their Creole man from the city made trouble with them and Gaama Dyankuso told them they had to leave." We realized from the details they provided that they were talking about Melville Herskovits, who reported in *Rebel Destiny* that Saamakas called him *Ame'ika Fandya* ("American Fringe"). We can only imagine that the shift to *African* Fringe was because he pressed so hard about finding Africanisms in Saamaka. In any case, it was a revelation to learn that the Herskovitses had been politely but firmly thrown out of Saamaka by the *gaama*, something we were able to confirm decades later when we read their previously private diaries.[11]

Sally's 1970s fieldwork led to a book on art, gender, and polygyny, and, before long, an ambitious NEH-funded exhibition, "Afro-American Arts from the Suriname Rain Forest," for which the two of us served as curators.[12] In preparation for the exhibition, we devoted part of our time in Saamaka to inventorying (and in some cases collecting) Saamaka textiles—a form of Saamaka art that had been badly neglected by Westerners, who focused their interest in art almost exclusively on men's woodcarving. When we told Gaama Agbago about the upcoming event, he was delighted and offered to show us the textiles that women had given him over the years. Together, we dragged seven massive trunks from his house to a shady spot where, with the help of Takite, we could examine their contents. For us, the exercise promised to open up an ethnographic gold mine, rich in materials that would help flesh out Saamaka art history. For Agbago, it was to be an emotional journey into his personal past.

FIGURE 23.1. Agbago. Photo: R. Price.

Takite helped open each carefully folded rectangle of cloth while Sally scribbled in her notebook, Rich manned the camera, and Agbago reminisced. This embroidered kerchief had been sewn by his mother, that cape was made by a late wife from Santigoon, that other was from his inauguration as *gaama*. For many of the cloths, however, these details weren't possible for him to retrieve. As with other men who'd opened their trunks for us, he'd lost track of specific origins for much of his collection, and the individual gifts had merged, weaving a generalized testimony to a lifetime of relationships.

When Agbago came to one small, round packet, his face lit up with a gentle smile. Turning his back to us, he tenderly undid the knot in the kerchief, and set aside the small pieces of cloth it held, one by one, counting softly in a language he'd heard in Guyane in the early years of the century. *Quinze!* Fifteen adolescent aprons that had been cut from their waist ties with his knife and slipped into his hunting sack. Fifteen

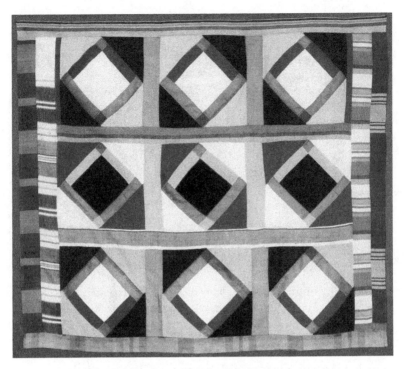

FIGURE 23.2. One of the shoulder capes sewn by Peepina
for Agbago. Photo: Antonia Graeber.

young girls who'd become women in his hammock. He recounted the
aprons to make sure he'd got the number right. "Dee ogi di mi du," he
remarked with a grin: "My little mischiefs."

Many of those youthful lovers' faces were now forgotten, but
Apumba had been with him for more than seventy years. He had spoken for her even before her breasts were full, and when she died earlier
in 1978 she had been the senior of his three wives, withered and frail,
but still sharp tongued and very much in charge.

When we told him about the exhibition that would introduce Americans to the arts of Saamakas, he announced that it would be only fitting
for him, as *gaama*, to make a contribution, and asked us to select four
pieces to display. After a brief consultation, we put aside three patchwork capes sewn by Peepina, his wife from Totikampu who died in 1967
and with whom he'd had many children, plus a beautifully embroidered
cape with appliqué'd borders. Agbago had no problem giving up the
first three, since Peepina had produced countless patchwork capes for

FIGURE 23.3. Remy Jungerman, 1988 wall painting
in his "Peepina" series. Paramaribo, Suriname.
Photo © Remy Jungerman.

him, but the fourth was special. It was sewn, he thought, by either his
mother or, more likely, Apumba. The embroidered cape would embellish his coffin someday, so we were free to photograph it, but we would
need to select an alternative for the exhibit.

Although they were no longer being worn, the capes and other garments that we collected from Agbago and other Saamakas, like the
ones we left behind, had not yet run the full course of their life histories. Peepina's beautiful patchwork creations, for example, were displayed in the exhibition as Agbago wished. The catalogue cover that
featured one of them was seen by people too numerous to estimate and
was even spotted a few times in made-for-TV movies. More recently,
that same patchwork cape has served as inspiration for an Amsterdam-based Surinamese artist, Remy Jungerman, whose whole "Peepina" series consists of creative variations on its composition and color scheme
in oil paintings, fabric and kaolin collages, and wall art.

After the exhibition traveled from Los Angeles to Dallas, it was scheduled to appear in Baltimore, where we were living, and we accepted an
invitation to host a group of Saamaka drummers, dancers, and singers,
who would put on performances there as well as Washington, DC, and

New York, the exhibit's next venue, over a ten-day period. Knowing how foreign the experience would be for the nine men and women who were chosen, some of whom had never been outside of Suriname, and how reluctant they would be to eat in restaurants for fear of menstrual pollution, we had them stay in our house, sleeping on mattresses on the floor, and cooking communal meals in the kitchen. We were especially pleased that Abatili was in the group, allowing us to reciprocate the hospitality he had shown us in Dangogo so many years before. The men quickly learned to navigate the neighborhood and enjoyed "going hunting" to buy things in local stores, while the women phrased the same outings as going to their gardens. One unanticipated pleasure during the group's stay was the involvement of a Baltimore troupe of African American dancers who, undeterred by the language barrier, befriended the Saamakas, coming to our house almost every evening, and often staying late into the night, for music and dancing.[13]

....

. . . And why haven't we continued working in Suriname?

In 1980, the political situation in recently independent Suriname suddenly took a turn for the worse. A coup d'état led by the army installed Desi Bouterse as commander in chief.[14] A civil war between the national government and Maroons broke out in 1986, pitting the national army of Suriname against a small guerrilla force known as the Jungle Commando, under the leadership of Ronnie Brunswijk, a Ndyuka Maroon who had served as a bodyguard for Bouterse. Most of the Jungles were young Ndyukas, but there were a number of Saamakas as well.[15]

At the same time, Agbago, critically ill in a Paramaribo hospital and told that his end was near, had an aid phone us in Paris to say that he'd like to see us once more before he passed away. We caught a flight to Paramaribo as quickly as we could, only to be told when we arrived that the *gaama* had been flown back to Asindoopo to die. We spent two days preparing for travel upriver to Saamaka (chartering a plane, buying presents), but at midnight, on the eve of our departure, two heavily armed Military Police banged on the door of our Paramaribo hotel room, pulled us from our bed, pushed us roughly into an MP vehicle, and drove us through forest and savannas of eastern Suriname, with another MP vehicle following close behind. Our captors refused to tell us why this was happening, and we had no reason to doubt that they planned to do us in. But after we arrived at the border town of Albina, where we were locked in a room for the rest of the night, they hustled us onto an early morning ferry to Guyane, first stamping our passports ONGELDIG ("invalid"), and telling us never to return.

We later learned that war had broken out between the Jungle Commandos and the government that weekend and, as well-known friends of the Maroons, we had been designated personae non gratae. When the U.S. Embassy asked for clarification about our expulsion, the Suriname government replied that it had been "an administrative error." But numerous friends in Paramaribo—people with political street smarts—suggested that incidents like the one we had experienced were clear signs from the military, and that we would be wise to keep our distance.

Gaama Agbago clung to life until 1989, dying quietly at the age of 102. We were badly torn between Rich's feeling that it was important to attend his funeral and Sally's cautionary stance following our scare with the military police. In the end, we didn't take the risk and had to content ourselves with videos and personal reports (see the next chapter).

In 1992, Rich flew to Costa Rica to testify on behalf of the Saamakas in a case being heard before the Inter-American Court of Human Rights that centered on the execution of seven unarmed Saamakas by Suriname government soldiers. At the end of the two-day trial, Suriname's highest judicial officer strolled over to him and extended his hand. "You know," he said in Dutch with a smile, "My colleagues and I [in the army] are well aware of your many writings and we hope you will come back to Suriname soon. Indeed, we will be preparing a *very special welcome* for you, whenever you arrive."[16]

Given the ominous tone of this invitation, we have restricted our continuing contact with Saamakas and other Maroons to Guyane, where the growing presence of Saamakas, following the disruption of their life in Suriname during the war, has given us opportunities to keep up with them, including those we knew in Dangogo. In 1990, while on a trip to collect objects in Aluku Maroon villages for a museum in Cayenne, we happened upon Kala's wife Anaweli, who kissed us profusely on both checks (à la française) and proudly showed us the large cement house she'd built with her recently acquired French welfare payments. She had left Kala some years earlier, she told us, no longer being able to take his tyrannical temper. And a few years later, while visiting the town of Régina, once home to a large population of immigrant Saamaka men, we heard a woman calling out to us excitedly in Saamakatongo: "Lisati! Sali!" It was Maame. Her hair was white, and she was surrounded by grandchildren, but her smile was the same one that she had so carefully suppressed when we took her photo in front of Kala's house in Dangogo. From her fridge, she brought out soda and beer. It was quite a reunion.

....

CHAPTER 24

Foto

Saamakas call Suriname's capital *Foto*. Indeed, Fort Zeelandia, guarding the broad riverine entrance to Paramaribo, has been a landmark since the Dutch takeover of the colony in 1667.

During much of our time in Suriname, the fort (which had been a prison earlier in the century) was home to the Surinaams Museum, where we often worked during our brief stays in Paramaribo, both in the storerooms of Maroon collections and in its excellent historical library (the former Koloniale Bibliotheek), taking pages and pages of notes and many photos. One memorable Sunday afternoon, Museum Director Jimmy Douglas, the former chief of police, invited us to join him and his wife in the fort's courtyard for a luncheon of peanut soup that he'd cooked himself. There he regaled us with stories of criminals he'd hanged in that very space, describing how he'd learned the proper formula for length-of-rope to weight-of-victim from his counterpart in Georgetown, Guyana. In the early 1980s, after the army-led coup d'état, the museum was hastily cleared out and the fort became the headquarters for the military. And in 1982 it was the site of the infamous "December Murders," when Desi Bouterse, then commander in chief (now the elected president of Suriname), tortured and killed fifteen prominent citizens in a single night—newspaper editors, lawyers, labor union leaders, and others.

During 1967 and 1968, we spent a total of some five weeks in Paramaribo, taking care of bureaucratic chores (immigration, police), buying supplies (from shotgun shells to canned sardines), interviewing various people who regularly interacted with Saamakas (missionaries and church officials, politicians, researchers, judges, storekeepers, district commissioners), reading books, manuscripts, and archives in the museum and at the Catholic and Moravian bishoprics, and visiting Saamaka villages that had been moved below Alcoa's artificial lake. We stayed at a small hotel run by an East Indian couple whose squeaky bedsprings often woke us at night, and moved only during the 1970s to slightly more upscale lodgings at the YWCA. Much of our food came from street carts, often East Indian roti, Javanese bami, or Chinese cornerstore sandwiches, though we sometimes treated ourselves to a meal at the Hong Kong, which featured loud soul music (James Brown) and liter jugs of Parbo beer.

Much of our time in the city was spent with Saamakas, either friends from upriver or their relatives who were living there. When we visited those few Saamakas we knew who lived there, we were taken aback by the grinding poverty (whole families in a tiny room, sleeping on the floor with no electricity or running water), the contrast between the beauty and dignity of their forest home and their new shantytown lives. We often realized just how different were many of our cultural assumptions. A Dangogo friend saw Sally about to cross the street and ran to grab her, not imagining that a woman could know how to avoid the traffic alone. And we noticed a middle-aged Saamaka woman shopping in a Chinese store wearing a black bra with her breasts hanging out underneath. When we shopped at the country's first supermarket with Amombebuka, he couldn't believe that we were allowed to walk down the aisles and just help ourselves to anything we wanted from the shelves. When we took Abatili and a couple of other Dangogo men to the cinema to see West Side Story they (not surprisingly, in retrospect) found both music and plot utterly boring and irrelevant. And when we examined an impressively diverse display of tape recorders with Dosili, we realized that the only feature he was interested in was the volume of the playback.[1]

We also spent a couple of days with two men from the largest Saamaka village, Ganze, which had been sunk by the lake, who shared their views of how the way life in that Christian village differed from the life they imagined in Dangogo. Though they were Western educated and spoke the city language at home with their children, they still used Saamaka expressions, saying "cross the river" for crossing the street, or when deciding to linger under a large tree while caught in a sudden downpour on our way to a soccer match, "it's not that we're going to a [First-Time] battle with the whitefolks."

But city people who interacted with Saamakas in their daily life taught us much as well. Ahmad El-Wanni, who owned the Jeruzalem Bazaar (the store that pretty much monopolized the sale of cloth to Maroons) kindly gave us eighty-nine cloth swatches, which Sally later used to elicit names from Saamakas, and described the process of procuring from China the 250,000 yards (in 750 patterns!) he sold each year. And an East Indian judge who occasionally encountered urban Maroons in his courtroom opened our eyes to the stereotypes that were current among urban Surinamers, arguing with us for hours that the Saamakas' staple food was millet, rather than rice; we never succeeded in convincing him otherwise.

During 1970s and 1980s visits, we worked quite a bit in the museum, going through its storeroom collections. We also spent many hours with sociologist Betty Sedoc, who had been appointed dean of Social Sciences at the new university, discussing plans for curriculum and research projects.[2]

After the military takeover in 1980, it was the bourgeois creole women who ran the YWCA who repeated to us the popular refrain that Surinamers should "let the boys have a chance," hoping for a brighter postcolonial future. And in 1986 it was one of El-Wanni's sons, then running the Jeruzalem Bazaar, who warned us, in whispers, for our personal safety on the very eve of our midnight expulsion from Suriname by the military police.

....

CHAPTER 25

Looking at Paper

"What do they do all day?" a visitor to Dangogo once asked Nai within our earshot. "They just keep looking at paper," she replied. Indeed, we often heard this explanation about why we tended to spend part of each day quietly inside our house, not something that Saamakas did. At the end of our stay in 1968, all that paper was put in trunks, carried downriver in a canoe, and shipped off to New Haven where Rich began drawing on it for a dissertation while Sally turned her attention to our upcoming life as parents.

It wasn't until fifty years after our first encounter with Saamakas and the publication of more than two dozen books about them that we decided to revisit the nitty-gritty of that ethnographic experience. The field data that we had carried with us from one home to another over the years, and which now sat in a row of four file cabinets in our house in Martinique, consisted not only of desiccated paper, frazzled at the edges, but also shoeboxes filled with tape cassettes,[1] bulging notebooks with transparent sleeves containing black and white negatives and contact sheets, plastic boxes holding color slides, manila envelopes with prints of various sizes, and more—including additional material from our returns to Saamaka in the 1970s.[2] We began by emptying three deep file drawers labeled "Sar fieldnotes 1960s" and set the contents on a table in our study. Thousands of single-spaced typed pages, each headed "rsp" or "shp" on the upper right and bearing scribbled tags in the left margin ("Apuku," "co-wives," "crop calendar," "cicatrization," "drum language," "address terms" . . .), were written in an indiscriminate thicket of English, Saamakatongo, and abbreviations thereof.[3] We *conjugal relations gifts* — Koopi's gifts, to A ateli, described by Sally, are in return for the gifts he gave her when he lai paka and took her. Beki notes that a woman didn't used to have to reciprocate at this stage unless the man came and took her from a long way off. Beki thanks Dofia profusely for gifts(Koopi's be). The thing about not having to make these gifts may be merely making them seem bigger, a way of gafá-ing...

general ogi — After GT opo, (see Sally's notes), Tioje announced to assembled people that next Ftiday Dgo would do its part in general mundu seeká Mamagadu ordered, to prevent ogi before jai.

basi ogi gadu — Refernece to Akonomisi as "di sembe abí hen buka"(that is, Nain's gadu's buka, ie the person who mbei it.

agric — Akundumini still cutting rice alibase.

Notes for Thursday 10/26

stealing — Asipei says if he doesn't sooto his door, people in his pisi will come steal his tobako.

beating "kumu" — If someone is fom unjustly, including say Elema or other kid, "di kumu f'en de ta suku".

address — Adelmo and Naina adrewss "suagi".

BM incident — Here is authorized version of Betemujee incident(see Sally's notes for some otter comments on it). When she arrived here, the door was locked. She tue lai at Nai's. Naina came and told her that she hadn't been here in a long while and probably didn't know that Djeni, her kambosa, had been cooking in Nai's since her own house roof was broken, and that it wouldn't be good for Bm to bbe there when Djeni showed up. Butm Naina said, Bm wouldn't come till next day so as long as she got out early in morning, it was ok.(Betemujee took this as jaká, Naina later claimed she was merely trying to be helpful, nice). Meanwhile, Maje broke latch on door for Bm. She then refused to go into house, saying that where she came from, they only broke latch when a person died and they couldn't find his key. Note that this incident, which happened quickly and was over when Dosili came and took her to her house soon after,

friction — has been told and retold ad nauseum since it occurred. Naina keeps denying responsibility, etc. Interesting thing is that they discuss this minor incident only, as if it were the real problem between them at Bm. Never any mention that Naina and others might have other reason for jaká-ing Bm. We think this kind of thinking is typical - Kala when he wanted to fight with me used sika as excuse, and always retold our differences in terms of that thing - which really had nothing to do with fundamental issue.

kapts — This afternoon, Konoi, Naina kosi Kala for all the sickness in Dgo. Of all kapts, he alone walks around, búja-ing all day, and never seeká azangpau etc, though everyone knows ogi ta ko. Kala never leads, just makes noise look at gangasa doti, etc.

social control — Scandal: Dosili almost fom Akonda: he kosi her tee a bigi to her face for stealing oranges from Kandamma's tree in Abat's pisi to sell at Djoemoe. They're not hers to take. First, she stripped a tree in another pisi, also not hers, but it wasn't quite so bad, Asipei says, because it belonged to a "baa" of her father's.

tree ownership + rights — Note that tree ownership often no longer corresponds to residence patterns, because trees outlive changing patterns of residnce.

FIGURE 25.1. A fieldnote page—RSP 536.

took a few days to scan them into pdfs in the hope that particular words would be roughly searchable in spite of all the typos and the graphic idiosyncrasies of our compact Hermes typewriter.

A 5×8-inch accordion file with pockets labeled A through Z fell apart when we picked it up. The contents, quickly transferred to a shoebox, consisted of a set of standardized data on every individual in Dangogo. We had used a template card with carefully excised rectangles designed to receive the data—age, parents, parents' clans and residence, detailed conjugal history, children born, children raised, coastal trips, residence history, garden camps, possession gods, formal friendships and, when known, the person who had supervised their rite de passage to adulthood. Conjugal history (sometimes requiring several cards) was entered through the holes of a second template card. And an additional set of cards contained less complete data on other people—mostly deceased relatives of the Dangogo residents, but also some of their spouses.

A mottled notebook labeled "Log Book 1967," eaten by insects on the cover but relatively intact inside, recorded six categories that we had filled in faithfully each day—food, weather, individual comings and goings (who made day trips to other villages, upriver camps, or the mission clinic; who was in the menstrual hut; etc.), ritual activities (oracle sessions, libations, various kinds of divination, etc.), special events (ancestral feasts, council meetings . . .), and our own activities. Halfway through the year we added the use of a template to keep track of how many people slept in Dangogo each night, distinguishing adult versus child, male versus female, and resident versus visitor. There were also two bulging manila envelopes containing densely filled 5×8-inch cards on which we had recorded the whereabouts of more than one hundred people each day between September 1967 and November 1968—whether they slept in Dangogo, were working in upriver garden camps, made trips to the mission clinic or other villages, and more.

The information on kinship relations that appeared on nearly every page of our fieldnotes had eventually been consolidated into multi-page genealogies, scotch-taped together left and right to create scrolls that allowed the connections over eight generations to be included.

And there was a notebook devoted to our coverage of material culture: a list of the twelve models of machetes, specifying what men owned each kind, entries for every kind of clothing, from gravediggers' kerchiefs and button earrings to embroidery stitches and different styles of patchwork capes, pages on every kind of ritual paraphernalia we'd heard of, and so on. For each object we had annotated the information we'd collected, the photos or sketches we'd made, and the details that were still needed. All this was part of a larger attempt to document Saamaka material culture—compensation for the fact that we had declined a 1967 request from Bill Sturtevant to make a collection for the Smithsonian, where he was a senior curator. It had been a tempting idea, but we decided that taking on the role of collectors could compromise the non-commercial relationship that we were taking pains to establish with our neighbors. So we said no. But then Bill proposed as an alternative that we make a *virtual* collection—an exhaustive inventory of the material life of Saamakas—including physical properties, historical antecedents, developments over time, production techniques, linguistic terms, hierarchies of value, conceptual associations, gender dimensions, ownership patterns, regional differences, and more . . . but stopping just short of acquiring the physical objects. So that is what we did.

And of course there was more to be had in the file cabinets—maps, loose memos, letters from the field, and other miscellanea. We also found a file box with almost two thousand 3 × 5–inch slips, arranged in 170 categories ("Snakegods," "Menstrual Seclusion," "Kinship Terms," "Hunting and Fishing," . . .), indexing the relevant pages of our fieldnotes and noting the specific information each one contained. Compiling it had been exceedingly time consuming, but in a pre-computer age, that's the sort of donkeywork that you had to do to keep track of such diverse information.[4]

It may be worth underlining the difficulties (better, impossibility) of recapturing or recapitulating the learning experience that fieldwork in another culture involves. Reading through our fieldnotes, we were struck by how much of the significance of particular comments depended on background knowledge of the things being referred to that was not explicitly spelled out, knowledge that readers who hadn't participated in our experiences wouldn't get. As we wrote up our day's activities, we were constantly building on assumptions about what we'd already seen, heard, and learned. Making sense of a note that "Seema worked on Djeni's house," for example, depended on knowing the re-

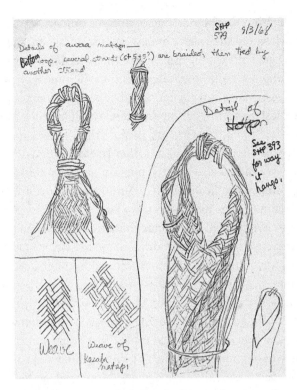

FIGURE 25.2. A fieldnote page—SHP 579. The weave of a
basketry press used to make awara palm oil compared
to that for a cassava press.

lationship between Seema and Dosili, and understanding that because
Djeni was pregnant, her husband Dosili had a taboo on doing this
work. When we already knew these sorts of things, we didn't need to
write them into our fieldnotes, and this was true even at the very beginning of our time in Saamaka. We were writing mnemonics for ourselves, not for outsiders.[5] In this book, we stick much more closely to
our fieldnotes than in any previous work, but as in Zeno's paradox, one
can never quite catch the turtle. What we attempt here is to get as close
as possible to those experiences of wonder, frustration, and learning,
remaining as faithful as we can to the fieldnotes while still retaining
coherence for those who haven't had the good fortune to experience
Saamaka life in person.

Re-reading the fieldnotes a half-century after they were written,
we've sometimes been surprised by the things that went unrecorded.

We searched in vain for a description of our original introduction to Kala, which would surely have been worth recording, but the first time he's mentioned he's simply fishing with Rich one day, as if we'd known him all along. Or again, our notes mention the time Sally was bitten twice by a scorpion hiding in her skirt, but nothing about the more serious medical problems she experienced. The 1967 daily-record book says "7/4–To Djumu, 7/15–To Foto [Paramaribo] + Barbados," without recording that after contracting amoebic dysentery from drinking river water, she was hospitalized at the mission and then told by the doctor to go someplace healthier than Suriname for a couple of weeks of recuperation. (If memory serves, we boiled river water for drinking throughout our stay but often enough found ourselves in social situations where we felt obliged to drink untreated water.) Or again, the 1968 log says: "8/12–8/20. We are in Djumu" without saying that she was hospitalized for a difficult miscarriage. And there's no mention of the warm twelve-ounce bottle of 7 Up that we somehow procured and shared to celebrate our fifth wedding anniversary, though we both remember how special it was. One lacuna that really surprised us was the silence in our notes about Rich's being credited with killing a deer during our first week in Dangogo and his doubts about being responsible for it (see chapter 2, "On Trial")—his fieldnotes simply describe the shooting and the butchering. Although that was a decisive moment for our integration into the village, neither the discussion of credit nor the doubts, which we both remember vividly, appear anywhere in our notes. And another drama—the receipt of a notice that Rich was being called up for military service in Vietnam and all the anxious scrambling to renew his deferment that ensued—is completely absent from our notes. Fieldnotes, like archives and memories, have many holes.

There are also self-created ethnographic holes. Although we participated widely in Saamaka life, we did not follow all possible paths. For example, Beki and other women tried hard to get Sally to practice the genital ablutions with herbs that women performed each morning to tighten and dry out their vaginas, but Sally rarely did so, just as she declined having cicatrizations cut. (It was only later that we learned about the more than one-hundred different species of plants that women use in these baths to insure "dry sex," an African-derived preference that causes women discomfort and pain during intercourse but is much appreciated by men.)[6]

Re-reading the fieldnotes after a half-century also brought home the seriousness of the anti-*bakaa* feelings expressed by Kala and others, the extent to which Saamakas were not merely playing a rhetorical game with the two young Americans. Consider, for example, the words of Pulitzer-Prize-winning novelist Alice Walker, talking in 2016 about her own childhood memories of the twentieth-century rural U.S. South:

Now I know about the hardships that my father, my grandfather, all of the black men went through. The women too, of course, but I was fascinated by the men. They were totally oppressed by the culture. Lynchings were frequent. I used to wonder why my father always had this look when he went off to town that said, I might not be back. He had to behave in this servile way. And if the white people were drunk, they would abuse him anyway.

The interviewer asks: "And that was their model for treating women?" Walker responds:

Enslavement culture was their only model for 300 years. They would be looking at the behavior of brutal white overseers. Did you realize that they used to behead people in our country? They put heads on spikes and lined the rivers to keep enslaved people in complete terror.[7]

It is clear from the notes that our respective roles in the field were molded by some combination of differing academic situations, gender expectations of the 1960s, and individual personalities. Rich had begun constructing a career in anthropology some five years earlier, conducting fieldwork during the summers in Peru, Martinique, Spain, and Mexico; he'd done graduate study in Paris and at Harvard; and he'd published several articles in leading anthropological journals in France and the United States. Sally had just finished her undergraduate degree at Harvard in French Literature, though she had learned the ropes of ethnographic fieldwork by accompanying Rich in all but his Peruvian experiences and had co-authored several publications about them.[8] By temperament, Rich was especially interested in historical research, while Sally's artistic bent led her to focus more on material culture, often filling her notes with sketches. And then there were ideas about gender, both our own upbringing in the 1940s and 1950s (Rich ran track, played basketball, and captained the soccer team in high school, while Sally was an accomplished seamstress and artist) and the firm Saamaka view of men as the ones who traveled to engage in work, and women as the ones who occasionally accompanied them. So that was also how we were generally seen—a man ("Lisati") with a job to do, joined by a woman ("Lisatimuyee" [Lisati's wife]) who provided company and domestic services.

Altogether, this meant that Rich spent a good deal of time in full-day interviews on a vast range of subjects, while Sally conducted fewer formal interviews, mainly on issues affecting women. Rich went hunting and fishing, attended oracle sessions and political meetings, and occasionally played soccer with the guys his age, while Sally spent more time hanging out with women, sewing with them on their doorsteps, washing clothes or dishes with them at the river, and using those informal settings to keep up with local news and gossip. She also served as a full-time buffer, sitting on the doorstep of our house on days when Rich was interviewing. As her notes say, "Interviewing in the village with people around is a real 2-man job. People who come to chat or greet us expect to be treated as well as if Rich weren't working. It's almost impossible for me to do any serious work." Rich's all-day interviews were sometimes interrupted by unforeseen events. Once, Asipei, who'd been providing information on who farmed where, looked through the glass panel in the back of our house and said quietly: "Grab your gun, there's a [large poisonous snake] on the path." The interview took a few-minutes break while Rich shot the eight-foot-long creature. (Years later we learned that in 1983 Asipei was fatally bitten by the same kind of snake, as he returned from his gardens in Mama Creek.)

Within a month or so of our arrival in 1967, we had settled in to something approaching a routine. Our activities ranged widely: Fishing, hunting, skinning animals, cleaning fish, cooking, washing clothes and dishes, and carrying water up from the river; visiting with people throughout the village, crossing the river to participate in events in the eastern side of Dangogo (rituals, oracle sessions, a childbirth), paddling downriver once in a while to Asindoopo or Dyuumu, attending long interrogations of Gaantata, spending as much as a few days a week on intensive interviews, scribbling notes in handwriting and then typing them up (making carbons and sending them back to the U.S. for safekeeping—we'd already heard enough stories about canoes sinking in the rapids); taking occasional photos (mostly when people requested them, and following their wishes for the pose—frontal, full body, and above all without a smile) that would be developed later in the city; and tape-recording drumming, secular and religious songs, folktale sessions, and more. Occasionally we took advantage of the chance to accompany friends on visits to far-off villages, sleeping with them there for a few days and getting a chance to see Saamaka life as it played out in another part of the river. This was especially useful when we were able to observe the life of people in the so-called transmigration villages who had recently been displaced by the artificial lake. Both in the large, new agglomeration of Boonsweki (over three thousand people!), with its row upon row of government-built wooden houses, and in the Christian villages downstream from the lake, we were able to experience a very different form of Saamaka life, where villagers were suddenly thrust into close contact with the social and cultural realities of the coastal region, where river water was not drinkable, and where bags of food doled out to families by the government were taking the place of the garden activities that had been such an important part of women's lives.

As we've mentioned in earlier chapters, we took several "time-outs" from the field. A few several-day visits to Paramaribo, always arranged with Gaantata's approval. The three weeks in newly independent Barbados in 1967, in a rented chattel house, that not only got Sally up to snuff after her amoebic dysentery but also gave us the opportunity to take stock and formulate hundreds of new questions based on what we'd learned so far. And the return to the United States from December 1967 to February 1968 to repeat that exercise at a different level, staying with Rich's parents and producing long lists of specifics that needed more detailed information. While we were there we also bought a small radio microphone for Rich to use at Gaantata interrogations. Beamed back to the tape recorder in our house, this allowed him to write up the contents of oracle sessions, which sometimes included as many as twenty complex problems over several hours and were far too long for him to remember in detail without the recordings.

During that trip we also visited the American Museum of Natural History in New York and went through the extensive Saamaka collection that had been made by physician/explorer Morton Kahn in the 1920s. One item that caught our attention was a pair of calfbands whose central bands were executed in a red-white-black zigzag design (in contrast to all the ones we'd seen in Saamaka, which sported simple bands of color in the middle).[9] Sally examined them with interest, and once we were back in Dangogo, created a pair for Beki's son Bane. This caused quite a stir, with women saying they'd never seen that complex design. Nai, however, was thrilled, telling us that she'd known this red-white-black zigzag style, which she said was called "turtle-back calf-bands," when she was a young girl.[10]

Other fragments of our "outside knowledge" of Saamaka culture also found their way into exchanges in the field. When Rich, in an interview with Asipei, mentioned Melville Herskovits's claim that the crescent moon motif in woodcarving represented the "male member" and thus carried a sexual message, Asipei seemed puzzled by the idea, and said he'd never heard anything like that. The next day he returned to our house looking a bit embarrassed, and said he had a question. With apologies for his ignorance, he wanted to know whether perhaps the erect penises of *white* men were curved and pointed like that.

Despite feeling enormously privileged to have lived in Dangogo and made Saamaka a precious part of our life, we often reflect that our time there deprived us of many of the defining experiences of our generation. During 1968, the radio we had in the field was powerful enough to pick up weekly news broadcasts beamed from Paramaribo in the Saamaka language by Dyangalampu, Gaama Agbago's Western-educated son. So that was how we learned of the assassinations, two months apart, of Martin Luther King and Robert Kennedy—both times Sally heard the news while in the menstrual hut. When the Soviet Union invaded Czechoslovakia, we tried to share the radio news with friends in Dangogo—Dosili shook his head in amazement for several days at the idea of waking up one morning, say in Dangogo, and finding tanks positioned all around the village. But we heard nothing of the My Lai massacre nor the rise of the Black Panther Party nor the violence at the Democratic Convention in Chicago nor the uprisings that marked May 1968 in Paris nor Tommie Smith and John Carlos raising their fists at the Mexico Olympics until our return to the States. If 1960s Saamaka has become a sort of dreamscape for us, our memories of that remarkable period in the United States come largely through the filter of Saamaka-language bulletins on a scratchy little radio deep in the South American rain forest.

....

CHAPTER 26

The End of an Era

On January 18, 1989, Gaama Agbago Aboikoni "went to sleep," as Saa-makas put it. At the age of 102, his heart had finally given out. We re-ceived the phone call at our home in Martinique, and for several days had heated debates about whether to fly to Suriname to pay our re-spects. In the end, we decided that in light of our expulsion by the army three years earlier and warnings about our safety should we ever try to return, it would be imprudent. In addition, the civil war remained in full swing, though a partial cease-fire had been declared in Saamaka territory during the funeral.

We later heard detailed descriptions of the events. Captain Kala, then about ninety, was immediately summoned to Asindoopo from Dangogo. When he arrived he went to the house where the *gaama* was lying in a hammock and ordered an assistant captain to call him by name three times. When there was no response, Kala told him to announce to the village, town-crier fashion, that *Gaama duumi*, "the *gaama* has gone to sleep." Abatili fired twelve gunshot salutes and set off to nearby vil-lages to spread the news, which quickly traveled downstream all the way to the city. That evening, local captains and the *gaama*'s family held a meeting to make the necessary plans, and asked Aduengi, Po-mala, Abatili, Akobo, and a few others to take charge of the upcoming events.

Over the next three months, several thousand people crowded into Asindoopo and nearby villages while preparations were being made for the burial. A team of Dutch and Surinamese anthropologists were among those present, gathering information for a book on the day-by-day events and celebrations.[1]

The day after the *gaama*'s death, firewood was gathered to heat water, and the bottom was cut out of one of Agbago's old canoes to create the *bungula* that would be raised and consulted about his succession and related matters. When the *gaama*'s body was placed on the *bungula*, the interrogation was conducted not with spoken words, as for a normal person's death or in a Gaantata oracle session, but instead through rhythms beaten out on the *apintii* drum. When his spirit was asked who should perform the washing of the body, it designated Akobo and Aduengi from Dangogo plus an assistant captain from the village of Pempe (the *gaama*'s father's clan). Using a combination of warm and cool river water, it took place in a shallow pit dug behind the council house of former *gaama* Dyankuso. Hair and nail clippings were taken and set aside to be used in later divination. The corpse was dressed in a breechcloth, pants, a shirt, a cape, and a bonnet, and then covered with decorated cloths, placed in a hammock, and laid out on the *bungula* in the cooking shed of Agbago's immediate predecessor, Gaama Atudendu. Meanwhile, Captain Kala went to the house where the *gaama*'s two wives were sitting and laid out the details of their mourning restrictions—what clothes to wear (including their dead husband's capes), how to cook, when to bathe, and so forth, until after the second funeral, many months later. For much of the following three months, every night and part of each day was given over to dancing, drumming, and singing, as people arrived from near and far bringing food and drink. The stated goal, as with all Saamaka funerals, was to "bury with celebration."

On the second and third day after the death, under the direction of Kala and Aduengi, men constructed the giant coffin—three meters tall and made of special woods—as women provided them with cooked delicacies, set out ceremoniously. By the third night, the *gaama*'s body had been laid in the coffin on top of layers and layers of decorated cloths and covered with colorful hammocks and cloths of every description, many taken from his personal trunks and dating from long-ago relationships with lovers, wives, and kinswomen. That night, the coffin was sealed and the outside decorated with additional cloths, some ancient, some new. It now lay in the house of mourning, watched over by the portrait of Queen Juliana and Prins

FIGURE 26.1. Gravediggers on the river. Photo: Martha Cooper.

Bernhard that had long occupied pride of place in the *gaama*'s council house.

Ten days after the death, divination with the *bungula* selected about a dozen gravediggers, with Pomala as their headman. Another thirty or so young men joined them when the work began the following day. As with all funerals, the gravediggers slept in a special house and traveled the river together. Their heads were tied with kerchiefs that rose to a point in front, and they were the rulers of the river throughout the period, taking whatever chickens or rum or other goods caught their fancy. As they left each morning, they were accompanied by Pomala's *apintii* playing—he was one of three Dangogo men who played the talking drum, the others being Doote and Peleki—and on their return, they blew horns and played drums even more noisily. It took them eight weeks to finish their task—a grave that measured five by four meters and nearly four meters deep, with a niche at one end for the massive coffin to be slipped in.

The night before the burial, in the presence of thousands of people including many officials and other visitors from the city, the massive

FIGURE 26.2. Lowering the coffin onto two canoes.
Photo: Martha Cooper.

FIGURE 26.3. The coffin on the river. Photo: Martha Cooper.

coffin was borne around the village three times on the heads of eight or nine men in a final farewell. Aduengi gave the *gaama* a special sendoff with a speech in archaic First-Time language. Captain Kala sang several *Adonke*, songs that had been sung by the First-Time ancestors, as close relatives from Dangogo, led by Akobo, danced around the coffin, their heads tied with white kerchiefs.

The burial took place three months after the *gaama* died. There had been countless rituals, council meetings, and entertainments before the final rites of separation that parted the *gaama* from his family, from various local deities, and from his nation. The coffin was brought to the landing place and set onto two side-by-side canoes. Gunshot salutes were fired from the riverbank and the *apintii* drum spoke as seventeen large canoes followed the coffin on its way to its final resting place. In the forest cemetery, three hundred visitors were permitted to witness the lowering of the coffin into the ground, near the graves of the *gaama*'s predecessors. After the grave was planked over with wood and covered by palm fronds, the *bungula* was placed on top.

That evening, family members and other villagers gathered to tell folktales before the house of mourning, and by the next day visitors were heading home. A week later, there were libations and a feast for

FIGURE 26.4. A dancer at the *gaama*'s funeral.
Photo: Martha Cooper.

the ancestors, prominent among them the *gaama*'s sister Nai, and a week after that, an all-night play and ancestor feast in Dangogo, the *gaama*'s birthplace.

The second funeral, which would normally have been held a year after the burial, was delayed by the civil war and finally took place nineteen months after the *gaama*'s death. The national army had burned down parts of Saamaka villages in 1990, and the ongoing war made travel difficult, so only a few hundred people, instead of the thousands who would otherwise have come, participated in the ceremonies. Nevertheless, many of the usual activities went forward. A group of men went hunting far upriver to provide game for the ancestral feasts. The river was drugged to furnish fish. Turtles were caught. The ritualized preparation of *apenkusu* (the lightly-fermented sugarcane juice that the First-Time ancestors loved) was prepared according to the normal rituals. Various festive dishes were cooked. The village was ritually cleansed. There were all-night dances and celebrations. Both of the *gaama*'s widows were ceremoniously brought out of mourning—the clothes they had been wearing were thrown in the river, as were the stools (after being broken) they had sat on, and they were given new clothes to wear. The special marks of a *gaama*'s funeral had been observed by the avoidance of several features of normal second funerals—playing Papa drums, chasing ghosts by masked dancers, and the ritual of "throwing the play in the water."

Abgago's second funeral was marked by countless other rituals, many of which were accompanied by the *apintii*, whose rhythms summoned particular people and classes of officials and commented in proverbs on the proceedings. There was a great deal of praying, as well as feasts for the ancestors. At the emotional high point of the ceremonies, during the final council meeting, Kala sang an *Adonke* to Boo—his mother, Nai's, and the *gaama*'s—bringing tears to many peoples' eyes.

The Dutch/Surinamese anthropologists who were present summed up their impressions of the man whose leadership was honored by this three-month-long homage:

> Gaama [Agbago] Aboikoni was a man with charisma. He radiated a natural authority and diplomacy. His eloquence and great knowledge of the culture made him loved by his people and respected by outsiders. Among the other Maroon *gaamas* he was known as *primus inter pares*.[2]

....

Looking back twenty-five years later, Agbago's death surely marked the end of an era—both for Saamakas and for the two of us.

Indeed, 2016 marks the fiftieth anniversary of our initial encounters with Saamakas, whose population has today grown close to 100,000 people.[3] Our earliest publications about them, written in the wake of the civil rights movement (when Rich began teaching at Yale, Bobby Seale and the Black Panthers were on trial just down the street), possessed the inherent moral uplift associated with these African American rebels who had broken the chains of slavery and built a new culture and society in the South American rainforest. We tried to show how non-literate people hitherto considered by outsiders (and by many anthropologists) to be "without history" had a vibrant intellectual life and a well-preserved knowledge of their early history. We tried to trace the extent to which people whose art had been assumed by outsiders to have been inherited directly from Africa were bursting with New World creativity and dynamism. On behalf of Saamakas, and doing our very best to express their perspectives, we wrote against the many essentialisms purveyed by outsiders, from Harvard-based Afro-centrists to various neo-Herskovitsians. As ethnographers writing about Saamaka culture and society, we saw ourselves engaged in an almost noble enterprise, telling stories that were in accord with those of the people whose lives we were studying, and providing a richly documented account of the lives of extraordinary African Americans.[4]

Then, as the situation of Saamakas began to change dramatically—and with it the kinds of issues that we were called on to describe and analyze—we were faced with less clear visions of how best to maintain our solidarity with the people we had come to care so much about. By the time that the civil war, which pitted Saamakas and other Suriname Maroons against the postcolonial national government, ended in 1992, a third of all Maroons had moved across the border to Guyane. And the two of us, as the most visible and activist academic supporters of the Saamakas, were condemned to continuing our work with Saamakas on the French side of the border.

The war brought stark changes to Saamaka. The forest and riverine world we'd known in the 1960s, 1970s, and early 1980s was home to Saamakas living in a state-within-a-state, where the *gaama* decided who could visit in the territory (until the mid-1970s, tourists were not welcome), money was rarely exchanged, hunting and fishing catches were shared among kin, most domestic items (from stools and combs to paddles and canoes) were carved by men for their wives, outboard motors were rare (only two in Dangogo in the 1960s), everyone slept in hammocks (there wasn't a single bed on the Pikilio in the 1960s), rice and vegetable gardens were a central part of women's lives, literacy was almost non-existent (during our 1960s fieldwork, only three men out of the several thousand in the region could read and write), all men (at least until the 1970s) wore breechcloths, and women cicatrized their bodies lavishly, went bare-breasted, and (until the mid-1970s) only rarely traveled beyond Saamaka territory. But by the 1990s that world was giving way to one in which a road, built for the national government by a Chinese contractor without the Saamakas' permission, gave city dwellers easy access to their villages, tourist camps and hotels (usually established by non-Saamakas) hosted outsiders on islands and other sites next to villages, evangelical and other new religions (even Baha'i) had arrived, fish and game, garden produce, and carved items had become commodities to sell for money, and Saamaka women were abandoning cicatrizations and had begun to travel almost as frequently as men to the capital and to neighboring Guyane. And as one elderly Saamaka man put it nostalgically, the day of "tits outside" was a thing of the past. Airstrips, which had first begun to be carved out of the forest in the 1960s and 1970s to ferry medical supplies and the occasional patient between the two missionary-run clinics in Saamaka territory and the city, now served Dutch visitors on jungle tours.

Today, significant numbers of Saamakas, like other Maroons, have dual residence between the coast and the interior. Many traditional villages along the Lawa and Tapanahoni rivers in eastern Suriname and the Saramacca River in the west have few residents other than the elderly, and many Saamaka villages have sharply diminished populations as well. A good half of Saamakas have left their villages for an uncertain existence in the cities of the coast and the others are adjusting to a life in which they are no longer undisputed masters of the realm for which their ancestors shed their blood. Meanwhile, the national government has invaded Saamaka territory, granting Chinese, Malaysian, American, and Canadian companies license to strip it clean of forest and mineral resources. Its aggressive plan is aimed at taking over the country's interior, and integrating its peoples—both Maroons and Amerindians—into the urban underclass of the national society, leaving their territories free for exploitation.

Yet the single most fundamental change, we imagine, has been in the realm of ideology and identity—Saamakas' (and other Maroons') feelings about themselves and the outside world. Given current circumstances, the unmitigated pride that Saamakas and other Maroons once had in First-Time values and in their own way of life is fast slipping away.

Today the great majority of the people we knew during our initial fieldwork, when we were in our twenties and thirties, have joined the ancestors,[5] and the ideological principles that had stood at the foundation of Saamaka life for two and a half centuries have lost much of their meaning. Tokens of modernity—from cell phones (which during the past decade have become ubiquitous) and ATMs (now found in several villages) to pornographic DVDs (widely available)—have become part of everyday life. Younger Saamakas have Facebook pages and smartphones, and use WhatsApp incessantly. Men routinely use chainsaws instead of axes for felling trees to make gardens. Women whose grandmothers couldn't travel beyond Saamaka territory except in the rare cases when their lineage leaders gave them permission now come and go to Paramaribo and Guyane as much as they wish. Many women have moved to the city to allow their children to continue schooling beyond fifth grade, and even in the villages of the interior, most have relocated their gardens closer to their villages so that their children can attend the rudimentary elementary schools that the government has built. Government interference in Saamaka affairs has increased markedly, and there is now a police post (with a couple of policemen from the city) in the village of the *gaama*, as well as in a few other villages downriver. The authority, both sacred and political, of traditional leaders has been greatly diminished. Outsiders have moved into Saamaka territory—Chinese storekeepers, Brazilian *garimpeiros*, Creole and Dutch tour operators, Cuban doctors, schoolteachers of various ethnicities, and several generations of Peace Corps volunteers,[6] as well as various evangelical and other religious leaders—each introducing new ideas, practices, and beliefs. Backbreaking, dangerous (and not very lucrative) artisanal gold mining in small mines run by Saamakas (sometimes with migrant Brazilians) has become the money-earning work of choice for young men, largely replacing the coastal wage labor of previous generations, and bringing with it prostitution, previously unheard of in Saamaka territory. AIDs has become a major problem. Several Saamaka-run radio stations now broadcast news and entertainment throughout the territory. Many Saamakas, both men and women, are engaged in the tourism industry—for example, working at tourist camps, running a small museum, and to some extent "performing their culture" when outsiders request it, in exchange for money.

Rogério Brittes, who conducted dissertation research in the Christian Saamaka village of Botopasi from 2011 to 2013, describes how villagers now prefer to import ready-made coffins from the city rather than constructing the traditional (complexly gabled) Saamaka coffins out of fear that they'll be ridiculed as being "too poor" to afford the modern ones. And during the 2013 "traditional" funeral of Gaama Belfon Aboikoni, instead of men going far upriver for a week of hunting to provide game and fish for the thousands of expected visitors, supermarket chicken was imported from the city. He writes:

> There is tourism, including luxury hotels, all along the Upper Suriname River; almost every village has at least one store, which sells imported food and other products; . . . almost all villages have [diesel] generators that provide [a few hours daily of] electricity; some have durotanks that store rainwater for periods of drought. . . . But the idea of progress is always on the horizon. There is a strong desire for more progress/modernization. As a twenty-something man remarked to me, "It's going to become like the city—it may take a hundred years, perhaps I won't see it, but this is going to turn into the city."[7]

Meanwhile, for the many Saamakas who now live in Guyane, changes have been even more radical. A majority of them do not have French residence papers and live in constant fear of deportation. Nonetheless, they reside in urban environments, their children go to French schools, hospital care is free, and low-level (often illegal) wage labor is available. There is daily interaction with a range of new kinds of people (shopkeepers, gendarmes, construction bosses, immigration officials, cultural promoters, schoolteachers, nurses, doctors) as well as neighbors of diverse ethnic origins (Europeans, Creoles, Brazilians, Haitians, Hmong, Amerindians). Their new neighbors also include an expanded Maroon universe, as Saamakas in Guyane share their new home with Ndyukas, Pamakas, and Alukus who, like them, are adjusting to unfamiliar social, cultural, and linguistic environments.[8]

It is in the context of these wrenching changes—specific to Suriname and Guyane but comparable to historical contingencies experienced by ex-primitives throughout the world during the same period—that our story must be situated. And we conclude that, in many significant ways, the difference between the Saamaka experienced by Melville and Frances Herskovits in the late 1920s and the Saamaka we encountered forty years later was less than that between Saamaka of the 1960s–1980s and the Saamaka of today. Yes, it took two or three weeks by paddle canoe (depending on the height of the river) in the Herskovits's day to get to the Saamaka capital while it was only a two- or three-day motor canoe voyage for us, but the tenor and tone of life in their time was relatively similar to that we experienced compared with the gap between our fieldwork period and today. Or so we imagine from our still excentric locations.

....

Since the millennium, several ethnographic projects have pulled us even further into our 1960s Saamaka dreamworld.

In 2000, we met an elderly Saamaka man named Tooy who had been living in Guyane for some fifty years, yet whose *imaginaire*—his thoughts, his dreams, his hopes—as well as his command of everything from ritual and drumming to history and esoteric languages, remained forever grounded in the Upper River Saamaka world where he grew up during the 1930s, 1940s, and 1950s. Tooy's identity centered on his home village and its spiritual possessions, the stretch of river and forest that surrounds it, the places where he hunted and gardened and gathered medicines, the world that his heroic ancestors first carved out deep in the Suriname rainforest more than three hundred years earlier. Rich learned more about Saamaka First-Time history and Saamaka ritual and other esoteric knowledge from Tooy than from even the most senior historians who taught him so much in Saamaka in the 1970s. In a sense, Rich and Tooy, who became the closest of friends, together managed to create a Saamaka world of the way-it-used-to-be, a shared nostalgia for something that each, for different reasons, felt was slipping away. We can imagine that had they met in Saamaka, the strong social controls mitigating against the feelings they developed for each other (the taboos on sharing deep historical and ritual knowledge with outsiders that are so strong in Saamaka) would have made the kinds of intellectual interactions that took place between them impossible. In any event, it was outside Saamaka territory, in an urban setting of the new millennium, that we added enormously to our knowledge about "traditional" Saamaka life and thought, in effect almost bracketing all the changes that had taken place during the past several decades and re-immersing ourselves in the Saamaka world of the mid-twentieth century.[9]

A second ethnographic project had a similar effect. Beginning in the 1990s, Saamakas back home faced a new and dire threat. By the millennium, the national government of Suriname had sold off most of Saamaka territory (legally, according to the postcolonial Suriname constitution) to Chinese, Canadian, and U.S. multinational gold mining and timber companies. The Saamakas organized and fought back, eventually petitioning the Inter-American Commission of Human Rights (in 2000) and winning a landmark decision (*Saramaka People v. Suriname*) before the Inter-American Court of Human Rights in 2007. The court's judgment required Suriname to change its laws (and, if necessary, its constitution) in order to grant the Saamaka People collective title to their traditional territory as well as considerable sovereignty over it— jurisprudence that henceforth applies to all indigenous peoples and Maroons in the Americas. Throughout the lengthy judicial process, Rich served as advisor to the Saamakas and as expert witness before the court. At its end, he felt obliged to write about the Saamakas' struggle and ultimate victory as well as his own discomfort with having had to emphasize—in order to help Saamakas win their battle—a "traditional" Saamaka world that he knew was in many respects rapidly disappearing—in a sense, our own dreamworld, as well as theirs.[10]

It is sad to have to report that as we write in 2016, the government of Suriname has continued to act as if the judgment of the court had never taken place—and its refusal to abide by the court's decision increasingly makes the 2007 judgment look like a Pyrrhic victory. The rights of Saamakas, as well as other Suriname Maroons and indigenous peoples, remain today under serious threat, despite the continued efforts of the Saamakas, their lawyers, the Inter-American Commission of Human Rights, and ourselves to persuade the government to comply with the orders of the court.

....

We often imagine returning to Upper River Saamaka, reconnecting with those people we knew who are still alive and with patterns of daily life that we'd become so familiar with, exploring the impact of all that has happened in the intervening decades, and trying to tease out the contours of what Amiri Baraka so aptly called "the changing same."[11] Our conversations in Guyane with Saamakas who've just returned from visiting their villages in the Suriname rainforest have told us a lot. Colleagues, doctoral students, and other visitors to Saamaka have also brought us insights about change. But there's so much more that we can only imagine, things we would need to experience in person in order to grasp the whole.

What kind of gossip goes on among women washing their clothes at the landing place? Or has that site, so crucial for sociability in the 1960s and 1970s, been left silent since the introduction of standpipes and running water? Does a woman who wakes up with a headache still walk up the hill to the ancestor shrine and speak to the dead for help? Does a man who has had repeated bad luck in hunting still visit a neighbor for divination? Do little boys still drive toy "canoes" along the ground, and do little girls still put dishes on their head for play trips to their "husband's village"? Is menstrual seclusion still treated with the same rigor and considered essential for keeping the village free of pollution? At night, does the river still come alive with the paddle canoes of men clandestinely visiting illicit lovers? Is adultery still the most common criminal offence, and how often is it still punished with a beating of the offending man by the husband's kin? What is urban life like for those Saamakas who now reside in and around the capital? What sort of lives have they fashioned as they join the urban under-class? To what extent and in what ways does their identity as Saamakas (in contrast to their identity as generic "Maroons") matter in the ethnic maelstrom of that city?

We hear stories from visitors (or read in their blogs and publications) about phenomena we can't fully evaluate. We've been told that there are many outhouses (usually private and locked) in the upriver villages, but that few of them function. Does that mean that men's preference for defecating in the river at night and women's for using large bread-nut leaves on trails in the forest persist? Some villages use only water imported from the city, we've heard, because of rampant pollution of the river, and mountains of plastic bottles now litter the edges of these settlements. Does that mean that freight canoes now bring bottles up-river by the thousands? We know that marijuana is widely grown and smoked and that some villages have homegrown Rastas. How has that changed sociability among kin and neighbors?

These days, our nostalgic dreams of pre–civil war Saamaka are often overshadowed by hints of new realities that come to us via Facebook, reports of visitors, e-mails, newspapers, and other media. Many of these realities more closely resemble nightmares. It is as if the Saamaka solidarity that lasted into the early years of the new millennium, and which fueled their victory before the Inter-American Court, has now degenerated into an each-man-for-himself ethic that has spread like a disease from the city. Since its 1980 coup d'état, Suriname has operated as either a dictatorship (from the 1980s into the 1990s) or a highly authoritarian "democracy" (narcocracy?) where corruption, banditry, patronage, and nepotism rule political life. Many Saamakas, including many of their leaders, now seem to be following the example of their city brothers in putting venal self-interest first. Party politics, with all its corruption, has spread from the city to the riverine world.

Recently, when asked by an interviewer about the future of Saamakas who currently live in traditional villages upriver, Vinije Haabo, a Western-educated Saamaka who lives in the Netherlands, offered a pessimistic prophesy:

> In twenty years' time there will hardly be any original inhabitants left in the Surinamese interior. Multiple mixed social groups will live there . . . Chinese, Brazilians, and other foreigners who are only there to extract the raw materials and leave as soon as possible. . . . I expect there'll be an exodus [of Saamakas and other traditional forest dwellers] and we'll see ghettos in the big cities just like in Africa and [elsewhere in] South America.[12]

His prediction certainly fits the Suriname government's latest proposals for the interior. These now include a road that runs through the heart of Saamaka and Ndyuka territories and connects with the Brazilian national highway system. Some plans call for a railroad as well.[13] Such projects would make the villages (and forest) in Saamaka and Ndyuka territory easily accessible to tourists, land speculators, miners, loggers, and other outsiders. Based on all available information, we now believe that the government's intention is to steamroller the rights of Maroons and indigenous people before the Inter-American Court or anyone else really takes notice, and to empty the forest of its current inhabitants in order to permit economic development that benefits the state and those in power.

The alternative view would be to suggest that Saamakas—drawing considerable strength from their culture, spirituality, and history of resistance as well as leaning on their victory before the court—will continue to insist on their own vision of the future with the same energy and single-mindedness that secured them a hearing before the court. They would decide, after weighing the pros and cons, what sorts of development would be undertaken within their territory and what sorts of development would be kept out. Their relationship to the government would become like that of many indigenous peoples around the world who consider themselves a "nation" even while recognizing (as the Saamakas always have) that they live within larger nation-states and must maintain cordial and collaborative relationships with them. In this scenario, Saamakas would remain largely masters of their collective fate, holding the upper hand in the continuing struggle that their ancestors began three centuries ago. However, as the years pass, and much to our distress, this scenario increasingly looks like little more than the stuff that dreams are made on.

NOTES

···

Preface

1. In 2010, the people known to outsiders as "Saramaka" requested to be recognized as "Saamaka," their own pronunciation of their name.

Chapter 1. Testing the Waters

1. Later, we learned that long ago two girls from a nearby village had drowned when their canoe sank at Mamadan. Eventually (some people say it was seventeen days, others three months, others a year) one of them appeared on a river rock in the rapids. When she had been ritually "cured" and could speak once again, she told of having been taken to the beautiful underwater palace of the Wenti-gods, where she was waited on by a bevy of young girls. She eventually returned, she said, because she missed salt (which Wentis do not eat) and begged them to bring her up to the surface. Older men have told us how, throughout the first half of the twentieth century when on their way to the coast to work, they would stop at the Wenti shrine at Mamadan and pour an offering of white kaolin water, and then, on their way back with their canoes laden with whitefolks' goods, they would pour offerings of sugarcane syrup. For more on Wentis, see chapter 14, "Agbago's Seagod."

Chapter 2. On Trial

1. Sally had sewn a pocket onto the inside of Rich's shoulder cape; her own notepads were harder to conceal, and she often had to rely on memory until she could get back to our house, since she felt uncomfortable writing in other peoples' presence. Clandestine note taking was standard ethnographic procedure at the time and was unquestioned from the perspective of professional ethics. Indeed, one rather complexly worked out technique for secretly taking fieldnotes in a pants pocket (using a two-inch piece of pencil and 2 × 3-inch pieces of paper

previously numbered, notched, and mounted on a tiny piece of cardboard), written by a future president of the American Anthropological Association, was published in the discipline's flagship journal and constituted recommended reading for graduate students about to undertake fieldwork throughout the 1960s (Sturtevant, "Technique for Ethnographic Note-Taking").

2. That shelf also held *Ulysses*, *Absalom, Absalom!* and *Under the Volcano*, if memory serves.

3. We later learned that his mother's brother, Pobosi, the greatest Saamaka *obiama* of the early twentieth century, had taught him the greater part of his knowledge. The Herskovitses saw Pobosi at Asindoopo in 1929, writing that he "had several broad stripes of white clay from wrist to shoulder of his right arm, and from knee to pelvis on the inner left thigh. Slung from one shoulder and reaching across to the opposite thigh was a white obia made of native fiber, and on his neck were several others. To these obias were added iron bands on his arms, while below his right knee and at the ankle of his right foot were other obias made of fiber and twisted black thread" (M. and F. Herskovits, *Rebel Destiny*, 188, 263).

Chapter 3. A Feast for the Ancestors

1. We were later told that this was because Boo, the person being honored by the feast, was her *neseki* (supernatural genitor).

Chapter 4. Going "Outside"

1. Martin, *Woman in the Body*, 111, 234.
2. Greer, *The Female Eunuch*, 42.
3. Leclerc, *Parole de Femme*, 48–49.
4. Buckley and Gottlieb, *Blood Magic*. See S. Price, "The Curse's Blessing."

Chapter 5. On Nai's Doorstep

1. Saamakas string a cord above the hammock, end to end, and drape a sheet over it to protect against bats. We did it faithfully and were never bitten.

2. People enjoyed giving names to each cloth pattern upon its first arrival in Saamaka. Some reflected the colors or pattern of stripes, but many more evoked local events such as a theft, a co-wife fight, a canoe sinking, or the installment of a chief, or news from beyond Saamaka (a concert by Miriam Makeba, the first moon landing). See S. Price, *Co-Wives and Calabashes*, 190–193, for forty-one examples of cloth names.

3. Although a couple of older women, including Ansebuka, smoked tobacco in clay pipes, as had been the custom in previous centuries, most Saamakas who used tobacco ingested it by snorting it in liquid form. They would first prepare the mixture by folding the green leaves into a banana leaf, heating it on a fire until it

softened and gave off liquid, put it in a calabash or tin can and sprinkled it with ashes. The mixture was squeezed with a thumb and then inhaled, one nostril at a time, and the excess wiped off with a rag.

4. Malaria was endemic in Saamaka. The Dutch doctor told Rich that on average one in four people had active malaria, though its incidence varied with the seasons. An official report showed that 187,750 pounds of malaria salt was being distributed per year in Upper River Saamaka.

5. Nai taught her a lot about comportment, but it was more often younger women such as Beki and Adiante's sister Komisaisi who coached her for more physical activities such as hulling rice or laundering a hammock.

6. Other women also surprised Sally on occasion with their willingness to share intimacies. Asipei's senior wife Akundumini, for example, offered to let her make a photographic inventory of her cicatrizations, including those on the most densely decorated parts of her body—her inner thighs.

7. For a fuller version of this folktale, see R. Price, *First-Time*, 13–14, and for the Saamakatongo original, R. Price, *Fesiten*, 20–23.

8. For a color photo of the hammock sheet, see S. and R. Price, *Afro-American Arts of the Suriname Rain Forest*, 77.

Chapter 6. Under Kala's House

1. Rich learned during another dinner that the captain also had a taboo on hearing the word *pusipusi* (house cat) while eating, a Komanti taboo stemming from his father's having been a renowned Komanti medium.

2. After that, the banknote story seemed to fade away. At least our fieldnotes are empty on its outcome.

3. For images of Kala and his staff, crowned with the arms and motto of the House of Orange, see R. Price, *Alabi's World*, 148.

Chapter 7. The Sika

1. In fact, the Matyau people were the first Saamakas to rebel and escape from slavery. In 1690 they burned their plantation and killed their *bakaa* master, Imanuël Machado—See R. Price, *First-Time*, 51–52.

2. More precisely, *Tunga penetrans*, a burrowing sand flea that is found on the coast of Suriname and in Guyane but not in Upper River Saamaka.

Chapter 8. What Month Is It?

1. The twelve Saamaka moons, in order, are Yailiba ("New Year's moon"), Bakayailiba ("After New Year's moon"), Gaanliba ("Big moon"), Pikideeweiliba ("Small dry season moon"), Sebitaaliba ("Pleiades moon"), Hondimaliba ("Hunter's

moon"), Baimatuliba ("Sweeps the forest moon"), Tanvuuwataliba ("The river's high moon"), Wayamakaliba ("Iguana moon"), Tenimu ("Tenth moon"), Elefumu ("Eleventh moon"), and Tualufumu ("Twelfth moon").

2. For more precise details, see R. Price, "To Every Thing a Season."

3. Schumann, "Saramaccanisch Deutsches Wörter-Buch," s.v. "jara."

4. "Dann" has disappeared from Saamaka vocabulary and its etymology remains a mystery.

5. It seems possible, if unlikely, that English influence on the plantation calendar persisted into the mid-eighteenth century, just as did the influence of the English language on that spoken on the plantations.

6. See Kyerematen, "Royal Stools of Ashanti."

Chapter 9. The Captain's "Granddaughter"

1. It was first published in S. and R. Price, *Afro-American Arts of the Suriname Rain Forest*, 53.

2. At that time, there was no feeling among Upper River Saamakas that women's breasts or children's nakedness should be covered, either in daily life or in photos.

3. When a Saamaka commits a crime or serious insult against a person, it's common for the victim, after death, to haunt the perpetrator's matrilineage forever in the form of a *kunu*, an avenging spirit. Every Saamaka is subject to a number of such spirits from the past, and divination in the case of illness or misfortune often instructs a person to enter into contact with one of them and make offerings to soothe its anger.

Chapter 10. Upriver

1. Women generally go to their garden camps once or twice a week to get firewood. Several kinds of trees are taboo for a variety of reasons (one because it would offend Apukus, another because it's used in the *kangaa* ordeal . . .). Saamaka men chuckle disparagingly at the Ndyuka practice of men participating in gathering firewood and harvesting cassava—tasks that clearly belong in the female sphere. Sally, like three other villagers, cooked on gas, rather than firewood.

2. *Clibadium surinamense.* On special occasions, a more powerful fish drug, *paundeku* (*Lonchocarpus chrysophyllus*), is used to drug the river. Drinking it mashed in water is also the most common means of Saamakas committing suicide.

3. The silk-cotton tree (*Ceiba pentandra*) and the similar bombax or kapok (*Bombax spp.*).

4. If the palm frond is still in place, the god has agreed, if not, another site must be found. Were this virgin forest rather than secondary growth, Abatili would leave a calabash with an offering on a forked stick for a week to see if the

god accepts it. For a more complex example of getting the god's permission to use a garden site, see R. Price, *Rainforest Warriors*, 18–19.

5. Ten years later Poi was already a wife and mother. (See the three photos of her—1968, 1974, 1978—on the dedication page of S. Price, *Co-Wives and Calabashes*.)

6. At certain times of the year, when most of the men in our neighborhood were absent, Rich provided the bulk of meat and fish for the women, who reciprocated with cassava cakes, okra, bananas, and other garden produce. The only product we bought regularly was rice, the Saamaka staple, since the garden Rich cleared and Sally planted at the edge of the village was only partially successful.

7. For a recording of Abatili singing tree-felling songs, see R. and S. Price, *Music from Saramaka*.

Chapter 11. At the Ancestor Shrine

1. According to records spanning several years from the hospital/clinic at Dyuumu, April is the year's low point for positive tests of malaria, with the final three months of the year having more than ten times that incidence. But this year was different.

Chapter 12. The Cock's Balls

1. Staehelin, *Die Mission der Brüdergemeine in Suriname*, III, ii, 265–266.

2. This ordeal—the thrusting of a ritually prepared feather through the tongue of the accused to determine truth or lies—seems directly traceable to the eighteenth-century Kingdom of Benin—Lindblom, *Afrikanische Relikte*, 92–93; Barbot, "Description of the Coasts of North and South-Guinea," 373.

Chapter 13. Nai's Rivergod

1. See R. Price, *Travels with Tooy*, 60–62, for more details on the sources in this and the following paragraph.

2. Gweyunga's name echoes that of one of the sons of the Dahomean god of the sea, Gbeyongo.

3. Tone children include other kinds of unusual births such as albinos, those with polydactyly, teeth, or Down syndrome, as well as breech births. In former times, Tone children like Nai were simply laid to rest at birth in the riverbank, for the waters to take away. Similarly, among Gweyunga's descendants in the village of Malobí, Tone priests were buried in a coffin that was released into the river and the water spirits would remove them from the coffin and carry them to their realm. This latter practice continued until the mid-twentieth century, when these priests began to be buried in the cemetery.

4. For examples, see R. Price, *Travels with Tooy*, 378.

5. At any time, each matrilineage has one *kunu* that it considers heavier than all others, its *gaan kunu*, its great avenging spirit.

6. We heard about Ma Tobosi and Zogia in fragments of prayers and conversations throughout our stay. Often, they seemed to contradict one another. What we present here is our best-guess composite.

7. This *kunu* also affects the lineage of Ma Tobosi's errant husband in Akisiamau, which brings the two villages together for certain palliative rituals.

8. What's in a name? Sometimes a dizzying flow of diasporic history. Brazilian anthropologist Luis Nicolau Parés, on the basis of his own fieldwork and a substantial ethnographic literature, pulls together some of the vagaries of a similar figure known as Tobosi in ancient Dahomey, as well as in contemporary Bahia, São Luis, and Haiti, outlining its most frequent attributes as a feminine, often childlike, freshwater god, a special kind of Vodu spirit treated with the greatest deference (Parés, "O triângulo das tobosi").

Chapter 14. Agbago's Seagod

1. Their towns include Gaanlolo, Oloni, Akinawebí, Kinazaan, Sinaibo, Laibeni, Gongongondome, Luwezaan, and Loonza, place names that sound strange, intriguingly "other," to Saamakas, roughly the way the place-names in Narnia mark that land as being clearly in another realm for English speakers.

2. Multi-media "plays" (*pee*), including singing, dancing, drumming, spirit possession, and other forms of performance, are a frequent and central part of Saamaka life.

3. As he carried Daute to shore, Todye sang, *Adyeunsu-oo, i miti kedye-ee, Adyeunsu. Adyeunsu baaa adyu, i miti kedye-ee kwekwe, Daute, odio-e mbaya-ee* ("Adyeunsu, there's been trouble, Adyeunsu. Brother Adyeunsu my father, there's been trouble, [exclamation], Daute, greetings my brother"). Adyeunsu is the Master of the Sea, a Wenti who is married to Ma Digbeonsu.

4. He once told Rich that her praise name was "Yaya Wedewe, hen da Yaya a Dande, Tyinaweebi, Anakiendukume kooade. Hen da Amame." For more on Yaya, see R. Price, *First-Time*, 160.

Chapter 15. Kala's Snakegod

1. *Alada* means the land of the dead in Papagadu language. Saamakas also refer to Alada as "Papa-country." Note that about 45 percent of the Saamakas' ancestors came from the Bight of Benin in ancient Dahomey and Togo, the so-called Slave Coast, which included the major slave-shipping ports of Allada/Ardra (the coastal kingdom of seventeenth-century Dahomey) and Grand and Little Popo (in neighboring Togo). See R. Price, *Travels with Tooy*, 291.

2. During our 1960s fieldwork, twenty-one of the forty-three gods in Dangogo were Papagadu.

3. Vodu and Dagowe are god names that appear in various parts of the African Diaspora, from Brazil to Haiti. All derive from the Bight of Benin, where snake-gods abound, with Dahomean Dangbe/Dagowe the best-known precursors.

4. The so-called Rainbow Boa (*Epicrates cenchria*), a smaller snake, and the Emerald Tree Boa (*Corallus caninus*) are also found there.

5. See R. Price, *Travels with Tooy*, 379–81.

Chapter 17. Playing for the Gods

1. This standard prayer reflected realities. The village food supply varied from week to week and even from one day to the next. It was not uncommon for women and sometimes men to eat plain rice for a meal and sometimes there was even a shortage of that. On the other hand, the variety of cultivated and wild fruits was considerable, and we rarely knew what the next day's menu might include.

2. See R. Price, *Travels with Tooy*, 160, for four photos, and 319–31, for Apuku language, proverbs, and songs.

Chapter 19. Sickness

1. We'd been protected from malaria by taking chloroquine as a prophylactic—it wasn't till one of our return trips in the 1970s that Rich contracted the disease.

2. See chapter 12, "The Cock's Balls," for a description of this day's divination.

3. We returned to the United States for three months to take stock, compile questions, and buy supplies.

Chapter 20. Death of a Witch

1. See van Wetering, "Witchcraft among the Tapanahoni Djuka." People found by divination to be witches were actually burned at the stake in Ndyuka well into the 1950s. Saamakas ended the practice early in the nineteenth century.

2. The remainder of this chapter is adapted from R. and S. Price, *Two Evenings in Saramaka*, 41–60.

3. Sisamai ("sister-in-law") can be used loosely, as a term of affection/solidarity, without genealogical specificity.

4. Normally, a woman in her fifties would be buried several weeks after her death. At the other extreme from Sindobobi in age and reputation, both Kandamma and Nai were kept above ground nearly three months when they died around 1970.

5. The full tales, as well as the interruptions and commentary that accompanied them, are available in R. and S. Price, *Two Evenings in Saramaka*. We have

also published the original transcriptions in the Saamaka language, see R. and S. Price, *Boo Go a Kontukonde*. The original recordings of five of these tales are available at http://kaona.fr/to/saao1, . . . saao2, . . . saao3, . . . saao4, ... saao5.

Chapter 21. Chasing Ghosts

1. Sally wore hers a month or two at a time during our stay and made calfbands for both of us, though Rich eventually removed his because they caused a mean fungus.

2. For examples, see R. Price, *Travels with Tooy*, 248–259, 367–375.

Chapter 22. Death of a Child

1. Now, a half century later, emboldened by all the Dungulali-Obia packets and liquids given to us by our friend Tooy, a senior Dungulali priest, we feel ready to put this story in print. For detailed information about Dungulali, see R. Price, *Travels with Tooy*, 15–22, 278–286, 331–341.

Chapter 23. Returns

1. Adiante Franszoon became a prize-winning student in the New Haven Adult Education program, gaining his high school equivalency in record time, and went on to complete a degree at New Haven Community College. When Rich joined the faculty at Johns Hopkins, Adi moved to Baltimore, rooming with graduate students and earning a BA in economics at the University of Baltimore. For years now, he has been supporting himself with the woodcarving skills he learned in Saamaka, producing high-quality furniture with Saamaka-style carving and selling it on the web and, on Saturdays and Sundays, at Washington's Eastern Market. Google him!

2. See for example, R. Price, *Maroon Societies*.

3. David Scott, "Modernity that Predated the Modern," 209.

4. Rich had his portable cassette recorder over his shoulder and switched it on as the captain greeted him. Kala later gave him permission to publish it.

5. Conversely, Bane had named his first daughter Sally.

6. Agbago told Rich that he hadn't wanted them to live in Saamaka, believing that they wouldn't adopt the local lifestyle the way we had and doubting that two women without husbands would be able to take care of themselves away from home. But he eventually gave in and they stayed, doing their best to spread God's word and teach literacy in the Saamaka language.

7. We had spent 1977–1978 at the Netherland Institute of Advanced Studies, near the archives in The Hague. For more detailed discussion of the exchanges with Saamaka elders, see R. Price, *First-Time*, 14–30.

8. Nonetheless, it did not really make it easier to elicit First-Time knowledge from wary elders, as people kept their own counsel about how much, and exactly what, they wished to share. All of their offerings resonated with the oft-cited ideological conviction that "First-Time kills." "Never tell another more than half of what you know"; "Those times—the days of war, the days of whitefolks' slavery—shall come again"; and "Never forget Nouna!" Rich had to keep telling himself that, as the Saamaka hunting proverb says, "if you don't stir up a hole, you won't find out what's in it," but he could never afford to forget its cautionary counterpart: "If you shake a dry tree, you'd better watch out for your head."

9. The tapes were a godsend when, thirty-five years later, we prepared a full version of First-Time in Saamakatongo, at the request of the Saamaka People, who bought three thousand copies for use in their schools. See R. Price, Fesiten.

10. This research led to both R. Price, First-Time and Alabi's World.

11. The Herskovitses' diaries also revealed that they were accompanied on their trip to the gaama's village by a cook from the city ("Coba," Jacoba Abensitt, whom Frances described as "a literate young woman"), a "professional bush guide"/manservant (Marcus J. Schloss), and Alexander M. W. Wolff, the manager of the Suriname Balata Company warehouse, who had often dealt with the gaama on business matters. All members of this colonial entourage spoke English and all were effectively disappeared from the Herskovitses' published writings, leaving the impression that the couple was alone "Among the Bush Negroes of Dutch Guiana" and working in the Saamaka language. See R. and S. Price, The Root of Roots.

12. See S. Price, Co-Wives and Calabashes; and S. and R. Price, Afro-American Arts of the Suriname Rain Forest. The exhibition was shown in Los Angeles, Dallas, Baltimore, and New York between 1980 and 1982 and directly inspired Sally's next major project—a critical exploration of perceptions of non-Western art in Europe and the United States (S. Price, Primitive Art in Civilized Places).

13. In 1992, we again participated in a visit of Saamakas to the United States, this time at the Smithsonian's Festival of American Folklife, a considerably less joyful experience. See R. and S. Price, On the Mall.

14. As we write in 2016 he is in his second term as democratically elected president of the country.

15. In August 1992 a "Peace Agreement" was reached between the government and the Jungles, officially ending the war. According to many observers, its main effect was to carve up the country into two major zones for the drug trade, with former Jungle leader Brunswijk getting the eastern part of the country and former dictator Bouterse the rest.

16. In 2007, when Rich again testified as expert witness for the Saamakas before the Inter-American Court, the attorney general of Suriname repeated and augmented these threats—see R. Price, Rainforest Warriors, 207–208.

Chapter 24. Foto

1. Saamakas have always been imbedded in modernity. The slave trade and plantation system were harbingers of industrial capitalism and the attitudes they engendered led Saamakas to embrace it on their own terms. From the liberation of tools and other European manufactures on their former plantations to their current appreciation of the latest inventions, from chainsaws to smartphones, Saamakas have always adapted outside manufactures to their own needs. On one of our first visits to Dangogo, early in our 1966 stay, Rich wrote: "One of the most striking things about Saamakas is their use of gadgets, machines, and manufactured items in general. They draw on the whole world: lots of stuff from West Germany (hunting equipment, fishing line, lanterns), England (cutlasses), USA (tools, guns, outboards), France (gunpowder, food), Holland (food, tape recorders, radios, magazines), Spain (gunpowder), Red China (cloth, flashlights, batteries), etc. etc. . . . I can imagine that Saamakas have always bought, traded, stolen such goods . . . Abatili showed me an electric lightbulb he'd bought. He said that now he just needed to buy a car battery and he'd have electric light."

2. Betty was among those publicly threatened by Bouterse just before the December Murders but she escaped with her family to Florida days before the event.

Chapter 25. Looking at Paper

1. The seven-inch reels we'd used for recording songs, folktales, oracle sessions, and more had been transferred to cassettes in the 1970s, and the reels themselves had been sent to the Archives of Traditional Music in Bloomington Indiana, to be stored in a climate-controlled environment. All the fieldnotes and other material from our work in Saamaka will eventually be made available to scholars at the Schomburg Center for Research in Black Culture in New York. We have already donated much of our material culture collection (mainly woodcarvings, textiles, and calabashes) to the Schomburg Center; the rest will follow in the coming years.

2. Our 1970s materials included hundreds of pages of typed fieldnotes as well as twenty notebooks filled with handwritten information from Rich's historical interviews (and their accompanying cassette recordings, now digitalized) and a similar stash of handwritten notes that Sally made during her dissertation research on art and gender.

3. Here and there our fieldnotes even included phrases in Tzotzil, the language of Zinacanteco Indians in Mexico, where we'd spent two summers just before going to Suriname. For example, Sally commented on one ancestral feast that, "Everyone was giving advice; there seemed to be no one h'kel ve'el." Our memory now faded, we asked Chiapas expert George Collier who reminded us that "h'kel ve'el" refers to the person in charge of overseeing a meal.

4. Some of our classmates in the 1960s were using "punch-card" or "edge-notch" sorting in their fieldwork. In that system fieldnotes were typed on 5 × 8-inch cards and notches were punched along the edges in positions that corresponded to particular categories of information. A skewer (or knitting needle) jabbed into the stack of 5 × 8's in a particular position would then retrieve the cards that held information on that category. It was understandably cumbersome, and in any case our notes were not typed in a way that would have allowed this approach. For an amusing description, see http://kk.org/thetechnium/one-dead-media/.

5. Not all anthropologists practiced the writing of fieldnotes as mnemonics for themselves. Sidney Mintz, for example, wrote carefully crafted sentences that seem designed for readers (perhaps other members of the People of Puerto Rico project) who did not share his experience: "October 8. 1948 . . . Dona Pola, who is a sister to Santos Oliver, with whom I live, lives in a larger house in front of ours" (cited in Giovannetti et al., *Antropologías del Caribe Hispano*, 34).

6. See for the most detailed inventory of such plants, van Andela et al., "Dry Sex in Suriname." In 2000, Saamaka women in Cayenne reiterated to Sally that these daily genital ablutions serve to tighten and dry the vagina and that they tend to make intercourse painful for women, but that women as well as men much prefer "dry sex." They told her bluntly, "No one likes wet pussy!"

7. Galanes, "Alice Walker and Colm Toibin."

8. Sally waited to begin graduate coursework until our children were in nursery school.

9. AMNH 26.72. See S. and R. Price, *Les arts des Marrons*, figure 4.19b.

10. By the time we returned to Saamaka in the 1970s, women up and down the river had picked up on what they were calling the "Dangogo style" calfbands and taken them to a whole new level, filling the entire object with complex designs in a veritable kaleidoscope of vivid colors.

Chapter 26. The End of an Era

1. This chapter draws on that book—Scholtens et al., *Gaama Duumi, Buta Gaama*. The images are courtesy of Martha Cooper, an American photojournalist who traveled to Suriname for the funeral, employing Adiante Franszoon as her guide.

2. Scholtens et al., *Gaama Duumi, Buta Gaama*. Four years after the funeral, anthropologist Ben Scholtens, senior author of that book, was murdered in Paramaribo, on the eve of his scheduled return to the Netherlands to defend his Ph.D. dissertation. The crime was never solved though there were strong suspicions that orders came from the top of the military regime because "he knew too much" about the army's atrocities during the civil war.

3. The populations of all six Suriname Maroon peoples have grown enormously since the time of our initial fieldwork. Today, the Saamaka and Ndyuka

each number nearly 100,000, the Pamaka and Aluku each 11,000, the Matawai 7,000, and the Kwinti 1,000. Maroons now make up 23 percent of the population of Suriname and 26 percent of the population of Guyane—within twenty years they are likely to constitute the largest "ethnic group" in each of these territories; see R. Price, *Maroon Population Explosion*.

4. For a full listing of these books and articles, see www.richandsally.net.

5. Of the ninety or so people we mention by name in this book, fewer than ten are still alive.

6. By 2013 the Peace Corps had departed definitively.

7. Brittes, "A Mása Gádu Kóndë," 319.

8. For an overview of the life of Maroons in Guyane, see R. and S. Price, *Les Marrons*.

9. See R. Price, *Travels with Tooy*.

10. For details on the Saamakas' legal struggle, see R. Price, *Rainforest Warriors*. Our continued reluctance to set foot in Suriname is strengthened by the threat that local laws pose for such writings. Freedom House, in its 2015 report, notes that "Suriname . . . has some of the most severe criminal defamation laws in the Caribbean. These include prison sentences of up to seven years for 'public expression of enmity, hatred, or contempt' toward the government, and up to five years' imprisonment for insulting the head of state" (https://freedomhouse .org/report/freedom-press/2015/suriname). Rich has also been involved, though more marginally, in the land rights struggle of rural Brazilians, encouraged by the *quilombo* provisions of the 1988 constitution—see R. Price, "Scrapping Maroon History" and "Reinventando a história dos quilombos."

11. This felicitous expression was first used by Amiri Baraka to refer to the development of African American music (Jones, *Black Music*).

12. Haabo, "The Future."

13. See van Dijck, "The IIRSA Guyana Shield Hub."

BIBLIOGRAPHY

van Andela, Tinde, Sanne de Korteb, Daphne Koopmansb, Joelaika Behari-Ramdasc, and Sofie Ruysschaertd. 2008. "Dry Sex in Suriname." *Journal of Ethnopharmacology* 116: 84–88.

Barbot, John. 1732. "A Description of the Coasts of North and South-Guinea." In *A Collection of Voyages and Travels*, edited by Awnsham Churchill and John Churchill. Vol. 5. London.

van Binnendijk, Chandra, and Paul Faber. 2000. *Beeldende kunst in Suriname: De twintigste eeuw.* Amsterdam: Koninklijk Instituut voor de Tropen.

Brittes W. Pires, Rogério. 2015. "A Mása Gádu Kóndë: Morte, Espíritos e Rituais Funerários em uma Aldeia Saamaka Cristã." Ph.D. diss., Museu Nacional, Universidade Federal do Rio de Janeiro, Brazil.

Buckley, Thomas, and Alma Gottlieb, eds. 1988. *Blood Magic: The Anthropology of Menstruation.* Berkeley: University of California Press.

van Dijck, Pitou. 2010. "The IIRSA Guyana Shield Hub: The Case of Suriname." Available at http://www.cedla.uva.nl/30_research/PDF_files_research/suriname_project/IIRSA.pdf.

Donicie, Antoon, and Jan Voorhoeve. 1963. *De Saramakaanse woordenschat.* Mimeo. Amsterdam: Bureau voor Taalonderzoek in Suriname van de Universiteit van Amsterdam.

van Eyck, J. W. S. 1828. "Algemeen verslag van den tegenwoordige staat en huisselijke inrigtingen, benevens de levenswijzen der bevredigde bosch-negers binnen deze kolonie." Manuscript. Koninklijk Instituut voor de Tropen, Amsterdam.

Galanes, Philip. 2016. "Alice Walker and Colm Toibin, and Their Trail of Words." Table for Three. *New York Times*, Jan. 23.

Giovannetti, Jorge L., Aníbal Escobar González, and Jesús Tapia Santamaría. 2015. *Antropologías del Caribe Hispano: Notas de campo sobre Cuba y Puerto Rico.* San Juan, PR: IINAS-DSA.

Greer, Germaine. 1971. *The Female Eunuch.* New York: McGraw-Hill.

Haabo, Vinije. 2010. "The Future." In *Paramaribo Span*, edited by Thomas Meijer zu Schlochtern and Christopher Cozier, 76. Amsterdam: KIT.

Herskovits, Melville J., and Frances S. Herskovits. 1934. *Rebel Destiny: Among the Bush Negroes of Dutch Guiana*. New York: McGraw-Hill.

Jones, LeRoy. 1967. *Black Music*. New York: William Morrow.

Kyerematen, A. 1969. "The Royal Stools of Ashanti." *Africa* 39: 1–9.

Leclerc, Annie. 1974. *Parole de Femme*. Paris: Grasset.

Lindblom, Gerhard. 1924. *Afrikanische Relikte und Indianische Entlehnungen in der Kultur der Busch-Neger Surinams*. Gothenburg: Elanders Boktryckeri Aktiebolag.

Martin, Emily. 1987. *The Woman in the Body: A Cultural Analysis of Reproduction*. Boston: Beacon Press.

Oates, Joyce Carol. 2015. "Inspiration and Obsession in Life and Literature." *New York Review of Books* 62(13): 80–85.

Parés, Luis Nicolau. 2001. "O triângulo das tobosi (uma figura ritual no Benin, Maranhão e Bahia)." *Afro-Asia* 25–26: 177–213.

Price, Richard, ed. 1973. *Maroon Societies: Rebel Slave Communities in the Americas*. New York: Doubleday/Anchor.

———. 1983. *First-Time: The Historical Vision of an Afro-American People*. Baltimore: Johns Hopkins University Press.

———. 1984. "To Every Thing a Season: The Development of Saramaka Calendrical Reckoning." *Tijdschrift OSO* 3: 63–71.

———. 1990. *Alabi's World*. Baltimore: Johns Hopkins University Press.

———. 1998. "Scrapping Maroon History: Brazil's Promise, Suriname's Shame." *New West Indian Guide* 72: 233–255.

———. 2000. "Reinventando a história dos quilombos: rasuras e confabulações." *Afro-Ásia* 23: 241–265.

———. 2008. *Travels with Tooy: History, Memory, and the African American Imagination*. Chicago: University of Chicago Press.

———. 2011. *Rainforest Warriors: Human Rights on Trial*. Philadelphia: University of Pennsylvania Press.

———. 2013. "The Maroon Population Explosion: Suriname and Guyane." *New West Indian Guide* 87: 323–327.

———. 2013. *Fesiten*. La Roque d'Anthéron: Vents d'ailleurs.

Price, Richard, and Sally Price. 1977. *Music from Saramaka*. Smithsonian Folkways 4225. Washington, DC.

———. 1991. *Two Evenings in Saramaka*. Chicago: University of Chicago Press.

———. 1994. *On the Mall*. Bloomington: Indiana University Press.

———. 2003. *Les Marrons*. Châteauneuf-le-Rouge: Vents d'ailleurs.

———. 2003. *The Root of Roots: Or, How Afro-American Anthropology Got Its Start*. Chicago: Prickly Paradigm Press. Available gratis at www.richandsally.net.

———. 2016. *Boo Go a Kontukonde*. La Roque d'Anthéron: Vents d'ailleurs.

Price, Sally. 1984. *Co-Wives and Calabashes*. Ann Arbor: University of Michigan Press.

———. 1989. *Primitive Art in Civilized Places*. Chicago: University of Chicago Press.

———. 1994. "The Curse's Blessing." *Frontiers: A Journal of Women Studies* 14 (2): 123–142.

Price, Sally, and Richard Price. 1980. *Afro-American Arts of the Suriname Rain Forest*. Berkeley: University of California Press.

———. 2005. *Les arts des Marrons*. La Roque d'Anthéron: Vents d'ailleurs.

Scholtens, Ben, Gloria Wekker, Laddy van Putten, and Stanley Dieko. 1992. *Gaama Duumi, Buta Gaama: Overlijden en opvolging van Aboikoni, grootopperhoofd van de Saramaka Bosnegers*. Paramaribo: Afdeling Cultuurstudies/Minov.

Schumann, C. L. 1778. "Saramaccanisch Deutsches Wörter-Buch." In *Die Sprache der Saramakkaneger in Surinam*, by Hugo Schuchardt (1914). *Verhandelingen der Koninklijke Akademie van Wetenschappen te Amsterdam* 14 (6): 46–116. Amsterdam: Johannes Müller.

Scott, David. 2004. "Modernity that Predated the Modern: Sidney Mintz's Caribbean." *History Workshop Journal* 58: 191–210.

Smith, Norval. 2002. "The History of the Suriname Creoles II: Origins and Differentiation." In *Atlas of the Languages of Suriname*, edited by Eithne B. Carlin and Jacques Arends, 131–151. Leiden: KITLV Press.

Staehelin, F. 1913–1919. *Die Mission der Brüdergemeine in Suriname und Berbice im achtzehnten Jahrhundert*. Herrnhut: Vereins für Brüdergeschichte in Kommission der Unitätsbuchhandlung in Gnadau.

Sturtevant, William C. 1959. "A Technique for Ethnographic Note-Taking." *American Anthropologist* 61: 677–678.

van Wetering, W. 1973. "Witchcraft among the Tapanahoni Djuka." In *Maroon Societies*, edited by Richard Price, 370–388. New York: Doubleday/Anchor.

INDEX

....

Abatili, 21, 28, 32, 33, 53, 58–60, 75–76, 77, 80, 82–85, 87, 119, 170, 175; relations with us, 8–11, 14, 25–26, 28–30, 48, 153–54, 192–93, 194, 199, 203, 215; sexual relations, 41, 42, 46, 48

Adiante, 73, 190

Aduengi, 96, 99, 127, 132, 134, 159–63, 167, 170, 174, 215, 216, 219

adultery. See sex and sexual relations

Afobaka dam and lake, 2, 3–4, 5, 11, 12, 203, 213

Afude, 123–31

Agbago (Gaama Agbago Aboikoni), x, 22, 23, 25, 30, 32, 57, 73, 74, 85, 108, 168, 185, 187, 190; conjugal relations, 44, 196–97; funeral of, 215–21; relations with us 6–7, 10–11, 21, 25–26, 28, 50, 60, 191, 195–98, 199, 200; role as gaama 4–5, 6, 13, 30, 87, 94–97, 112, 156, 161, 186, 197. See also Wenti (seagod)

agida drum. See snakegods

Agumii, 128, 129, 153

Akisiamau, 58, 74, 93, 97, 105, 125, 133, 168, 194

Akobo, 9, 19, 32, 33, 41, 74, 77, 78, 82, 86, 87, 91, 128, 144–50, 152–54, 170–72, 184, 215, 216, 219

Akonda, 45, 47, 80, 122, 123–131, 182, 184, 193

Akonomisi, 97, 110, 116, 120, 124, 145, 146, 150, 151, 153

Akundumini, 50n6, 185, 195

Aluku Maroons, 2, 71, 73, 200, 225

Amerindians, 54, 56, 95, 223, 225

Amombebuka, 56, 58–59, 75, 80, 85, 120, 144–49, 179, 203

anaconda god. See snakegods: Watawenu

Analisi, 28–29, 32, 33

Anaweli, xi, 15, 42, 60, 71, 72, 114, 146, 200

ancestors, 6, 87, 101; feasts for, 9, 11, 19, 21, 28–33, 86, 155, 174, 176, 178, 186, 219–21. See also ancestor shrines

ancestor shrines, 22, 25, 168; Awoonenge, 17, 24, 34; Bongootu Pau, 17, 18, 25, 86–92, 96, 101, 124, 129, 148, 159

animals, 10, 11, 19, 21, 23, 28, 30, 36, 40, 42, 43, 45, 47, 50, 53, 64, 82, 85, 86, 121, 149, 153, 170–72, 173, 178, 183

Ansebuka, 47–49, 157, 172–78, 180, 184, 186, 188

Antonisi, 162, 171–72

Apaasu, Assistant Captain, 27, 91–92, 121, 132, 134, 136, 144, 146, 157–65, 167–70, 174–76 *apintii* (talking drum). *See* drums and drumming

apron girls, 37, 46, 53, 71, 74, 196–97

Apuku (forest spirit), 11, 24, 28, 30, 45, 53–54, 63, 80, 85, 86, 93, 102, 120, 128–31, 138, 148–49, 156, 165, 169, 176–77

Apumba, xi, 50, 74, 75, 85, 197

Asabosi, 155–72, 174

Aseni, 26, 92, 95–96, 132, 140, 146, 149

Asensi, 104, 179–80, 184

Asindoopo, x, 4, 7, 10, 13, 21–23, 25, 54, 87, 179, 186, 193–95, 199

Asipei, 17, 21, 50, 62, 80, 87–91, 94–95, 101, 107, 112, 121, 123, 128, 141, 147, 148, 150, 156–57, 170, 183, 214

Asopi, 14, 161, 163

Atudendu, Gaama, 6, 87, 91, 94, 102, 115, 121, 145, 216

avenging spirit. See *kunu* (avenging spirit)

Baala (elderly *obiama*), 22–23

Baala (younger man), 23–24, 132, 134–36

Bane, 9, 43, 144–47, 153

Beki, 9, 32, 35–36, 38, 43, 56, 63, 73, 74, 77, 82, 86, 87, 91, 92, 101, 119, 120, 145–49, 153–54, 210, 214

Binotu, 123–25, 146

Bongootu, 18, 86–87, 89–91, 96, 124, 140

Boo, 19, 28–33, 74, 145, 221

Botopasi, 37–38, 43, 59, 113, 128, 225

Bouterse, Desi, 199, 202

bungula. See divination

calfbands, 45, 78, 123, 174, 213–14

calabashes: carving of, 7, 11, 45; in meals, 30, 51, 54, 81, 85; in play, 38, 81; in ritual, 22, 23, 31–32, 75–76, 86, 87, 90, 92, 99, 104, 114, 119, 129,

134–35, 137, 138, 142, 150–51, 153, 159, 165, 168–69, 177, 187; trees, 9, 38

canoes, 9, 14, 24, 28, 30, 35, 36, 46, 51, 52, 54, 55, 56, 75, 76, 77, 91, 94, 104, 107, 109, 110, 116–17, 121, 125, 128, 141, 154, 156, 158, 159, 165–66, 168, 169, 174, 178, 180, 186, 193, 205, 212, 216, 219, 222, 226

Cayenne. *See* Guyane (French Guiana)

childbirth. *See* pregnancy and childbirth

children, 7, 30, 32, 38, 42–43, 78, 80–81, 116, 118, 170, 178, 179–89, 193–94. *See also* sex and sexual relations

Christian villages, xi, 37, 59, 203, 213. *See also* Botopasi

cicatrization, 9, 36, 50n6, 52, 210, 223

civil war (1986–1992), ix, 199–200, 220, 22

cloth and flags, 3, 24–27, 32, 75, 93, 94, 96, 99, 119, 134, 136, 139, 150, 156, 160, 162, 173, 176, 204

clothing, 5, 6, 8, 20, 30, 31, 42, 98, 99, 133, 135, 137, 138, 150, 151, 157, 160, 162, 164–65, 167, 172, 174, 175, 188, 191, 193, 195–98, 213–14, 216, 217, 219, 221, 222–23

conjugal relations, 41–42, 46, 48, 87–92, 93, 156, 158, 179, 216, 221

cooking. *See* food and food preparation

co-wives, xi, 43–44, 54, 81, 111, 128, 129

dance and dancing, 11, 24, 32, 38, 75, 82, 97, 103, 116–18, 120, 132, 134, 136–38, 151, 162, 168, 171, 174–76, 178, 216, 219, 221

Dangogo, x, 9, 10, 13, 17, 28, 34, 37, 86, 93, 105, 113, 138, 155, 173, 179, 186, 190, 192, 207, 220

Daume, 33, 93, 125

divination, 47, 54, 74, 80n4, 108, 110,
153, 184; with a bottle cap, 27, 129,
141; with cocks, 92–93, 97, 100–102,
117, 124, 134, 148, 149, 151, 152;
with coffin or bungula, 125, 159–61,
163–69, 173, 189, 193, 216, 217, 219;
with kangaa, 38, 101; with mafiakata,
38, 45, 120, 125, 144. See also oracles

Doote, 18–20, 24–25, 28, 30, 63, 91, 92,
97, 101–102, 123–27, 129–32, 134, 136,
148, 149, 150, 151, 153, 173–74, 187,
190, 217

Dosili, 9, 28, 32, 40, 41, 46, 51, 52, 59,
60, 75–76, 77, 80, 85, 92–99, 120,
153–54, 157, 161, 170, 175, 203, 209,
214

dreams, 40, 122, 145, 149–50, 152, 179

drums and drumming 23, 24, 94, 103,
116, 117, 132–38, 150, 151, 152, 161,
162, 166, 168, 169, 171, 174, 175–76,
178, 185, 187, 213, 216; apintii, 132,
172, 175, 190, 216, 217, 219, 221

Dungulali-Obia, 87, 147, 150, 186–88

Dyam, 19, 33, 43, 80–81, 86

Dyamati, 33, 74, 119

Dyankuso (Gaama), 22, 74, 88, 91, 145,
195, 216

Dyeni, 9, 42, 46, 92–99, 132, 137, 185, 208

Dyuumu, 7, 21, 59, 91, 185, 190; clinic
and hospital, 86, 91, 94, 95–97, 112,
144, 146, 147, 148, 150, 182–83, 188,
193, 194, 210; school, 112–13, 182

election and assassination attempt
(1968), 13–14, 21–23

Elima, 9, 43, 113, 118, 119, 130, 145,
146, 150

Emma, 37–38, 75

faagi. See menstruation and menstrual
seclusion

Faanselia, 132, 133, 136

Faansisonu, Headcaptain, 23, 24, 30,
32, 56–57, 94, 112, 115, 124, 126, 139,
141, 142, 159–60, 169, 170, 174, 188,
194

feminism, 38–39

fieldnotes, xi, 7, 10, 21, 36, 43, 60, 79,
86, 92, 144, 185, 202, 205–14

fieldwork, 1–3, 6–11, 13–15, 19–21,
24–27, 34, 36, 38, 49, 51, 58–61, 75,
79, 103, 130, 153–54, 174n1, 180, 185,
189–95, 202–3, 205–14

First-time, 5, 15, 17, 21, 27, 34, 50, 57,
59, 94, 95, 103, 147, 175, 190–91, 193,
194, 204, 219, 223

fishing. See hunting and fishing

folktales, 9, 50, 169–72, 205n1, 213, 219

food and food preparation, 29–31, 35,
38, 40, 42, 43, 45, 58, 78, 86, 134n1,
135, 151–52, 161, 165–66, 167, 173–74,
175, 178, 192, 220–21

forest spirits. See Apuku (forest spirit)

French Guiana. See Guyane

funerals, 5, 11, 25, 28, 50, 52, 125, 139,
145, 157–78, 179–80, 193, 215–21

Gaanlio, 6, 22, 52, 56, 112

Gaanseei, 160, 166, 169, 172

Gaantata. See oracles

Gaduansu, 47, 91, 135

Gadya, xi, 43–44, 75, 85, 123, 185

garden camps, 36, 52, 76, 156, 158,
168, 180. See also Kpokasa

gardening, 63, 64, 76, 222, 224; burning fields, 66, 85, 129; crops, 65–66,
78, 79–80; cutting underbrush,
65, 82, 192; planting and harvesting, 64–66, 77, 78, 85, 123, 130; site
selection, 65, 77, 80; tree-felling 19,
66, 82–85, 192

gender, 9, 19, 35, 43, 77, 97, 81, 113, 116,
132, 133, 138, 146, 195, 211–12, 224

gift-giving, 11, 50, 123; conjugal, 42, 56, 78, 81, 99, 180

Godofutu, 44, 101, 133, 137

Guyane, 15, 18, 53, 55–56, 85, 101, 109, 110, 115, 128, 138, 174, 186–87, 196, 200, 222–23, 226

Herskovits, Melville and Frances, 1, 6, 11, 23n3, 34, 103, 195, 214, 226

human rights abuses, 2, 5, 199–201, 202, 204, 213, 220, 223, 227. See also Afobaka dam and lake

hunting and fishing, 11, 13, 14, 15, 21, 23, 28, 36, 40–41, 42, 43, 47, 50, 52–53, 60, 64, 73, 75, 78, 82–84, 93, 104, 105, 120, 130, 149, 158, 172, 173, 192, 208, 210, 212, 220, 222, 225

illnesses and injuries, 1, 24, 33, 45, 51–52, 86, 101, 105, 120, 141, 144–54, 155, 162, 172, 179, 182–83, 185, 224; malaria, 45–46, 91, 97, 144, 147, 148, 150, 192, 210; mental illness, 22, 123–31, 143

Ina, 9, 14, 74, 77, 85

Inter-American Court of Human Rights, 200–201, 227–29

jaguars, 3, 10, 171, 176

Kaadi, xi, 36, 43–44

Kabuesi, 32, 122, 158, 160, 166, 167, 169, 170, 174, 175, 179, 180, 182, 183, 185

Kahn, Morton, 34, 213

Kala (Dangasi), x, 14–19, 23, 28, 30, 32, 33, 35, 40–41, 42, 51–57, 74, 75–76, 85, 88, 92, 102, 103, 114, 115–16, 119, 122, 124, 125, 127, 139, 140, 141, 155, 192, 193, 194, 200–201, 210, 215, 216, 221; calendrical reckoning, 61–63, 66; relations with us, 21, 24–27,

58–61, 132, 142, 211; relations with women 71–73, 87–92

Kandamma, 28, 151, 153, 158, 167, 170–72

kangaa. See divination

Kasindo, Assistant Captain, 49, 71, 73, 86, 87, 96, 110, 114, 119, 123, 124, 125, 126, 127, 128, 130, 131, 142, 147, 149, 150, 151, 152, 153, 157, 170, 178, 180, 184, 186

Kasolu, 162–63, 170–72

Kesegogo, 134, 135, 136, 137, 138

Ketema, Captain, 28, 31–32

kin terms, xi, 16, 171, 208

Kodyi, 18, 108, 186–87

Komanti, 54n1, 92, 95, 102, 136, 144, 147, 149, 176, 194

Konoi, 45, 46, 63, 91, 92, 102, 120, 126, 139, 140, 170

Kpokasa, 9–10, 34, 63, 74–85, 92, 101, 102, 149

kunu (avenging spirit), 71, 104, 119, 125, 133, 141, 142, 143, 146, 147, 157, 166; Ma Faansina, 87–92

labor trips, 6, 17, 28, 42, 55, 101, 108–9, 112, 171, 173, 174, 224

Langu, 22–23

languages, ix, 2, 13, 58–60, 108, 203–4; ritual, 94–95, 103, 114, 119, 137, 192; Saamakatongo, ix, 5, 9, 11, 60, 67–69, 90, 214; Sranantongo, 5, 6, 11, 110, 152, 203

libations. See prayers and libations

Line, 6, 14, 22, 28–30

Lukunya. See snakegods: Papagadu (Vodu)

Maame, xi, 15, 60–61, 63, 71–73, 114, 141, 201

Ma Faansina. See kunu (avenging spirit)

mafiakata. See divination
Malobi, 104, 105, 146, 147, 179
Mamadan, 4, 12
Mamagadu. *See* oracles
Matawai Maroons, 53, 104
Ma Tobosi, 104–5, 147
Matyau clan, 41, 60, 74, 112, 194
meals, 9, 21, 51–57, 81
medicinal and ritual leaves and plants, 9, 22, 75, 80, 86, 97, 98, 101, 103, 119–20, 124, 126, 129, 130, 131, 133, 136, 146, 149, 150, 156, 159, 169, 187, 188, 210
menstruation and menstrual seclusion, x, 16–17, 34–39, 47, 73, 75, 92, 107, 112, 129, 142, 183, 192, 199, 208, 214
Michels, District Commissioner Jan, 3, 13, 57
Mintz, Sidney W., 2, 191, 209n4
money, 21, 26, 47, 54, 56, 109, 112, 113, 115, 118, 140, 182, 223, 224
Moravians, 4, 13, 66, 101, 112–13, 203
museums, 191, 195, 197–99, 200, 202–3, 204, 208, 213, 224

Nai, x–xi, 15, 25, 32, 33, 36, 38, 40–50, 57, 63, 71, 74, 75–77, 86, 87, 90–94, 97, 98, 102, 103–4, 113, 122, 124, 128, 130, 131, 133, 135, 139–41, 144, 146–51, 153, 155, 157, 167, 169, 179–80, 184–85, 214, 220; relations with us 9, 28–29, 37, 47–50, 77, 107, 193. *See also* Tone (river god)
Naina, 9, 32, 44, 74, 77–78, 82, 86–87, 91, 92, 97, 110, 119–20, 145, 150, 151, 153, 184
namesake (*neseki*), xi, 32n1, 50, 93, 95–96, 104–5, 120, 125–26, 145, 175, 193

Ndovie. *See* snakegods: Papagadu (Vodu)
Ndyuka Maroons, 2, 18, 72, 104, 155, 225

obia, 20, 21, 22–23, 27, 28, 33, 48–49, 75–76, 80, 86, 92, 93, 97, 99, 124, 127, 129, 130, 136, 139–42, 146, 148, 149, 170, 171, 176, 180, 182, 183. *See also* Dungulali-Obia; witchcraft
oracles: Mamagadu, 18–19, 94, 97, 99, 100, 125–26, 130, 138, 149, 150, 185; Gaantata, 18–19, 24–27, 28, 55, 63, 77, 94, 97, 100, 102, 104, 107, 115, 123–24, 126–31, 133, 138, 139, 140, 142–47, 149, 152, 167, 168, 183, 212, 213, 216. *See also* divination

Papagadu. *See* snakegods
Paramaribo, 2, 13, 14, 163, 194, 202–4, 213
payments for rituals, 24–26, 45, 93, 94, 111, 118, 119, 136, 139–40, 142, 148, 152–53, 156, 172, 175–76, 178, 183, 184; *madyomina*, 49, 76, 92, 96, 104, 134, 136, 141, 152, 153
Peepina, 21, 87, 197–98
Peleki, 185, 190, 194, 217
Pengel, Prime Minister Johan Adolf, 13–14
Pikilio, x, 6, 9, 11, 25, 47, 55, 74, 112, 139
Pobosi, 22n3, 108, 110
Poi, 9, 38, 43, 80, 81, 144–47, 153
polygyny, 37, 41–42, 52, 54. *See also* co-wives
Pomala, 63, 98, 132, 134–35, 139, 147–49, 157–59, 186, 215, 217
Pompia, 151–53, 170
population figures, x, 2, 7, 221, 222, 223
possession, 11, 24, 38, 80, 87, 114, 117, 118–20, 132–38, 151, 152, 153

pottery, 45, 97, 98, 104, 105, 119, 133, 135, 148, 150, 173

prayers and libations, 4, 5, 6, 17, 18, 25, 28, 31–32, 47, 56, 75–76, 78, 85, 86–92, 95–96, 99, 101, 123, 125, 132, 133, 135, 136, 140, 144–45, 147–48, 152, 153, 160–62, 166, 172, 174, 178, 185, 188, 219, 221

pregnancy and childbirth, 9, 19, 24, 25, 37, 38, 46–47, 71, 92–99, 100–101, 103, 107, 109–12, 141, 157, 183, 185

proverbs, x, 91, 94, 192–93

river travel, 3–6, 14, 28, 77, 212, 226

Safeli, 170, 179–89
school. See Moravians
seagods. See Wenti (seagods)
Seena, 9, 43, 86, 92, 146, 151, 209
sex and sexual relations, 42, 46, 49, 51–54, 93, 105, 162, 182, 196–97, 210, 214, 224; adultery 46, 93, 101, 180, 186, 192, 193; among children, 38, 43. See also polygyny
siba. See witchcraft
Sindobobi, 155–72, 173–78, 184
Sido. See Wenti (seagod)
snakegods, 11, 28, 38, 80, 116, 169, 208; Gaan-sembe-u-matu, 116; Papagadu (Vodu), 85, 86, 102, 105, 110, 114–22, 123, 125, 132–38, 145–47, 150–54, 165, 176, 177; Watawenu, 97, 115, 116, 120, 122
snakes, 20, 22, 29, 36, 82, 116, 119, 121, 172, 188, 192, 212
songs, singing: secular, 32, 77, 111, 170–72, 216; ritual, 85, 102, 103, 112n3, 114, 117, 122, 128, 133, 134,

150, 161, 162, 166, 168, 171, 174–75, 187, 195, 205n1, 213, 219, 221

sorcery. See witchcraft
stereotypes of Maroons, 3, 17, 26, 204

taboos, 30, 36, 40, 54, 77, 78, 101, 141, 165, 178, 187, 192, 209
Takite, 20, 50, 77, 80, 85, 86, 157, 159–60, 162, 170, 186, 187, 195
Tampaki, 109, 187
Tando, 26, 32, 54–55, 101–2, 115, 140, 146, 147, 148, 174, 176, 187
textile arts and sewing, 44, 50, 78, 98, 195–98, 212, 214, 216
Tioye, 127, 146, 149, 157, 167
Tita, 86–87, 132–33, 134, 136, 138
tobacco, 45, 47–48, 80, 119, 123–26, 175, 182, 188
Todye. See Wenti (seagod)
Tone (river god), 47, 97, 102, 103–7, 119, 133, 145–48, 150–53, 171, 179, 186
Tooy, 116–17, 122, 138, 226–27
tourism, 191, 223, 224, 229
trees, 9, 18, 19, 66, 77, 79, 80, 82, 84, 85, 129, 130, 140, 149, 166, 182, 224
Tuliobuka, 6, 112
turtles, 30, 173, 178, 214, 220

Wenti (seagod), 4, 95, 108–13, 147; Sido, 110, 114, 116, 119, 150–53; Todye, 108–13
witchcraft, sorcery, siba, and evil obias, 43–44, 55, 74, 94, 105, 111–12, 124, 125, 126, 127, 130–31, 155–72
woodcarving, 7, 9, 21, 30, 42, 50, 55, 99, 170, 191, 195, 214, 222, 223

Yegi, 132, 136, 137